Student Solutions Manual

STATISTICS FOR BUSINESS AND ECONOMICS

Sixth Edition

Paul Newbold
William L. Carlson
Betty Thorne

Dr. Steven C. Huchendorf
University of Minnesota

PEARSON
Prentice
Hall

Upper Saddle River, New Jersey 07458

VP/Editorial Director: Jeff Shelstad
AVP/Executive Editor: Mark Pfaltzgraff
Assistant Editor: Barbara Witmer
Associate Director Manufacturing: Vincent Scelta
Production Editor & Buyer: Wanda Rockwell
Printer/Binder: Integrated Book Technology, Inc.

10 9 8 7 6 5 4 3 2
ISBN 0-13-188098-5

Contents

Chapter 1   Why Study Statistics? 1

Chapter 2   Describing Data: Graphical 2

Chapter 3   Describing Data: Numerical 19

Chapter 4   Probability 31

Chapter 5   Discrete Random Variables and Probability Distributions 41

Chapter 6   Continuous Random Variables and Probability Distributions 61

Chapter 7   Sampling and Sampling Distributions 72

Chapter 8   Estimation: Single Population 82

Chapter 9   Estimation: Additional Topics 91

Chapter 10 Hypothesis Testing 99

Chapter 11 Hypothesis Testing II 107

Chapter 12 Simple Regression .117

Chapter 13 Multiple Regression 137

Chapter 14 Additional Topics in Regression Analysis 169

Chapter 15 Nonparametric Statistics 185

Chapter 16 Goodness-of-Fit and Contingency Tables 189

Chapter 17 Analysis of Variance 199

Chapter 18 Introduction to Quality 213

Chapter 19 Time Series Analysis and Forecasting 226

Chapter 20 Additional Topics in Sampling 251

Chapter 21 Statistical Decision Theory 258

Chapter 1:

Why Study Statistics?

1.2   Various answers. Marketing decisions under uncertainty could include pricing decisions, promotion decisions, advertising decisions, packaging decisions, etc.

1.4   a. Various answers. A population parameter could be the true overall population mean income of all families living in West Palm Beach, Florida
      b. Various answers. A population parameter could be the true overall population standard deviation of all stocks traded on the New York Stock Exchange.
      c. Various answers. A population parameter could be the true population mean costs of all medical insurance claims received by a company in a given year.
      d. Various answers. A population parameter would be the true population mean values of all accounts receivable for a corporation.

1.6   a. The population consists of all of the airline's scheduled flights at Orlando International Airport.
      b. The sample consists of the randomly selected 200 flights
      c. The statistic is the 1.5% that were found to depart later than the scheduled time for the 200 randomly selected flights
      d. 1.5% is a sample statistic

1.8   a. Descriptive – to describe information about a one-week sample
      b. Inferential statistics – to estimate the true percentage of all employees who arrive to work late
      c. Inferential statistics – to predict the relationship between years of experience and pay scale.

Chapter 2:

Describing Data: Graphical

2.2   a. Categorical data. The measurements levels are qualitative – nominal.
            Yes/no response
        b. Categorical data. The measurement levels are qualitative - nominal.
        c. Numerical data. Dollar amounts are generally considered continuous,
            even though we may truncate dollar amounts and treat dollar amounts
            as if they were the same as discrete.

2.4   a. Categorical – Qualitative – ordinal
        b. Numerical – Quantitative – discrete
        c. Categorical – Qualitative – nominal
        d. Categorical – Qualitative – nominal

2.6   a. Categorical – Qualitative – nominal
        b. Numerical – Quantitative - discrete
        c. Categorical – Qualitative – nominal: yes/no response
        d. Categorical – Qualitative – ordinal

2.8   a. Various answers - Categorical variable with ordinal responses: Health
            consciousness
        b. Various answers – Categorical variable with nominal responses: Gender

2.10   Pareto diagram – possible defects for a product line; Category "Other"
         combines Defects F & G

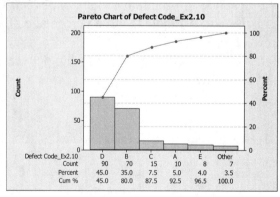

2.12   Component (stacked) bar chart – age and time to complete a task

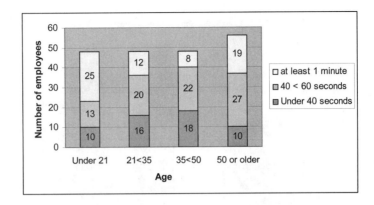

2.13   a. Bar chart of endangered wildlife species in the U.S.

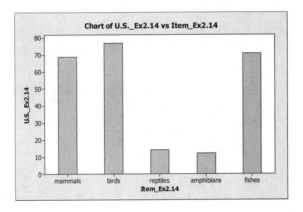

    b. Bar chart of endangered wildlife species outside the U.S.

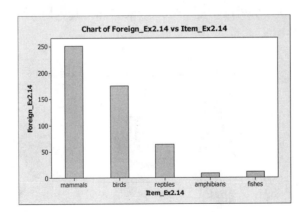

c.   Bar chart to compare the number of endangered species

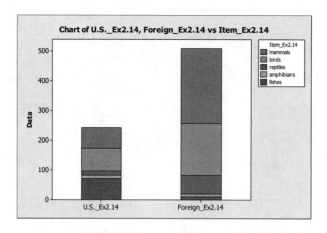

2.16   Describe the data graphically

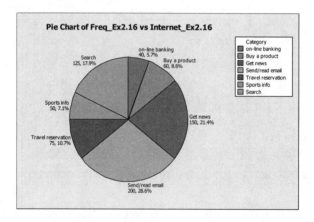

2.18   a. Component (stacked) bar chart of gender and level of health
        consciousness

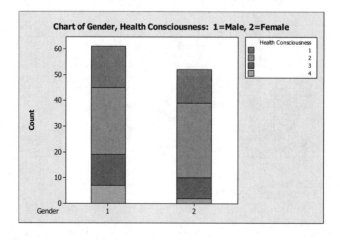

b. Component (stacked) bar chart of desire for protein supplement and level of health consciousness

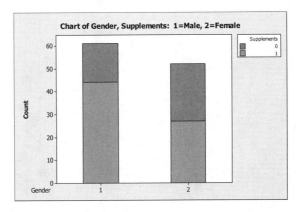

2.20   Time series plot of mobile phone usage (in minutes)

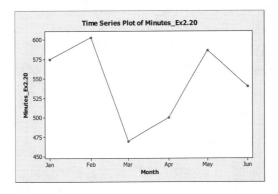

2.21   a. Time series plot of degrees awarded

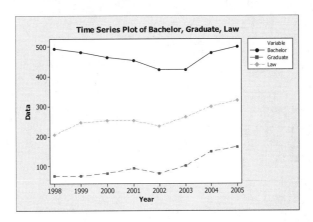

b. The number of law and graduate degrees awarded is increasing. The number of bachelor degrees awarded declined from 1998 to 2004 with a slight increase in 2005. Enrollment restrictions may be in order if class sizes are becoming too large or if crowding conditions occur.

2.24   Time series plot of Value

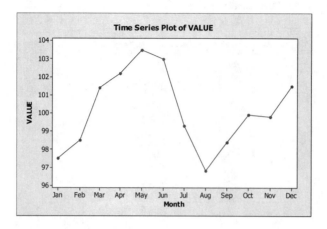

2.26   Time series plot of Dow Jones Industrial Average

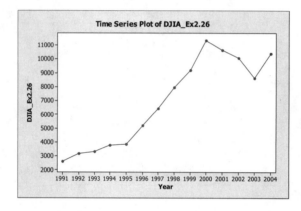

2.28   Time series plot of Housing Starts data

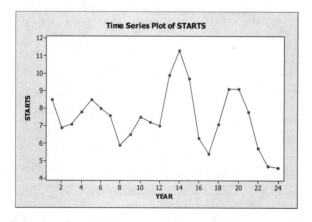

2.30   a. 5 – 7 classes
        b. 7 – 8 classes
        c. 8 – 10 classes
        d. 8 – 10 classes
        e. 10 – 11 classes

2.32   a. frequency distribution

Bin	Frequency
10 < 20	5
20 < 30	3
30 < 40	8
40 < 50	3
50 < 60	5
60 < 70	4

b. histogram and c. ogive

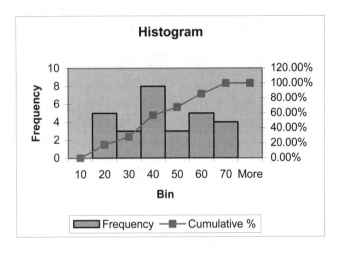

d. stem-and-leaf display

Stem-and-Leaf Display: Data_Ex2.32
```
Stem-and-leaf of Data_Ex2.32  N  = 28
Leaf Unit = 1.0

   2    1  23
   5    1  557
   7    2  14
   8    2  8
   9    3  2
  (6)   3  567799
  13    4  0144
   9    4
   9    5  14
   7    5  699
   4    6  24
   2    6  55
```

2.34

Classes	Frequency	a. Relative Frequency	b. Cumulative Frequency	c. Relative Cumulative Frequency
0<10	8	16.33%	8	16.33%
10<20	10	20.41%	18	36.74%
20<30	13	26.53%	31	63.27%
30<40	12	24.49%	43	87.76%
40<50	6	12.24%	49	100.00%
Total	49	100.00%		

2.36   For the file Water - construct a frequency distribution, cumulative frequency distribution, histogram, ogive and stem-and-leaf display. Various answers – one possibility is to use 7 classes with a width of .1.

Bin	Frequency	Cumulative %
3.5 < 3.6	0	1.33%
3.6 < 3.7	8	12.00%
3.7 < 3.8	29	50.67%
3.8 < 3.9	22	80.00%
3.9 < 4.0	13	97.33%
4.0 < 4.1	1	98.67%
4.1 < 4.2	1	100.00%

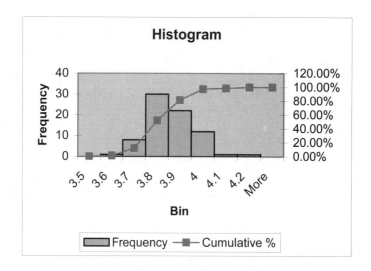

Stem-and-Leaf Display: Weights

```
Stem-and-leaf of Weights  N  = 75
Leaf Unit = 0.010

    1    35  7
    3    36  34
    9    36  577799
   21    37  111122344444
  (17)   37  55566777777889999
   37    38  0111112222244
   24    38  556677899
   15    39  01334444
    7    39  56689
    2    40
    2    40  6
```

2.38   a. Histogram and c. Ogive of the **Returns** data

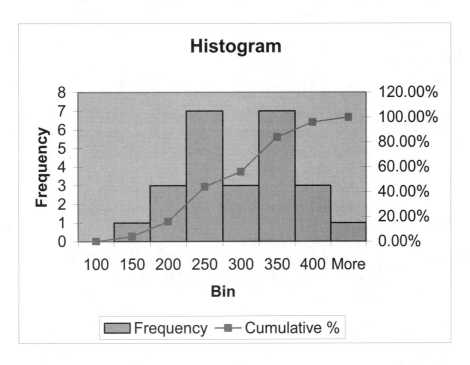

b. stem-and-leaf display

Stem-and-Leaf Display: Returns
```
Stem-and-leaf of Returns  N  = 25
Leaf Unit = 10

   1    1   3
   1    1
   1    1
   4    1   899
   7    2   001
   7    2
  12    2   44445
  12    2
 (2)    2   89
  11    3   00001
   6    3   22
   4    3
   4    3   6
   3    3   89
```

2.40   Scatterplot

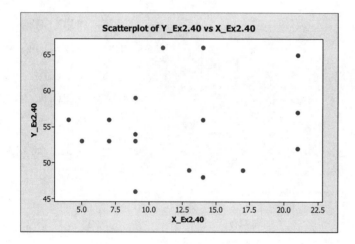

2.42   a. cross table for subcontractors and parts supplied

Subcontractor	Defective Parts	Non-defective Parts	Parts Supplied
A	4	54	58
B	10	60	70
C	6	66	72
Total	20	180	200

b. bar chart

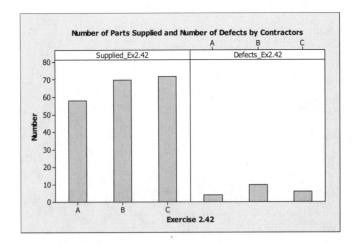

2.44   Acme Delivery – relation between shipping cost and number of delivery
        days

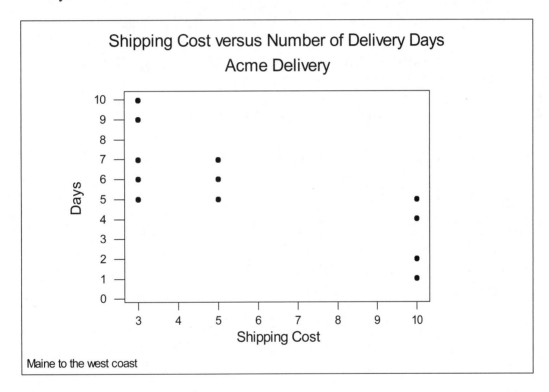

The relationship appears to be negative; however there is significant variability in
delivery time at each of the three shipping costs – regular, $3; fast, $5; and
lightning, $10.

2.46   Scatterplot of Citydat – taxbase versus comper

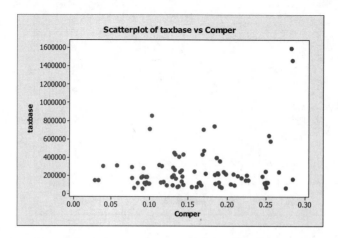

No relationship between the two variables and hence no evidence that emphasis on attracting a larger percentage of commercial property increases the tax base. The two outlier points on the right side of the plot might be used to argue that a very high amount of commercial property will provide a larger tax base. That argument, however, is contrary to the overall pattern of the data.

2.48   a. Time series plot with vertical scale from 5000 to 5700.

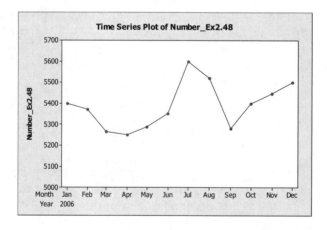

b. Time series plot with vertical scale from 4000 to 7000.

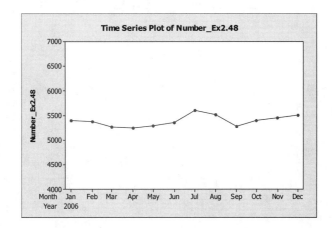

c. Differences between the two graphs include the variability of the data series. One graph suggests greater variability in the data series while the other one suggests a relatively flat line with less variability. Keep in mind the scale on which the measurements are made.

2.50   Draw two time series plots for Inventory Sales with different vertical ranges.

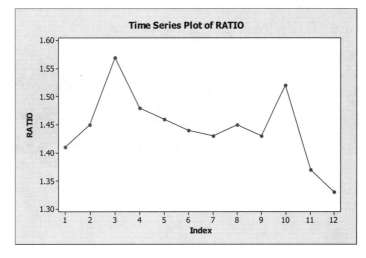

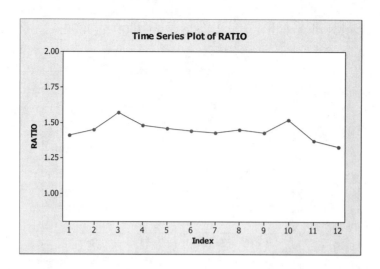

Differences between the two graphs include the variability of the data series. One graph suggests greater variability in the data series while the other one suggests a relatively flat line with less variability. Keep in mind the scale on which the measurements are made.

2.52   a.   Draw a histogram of 20 forecasted earnings per share.

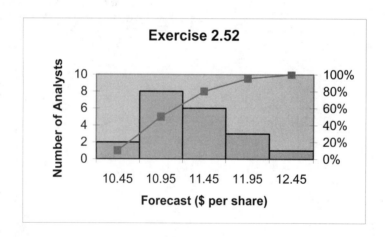

Answer to b., c. and d. are:

	(b)		(c)	(d)	
Forecast of Earnings Per Share	Frequency	Relative Freq.	Cumulative Freq.	Cumulative %
9.95	2	0.1	2	10.00%
10.45	8	0.4	10	50.00%
10.95	6	0.3	16	80.00%
11.45	3	0.15	19	95.00%
11.95	1	0.05	20	100.00%

d.   Cumulative relative frequencies are in the last column of the table above. These numbers indicate the percent of analysts who forecast that level of earnings per share and all previous classes, up to and including the current class. The third bin of 80% indicates that 80% of the analysts have forecasted up to and including that ≤ 11.45 level of earnings per share.

2.54   Time-series of quarterly rates of return – Stock funds:

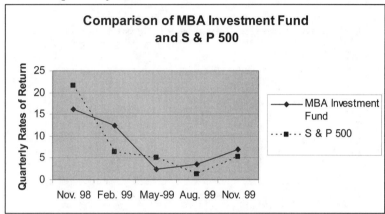

2.56   County Appraiser's Office – Data Entry Process
    a. Pareto diagram

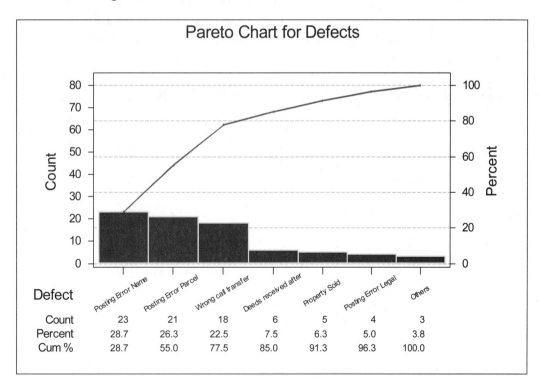

b. Recommendations should include a discussion of the data entry process. The data entry was being made by individuals with no knowledge of the data. Training of the data entry personnel should be a major recommendation. Increasing the size of the monitors used by the data entry staff would also reduce the number of errors.

2.58   Weekly traffic increase for the top five Health, Fitness & Nutrition Internet sites

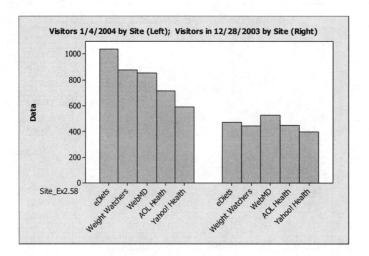

Weekly traffic increases from 2003 to 2004 could come about because the total number of users of the Internet has increased, an increasing awareness of health Internet sites, or an aging baby boom population that is more concerned about health issues.

2.60   Plot the data for advertising expenditures and total sales.

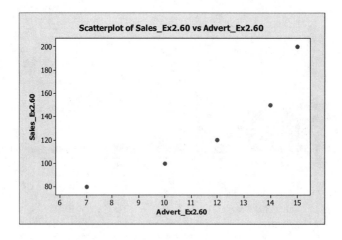

2.62   Plot the batting averages vs. hours spent per week in a weight-training program.

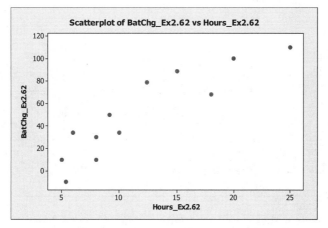

It appears that the number of hours spent per week in a special weight-training program is positively related to the change in their batting averages from the previous season.

2.64   a. Describe the new product data with a cross table

Age	Friend	Newspaper	Subtotal
<21 years	30	20	50
21-35	60	30	90
35+	18	42	60
Subtotal	108	92	200

b. Describe the data graphically

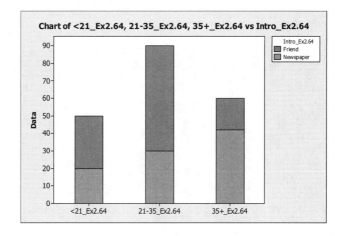

2.66   a. Construct cross tables from the Smoothies data file – gender and level
            of health consciousness

Health Consciousness	Male	Female	Subtotal
Very	16	13	29
Moderately	26	29	55
Slightly	12	8	20
Not very	7	2	9
Subtotal	61	52	113

    b. Do you like a protein supplement in your smoothie?

Health Consciousness	No	Yes	Subtotal
Very	12	17	29
Moderately	19	36	55
Slightly	9	11	20
Not very	2	7	9
Subtotal	42	71	113

2.68   a. Cross table of method of payment and day of purchase for Florin data
            file.

Payment	M	T	W	Th	F	S	Tot
Am Ex	7	0	3	4	3	6	23
MC	1	4	4	2	4	9	16
Visa	6	6	4	5	8	10	24
Cash	3	1	0	0	3	9	16
Other	2	0	4	4	7	6	23
Subtotal	19	11	15	15	25	40	125

    b. Pie chart of rose color preference

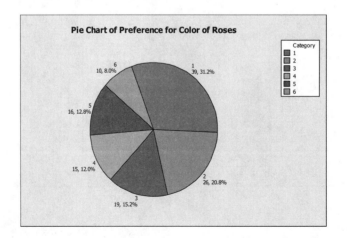

Chapter 3:
Describing Data: Numerical

3.2   Number of complaints: 8, 8, 13, 15, 16
     a. Compute the mean number of weekly complaints

$$\bar{x} = \sum \frac{x_i}{n} = \frac{60}{5} = 12$$

     b. Calculate the median = middlemost observation = 13
     c. Find the mode = most frequently occurring value = 8

3.4   Department store % increase in dollar sales: 2.9, 3.1, 3.7, 4.3, 5.9, 6.8, 7.0, 7.3, 8.2, 10.2

     a. Mean $\bar{x} = \sum \frac{x_i}{n} = \frac{59.4}{10} = 5.94$

     b. Median = middlemost observation: $\frac{5.9 + 6.8}{2} = 6.35$

     c. The distribution is relatively symmetric since the mean of 5.94 is relatively close to the median of 6.35. Since the mean is slightly less than the median, the distribution is slightly skewed to the left.

3.6   Demand for bottled water: 40, 43, 50, 55, 60, 62, 65

     a. Describe central tendency. $\bar{x} = \sum \frac{x_i}{n} = \frac{375}{7} = 53.57$. The mean demand for one-gallon bottles is 53.57 which is the balancing point of the distribution. The median of 55 indicates that half of the distribution had larger sales than 55 bottles and half had smaller sales. No unique mode exists in the distribution

     b. Comment on symmetry or skewness. Since the mean is slightly less than the median, the distribution is slightly skewed to the left.

3.8   Ages of 12 students
     a. $\bar{x} = \sum \frac{x_i}{n} = \frac{307}{12} = 25.58$
     b. Median = 22.50
     c. Mode = 22

3.10 a. $\bar{x} = \sum \frac{x_i}{n} = \frac{282}{33} = 8.545$
     b. Median = 9.0
     c. The distribution is slightly skewed to the left since the mean is less than the median.

3.12   The variance and standard deviation are:

$$s^2 = \frac{\sum (x_i - \bar{x})^2}{n-1} = \frac{36}{7} = 5.143 \quad \text{and} \quad s = 2.268$$

3.14   Calculate the coefficient of variation:

$$\bar{x} = 9; \quad s^2 = \frac{\sum (x_i - \bar{x})^2}{n-1} = \frac{10}{4} = 2.5; \quad s = 1.581;$$

$CV = [1.581/9] \times 100\% = 17.57$

3.16   a.   IQR = 24.25; $Q_1 = 49.5$; $Q_3 = 73.75$

   b.   8th decile = 80th percentile = 18.4th observation = 76 + 0.4(79-76) = 77.2

   c.   92nd percentile = 21.26th observation = 83 + 0.16(87-83) = 83.64

3.18   Use Chebychev's theorem to approximate each of the following:

   a.   Between 190 and 310. At least 88.9% of the observations are within 3 standard deviations from the mean

   b.   Between 210 and 290. At least 75% of the observations are within 2 standard deviations from the mean

   c.   Between 230 and 270. At least 0% of the observations are within 1 standard deviation from the mean

3.20   Compare the annual % returns of stocks vs. U.S. Treasury bills.

Descriptive Statistics: Stocks_Ex3.20, TBills_Ex3.20

Variable	N	N*	Mean	SE Mean	TrMean	StDev	Variance	CoefVar	Minimum
Stocks_Ex3.20	7	0	8.16	8.43	*	22.30	497.39	273.41	-26.50
TBills_Ex3.20	7	0	5.786	0.556	*	1.471	2.165	25.43	3.800

Variable	Q1	Median	Q3	Maximum	Range	IQR
Stocks_Ex3.20	-14.70	14.30	23.80	37.20	63.70	38.50
TBills_Ex3.20	4.400	5.800	6.900	8.000	4.200	2.500

   a.   Compare the means of the populations

$$\mu_{stocks} = \frac{\sum x_i}{N} = \frac{57.12}{7} = 8.16 \quad \mu_{Tbills} = \frac{\sum x_i}{N} = \frac{40.502}{7} = 5.786$$

The mean annual % return on stocks is higher than the return for U.S. Treasury bills

b. Compare the standard deviations of the populations

$$\sigma_{stocks} = \sqrt{\sigma^2} = \sqrt{\frac{\sum(x_i - \mu)^2}{N}} = 20.648$$

$$\sqrt{\frac{(4.0-8.16)^2 + (14.3-8.16)^2 + (19-8.16)^2 + (-14.7-8.16)^2 + (-26.5-8.16)^2 + (37.2-8.16)^2 + (23.8-8.16)^2}{7}}$$

$$\sigma_{Tbills} = \sqrt{\sigma^2} = \sqrt{\frac{\sum(x_i - \mu)^2}{N}} = 1.362$$

$$\sqrt{\frac{(6.5-5.8)^2 + (4.4-5.8)^2 + (3.8-5.8)^2 + (6.9-5.8)^2 + (8.0-5.8)^2 + (5.8-5.8)^2 + (5.1-5.8)^2}{7}}$$

The variability of the U.S. Treasury bills is much smaller than the return on stocks.

3.22 a. range = 4.11 – 3.57 = 0.54, standard deviation = 0.1024, variance = 0.010486

b. Five number summary:

	Min	Q1	Median	Q3	Max
	3.57	3.74	3.79	3.87	4.11

c. IQR = Q3 – Q1 = 3.87 – 3.74 = .13. This tells that the range of the middle 50% of the distribution is 0.13

d. Coefficient of variation = s / $\bar{x}$ = 0.1024 / 3.8079 = 0.02689 or 2.689%

3.24 a. Standard deviation(s) of the assessment rates:

$$s = \sqrt{s^2} = \sqrt{\frac{\sum_{i=1}^{n}(x_i - \bar{x})^2}{n-1}} = \sqrt{\frac{583.75}{39}} = \sqrt{14.974} = 3.8696$$

b. The distribution is mounded. Therefore, the empirical rule applies. Approximately 95% of the distribution is expected to be within +/- 2 standard deviations of the mean.

3.26 a. mean without the weights $\bar{x} = \sum \frac{x_i}{n} = \frac{21}{5} = 4.2$

b. weighted mean

w_i	x_i	$w_i x_i$
8	4.6	36.8
3	3.2	9.6
6	5.4	32.4
2	2.6	5.2
5	5.2	26.0
24		110.0

$$\bar{x} = \frac{\sum w_i x_i}{\sum w_i} = \frac{110}{24} = 4.583$$

3.28   Find the weighted mean per capita personal income

State	Pop	Income	$w_i x_i$
AL	4,500,752	26,338	118,540,806,176
GA	8,684,715	29,442	255,695,379,030
IL	12,653,544	33,690	426,297,897,360
IN	6,195,643	28,783	178,329,192,469
NY	19,190,115	36,574	701,859,266,010
PA	12,365,455	31,998	395,669,829,090
TN	5,841,748	28,455	166,226,939,340
	69,431,972		2,242,619,309,475

$$\bar{x} = \frac{\sum w_i x_i}{\sum w_i} = \frac{2,242,619,309,475}{69,431,972} = 32,299.519$$

3.30   Based on a sample of n=50:

m_i	f_i	$f_i m_i$	$(m_i - \bar{x})$	$(m_i - \bar{x})^2$	$f_i(m_i - \bar{x})^2$
0	21	0	-1.4	1.96	41.16
1	13	13	-0.4	0.16	2.08
2	5	10	0.6	0.36	1.8
3	4	12	1.6	2.56	10.24
4	2	8	2.6	6.76	13.52
5	3	15	3.6	12.96	38.88
6	2	12	4.6	21.16	42.32
Sum	**50**	**70**			**150**

a. Sample mean number of claims per day = $\bar{X} = \dfrac{\sum f_i m_i}{n} = 70/50 = 1.40$

b. Sample variance = $s^2 = \dfrac{\sum f_i(m_i - \bar{x})^2}{n-1} = \dfrac{150}{49} = 3.0612$

Sample standard deviation = $s = \sqrt{s^2} = 1.7496$

3.32 Estimate the sample mean and sample standard deviation

m_i	f_i	$f_i m_i$	$(m_i - \bar{x})$	$(m_i - \bar{x})^2$	$f_i(m_i - \bar{x})^2$
10.2	2	20.4	-0.825	0.681	1.361
10.7	8	85.6	-0.325	0.106	0.845
11.2	6	67.2	0.175	0.031	0.184
11.7	3	35.1	0.675	0.456	1.367
12.2	1	12.2	1.175	1.381	1.381
	20	220.5			5.138
x-bar=	11.03			variance =	0.2704

a. sample mean = $\bar{X} = \dfrac{\sum f_i m_i}{n} = 220.5/20 = 11.025$

b. sample variance = $s^2 = \dfrac{\sum f_i(m_i - \bar{x})^2}{n-1} = 5.138/19 = 0.2704$

sample standard deviation = $s = \sqrt{s^2} = 0.520$

3.34 Calculate mean and standard deviation of mobile phone usage from Example 3.9

Minutes	m_i	f_i	$f_i m_i$	$(m_i - \bar{x})$	$(m_i - \bar{x})^2$	$f_i(m_i - \bar{x})^2$
220<230	225	5	1125	-36.545	1335.57	6677.851
230<240	235	8	1880	-26.545	704.6612	5637.289
240<250	245	13	3185	-16.545	273.7521	3558.777
250<260	255	22	5610	-6.5455	42.84298	942.5455
260<270	265	32	8480	3.45455	11.93388	381.8843
270<280	275	13	3575	13.4545	181.0248	2353.322
280<290	285	10	2850	23.4545	550.1157	5501.157
290<300	295	7	2065	33.4545	1119.207	7834.446
		110	28770			32887.27

a. $\bar{x} = \dfrac{\sum f_i m_i}{n} = \dfrac{28770}{110} = 261.54545$

b. $s^2 = \dfrac{\sum f_i(m_i - \bar{x})^2}{n-1} = \dfrac{32887.27}{109} = 301.718 \quad s = \sqrt{s^2} = 17.370$

3.36   a. compute the sample covariance

x_i	y_i	$(x_i - \bar{x})$	$(x_i - \bar{x})^2$	$(y_i - \bar{y})$	$(y_i - \bar{y})^2$	$(x_i - \bar{x})(y_i - \bar{y})$
12	200	-7	49	-156	24336	1092
30	600	11	121	244	59536	2684
15	270	-4	16	-86	7396	344
24	500	5	25	144	20736	720
14	210	-5	25	-146	21316	730
95	1780	0	236	0	133320	5570
$\bar{x} = 19.00$	$\bar{y} = 356.0$		$s_x^2 = 59$		$s_y^2 = 33330$	Cov(x,y) = 1392.5
			$s_x = 7.681146$		$s_y = 182.5650569$	

$$Cov(x,y) = \frac{\sum (x_i - \bar{x})(y_i - \bar{y})}{n-1} = \frac{5570}{4} = 1392.5$$

b. compute the sample correlation coefficient

$$r = \frac{Cov(x,y)}{s_x s_y} = \frac{1392.5}{(7.6811)(182.565)} = 0.9930$$

3.38   a. $Cov\ (x,y) = 4.268$

      b. $r = 0.128$

      c. Weak positive association between the number of drug units and the number of days to complete recovery. Recommend low or no dosage units.

3.40   a. compute $b_1 = \dfrac{Cov(x,y)}{s_x^2} = \dfrac{3.25}{5} = 0.65$

      b. compute $b_0 = \bar{y} - b_1\bar{x} = 7 - 0.65(4) = 4.4$

x_i	y_i	$(x_i - \bar{x})$	$(x_i - \bar{x})^2$	$(y_i - \bar{y})$	$(y_i - \bar{y})^2$	$(x_i - \bar{x})(y_i - \bar{y})$
1	5	-3	9	-2	4	6
3	7	-1	1	0	0	0
4	6	0	0	-1	1	0
5	8	1	1	1	1	1
7	9	3	9	2	4	6
20	35	0	20	0	10	13

      c.   What is the equation of the regression line?

$$\hat{y} = b_0 + b_1 x = 4.40 + .65x$$

3.42   a. Describe the data numerically (covariance and correlation)

$$\text{Covariance} = C\text{ov}(x,y) = \frac{\sum (x_i - \bar{x})(y_i - \bar{y})}{n-1} = \text{-598.5714286} / 6 = \text{-99.762}$$

$$\text{Correlation} = \frac{Cov(x,y)}{s_x s_y} = \frac{-99.76190476}{(2.340126)(45.98136)} = -0.927136$$

x_i	y_i	$(x_i - \bar{x})$	$(x_i - \bar{x})^2$	$(y_i - \bar{y})$	$(y_i - \bar{y})^2$	$(x_i - \bar{x})(y_i - \bar{y})$
10	100	2.857142857	8.163265	-38.5714	1487.755	-110.2040816
8	120	0.857142857	0.734694	-18.5714	344.898	-15.91836735
5	200	-2.142857143	4.591837	61.42857	3773.469	-131.6326531
4	200	-3.142857143	9.877551	61.42857	3773.469	-193.0612245
10	90	2.857142857	8.163265	-48.5714	2359.184	-138.7755102
7	110	-0.142857143	0.020408	-28.5714	816.3265	4.081632653
6	150	-1.142857143	1.306122	11.42857	130.6122	-13.06122449
50	970		32.85714		12685.71	-598.5714286

b. Compute and interpret $b_1 = \frac{Cov(x,y)}{s_x^2} = $ -99.7619 / 5.4762 = -18.217. For a

one dollar increase in the price per gallon of paint, we estimate that the quantity sold per seven days of operation would decrease by 18.217 gallons of paint.

c. Compute and interpret $b_0 = \bar{y} - b_1 \bar{x} = 138.5714 - (-18.217)(7.1429) = 268.70$.

If the price of the paint were \$0 per gallon, we would expect to sell 268.7 gallons per seven days of operation. Interpret with caution - note that we are extrapolating the results beyond the observed data.

d. How gallons would be sold if the price is \$7 per gallon?

$\hat{y} = b_0 + b_1 x = 268.7 - 18.217(7) = 141.181$ gallons sold per seven days of operation

3.44   a. Compute covariance and correlation between retail experience (years) and weekly sales (hundreds of dollars)

x_i	y_i	$(x_i - \bar{x})$	$(x_i - \bar{x})^2$	$(y_i - \bar{y})$	$(y_i - \bar{y})^2$	$(x_i - \bar{x})(y_i - \bar{y})$
2	5	-1.875	3.515625	-5.75	33.0625	10.78125
4	10	0.125	0.015625	-0.75	0.5625	-0.09375
3	8	-0.875	0.765625	-2.75	7.5625	2.40625
6	18	2.125	4.515625	7.25	52.5625	15.40625
3	6	-0.875	0.765625	-4.75	22.5625	4.15625
5	15	1.125	1.265625	4.25	18.0625	4.78125
6	20	2.125	4.515625	9.25	85.5625	19.65625
2	4	-1.875	3.515625	-6.75	45.5625	12.65625
31	86		18.875		265.5	69.75
$\bar{x}$ = 3.875	$\bar{y}$ = 10.75		s_x^2 = 2.6964		s_y^2 = 37.9286	Cov(x,y) = 9.964286
			s_x = 1.64208		s_y = 6.15862	

$$\text{Covariance} = C\text{ov}(x,y) = \frac{\sum(x_i - \bar{x})(y_i - \bar{y})}{n-1} = 69.75 / 7 = 9.964286$$

$$\text{Correlation} = \frac{Cov(x,y)}{s_x s_y} = \frac{9.964286}{(1.64208)(6.15862)} = .9853$$

b. Compute the regression coefficients $b_1 = \dfrac{Cov(x,y)}{s_x^2} = 9.964286 / 2.6964 = $ 3.6954 and $b_0 = \bar{y} - b_1\bar{x} = 10.75 - (3.6954)(3.875) = $ -3.5697

c. The regression equation provides an estimation of the impact that additional retail experience has on weekly sales (in hundreds of dollars). It appears that as retail experience increases, the weekly sales also increase. This estimate is based on retail experience between 2 and 6 years with weekly sales of $400 to $2,000.

3.46   Air Traffic Delays (Number of Minutes Late)

m_i	f_i	$f_i m_i$	$(m_i - \bar{x})$	$(m_i - \bar{x})^2$	$f_i(m_i - \bar{x})^2$
5	30	150	-13.133	172.46	5173.90
15	25	375	-3.133	9.81	245.32
25	13	325	6.867	47.16	613.11
35	6	210	16.867	284.51	1707.07
45	5	225	26.867	721.86	3609.30
55	4	220	36.867	1359.21	5436.84
	83	1505			16785.54
x-bar=	18.13			variance =	204.7017

a. Sample mean number of minutes late = 1505 / 83 = 18.1325
b. Sample variance = 16785.54/82 = 204.7017
sample standard deviation = s = 14.307

3.48   a. Scatter Plot of Quantity of Cotton Produced (Cottonq) and Wholesale Price Index

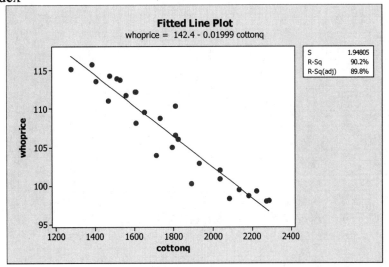

b. $\hat{y} = 142.398 - 0.0199937x$;   marginal effect is -.0199937

c. Estimate the relationship between exported cotton fabric and the production of cotton.

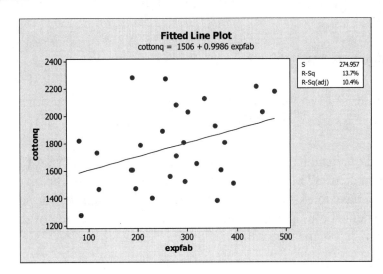

3.50 a. Describe the direction and strength of the relationship between SAT Math score and GPA at time of graduation.

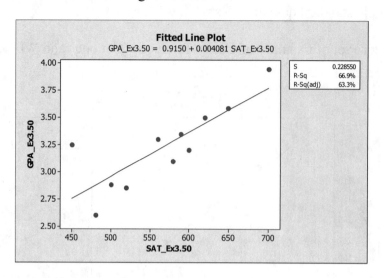

Correlations: SAT_Ex3.50, GPA_Ex3.50
Pearson correlation of SAT_Ex3.50 and GPA_Ex3.50 = 0.818

Direction is positive with a relatively strong (r =0.818) correlation between the two variables. There is a positive relationship between the Math SAT score and the GPA at the time of graduation.

b. Compute and interpret $b_1 = 0.004081$. For a one point increase in the Math SAT score, we estimate that GPA at the time of graduation will increase by .004081.

c. Compute $b_0 = 0.9150$

d. If Math SAT = 530, predict the student's college GPA at time of graduation
$\hat{y} = b_0 + b_1 x = .915 + .004081(530) = 3.078$

e. Based on this data, can you predict GPA for a 375 Math SAT?
The value of 375 for the Math SAT score is outside of the observed data. We would have to extrapolate beyond the observed data in order to make a statement about the graduating GPA. The results outside of the observed data are much less meaningful.

3.52 a. Describe the data graphically between graduating GPA vs. entering SAT Verbal scores

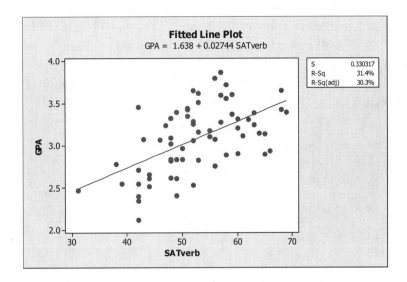

b. Describe the data numerically

Covariances: GPA, SATverb
```
                 GPA      SATverb
GPA         0.169284
SATverb     1.791637   65.293985
```
Correlations: GPA, SATverb
```
Pearson correlation of GPA and SATverb = 0.560
P-Value = 0.000
```
Regression Analysis: GPA versus SATverb
```
The regression equation is
GPA = 1.64 + 0.0274 SATverb
```

c. Estimate a graduation GPA for a student with a verbal score of 52
GPA = 1.64 + 0.0274 SATverb = 3.06

3.54 Mean of $295 and standard deviation of $63.
  a. Find a range in which it can be guaranteed that 60% of the values lie.
      Use Chebychev's theorem: at least 60% = $[1-(1/k^2)]$. Solving for k = 1.58. The interval will range from 295 +/- (1.58)(63) = 295 +/- 99.54. 195.46 up to 394.54 will contain at least 60% of the observations.
  b. Find the range in which it can be guaranteed that 84% of the growth figures lie
      Use Chebychev's theorem: at least 84% = $[1-(1/k^2)]$. Solving for k = 2.5. The interval will range from 295 +/- (2.50)(63) = 295 +/- 157.5. 137.50 up to 452.50 will contain at least 84% of the observations.

3.56   Tires have a lifetime mean of 29,000 miles and a standard deviation of 3,000 miles.

a. Find a range in which it can be guaranteed that 75% of the lifetimes of tires lies. Use Chebychev's theorem: at least 75% = $[1-(1/k^2)]$. Solving for k = 2.0. The interval will range from $29,000 \pm (2.0)(3000) = 29,000 \pm 6000 = 23,000$ to 35,000.

b. 95%, solve for K = 4.47. The interval will range from $29,000 \pm (4.47)(3000) = 29,000 \pm 13,416.41 = 15,583.59$ to 42,416.41.

Chapter 4:

Probability

4.2   a. *A* intersection *B* contains the sample points that are in both *A* and *B*. The intersection = (E_3, E_9).

       b. *A* union *B* contains the sample points in *A* or *B* or both. The union = $(E_1, E_2, E_3, E_7, E_8, E_9)$

       c. *A* union *B* is not collectively exhaustive – it does not contain all of the possible sample points.

4.4.   a. *A* intersection *B* = (E_3, E_6)

       b. *A* union *B* = $(E_3, E_4, E_5, E_6, E_9, E_{10})$

       c. *A* union *B* is not collectively exhaustive – it does not contain all of the possible sample points.

4.6   a. $(A \cap B)$ is the event that the Dow-Jones average rises on both days which is O_1. $(\overline{A} \cap B)$ is the event the Dow-Jones average does not rise on the first day but it rises on the second day which is O_3. The union between these two will be O_1 or O_3 either of which by definition is event *B*: the Dow-Jones average rises on the second day.

       b. Since $(\overline{A} \cap B)$ is the event the Dow-Jones average does not rise on the first day but rises on the second day which is O_3 and because *A* is the event that the Dow-Jones average rises on the first day, then the union will be O_2, either the Dow-Jones average does not rise on the first day but rises on the second day or the Dow-Jones average rises on the first day or both. This is the definition of $A \cup B$.

4.8.   The total number of outcomes in the sample space, $N =$

$$C_2^{12} = \frac{12!}{2!(12-10)!} = 66.$$

The number of ways to select 1 A from the 5 available, $C_1^5 = \frac{5!}{1!(5-1)!} = 5$.

The number of ways to select 1 B from the 7 available, $C_1^7 = \frac{7!}{1!(7-1)!} = 7$.

The number of outcomes that satisfy the condition of 1A and 1 B is 5 X 7 = 35. Therefore, the probability that a randomly selected set of 2 will include 1A and 1 B is $P_A = \frac{N_A}{N} = \frac{C_1^5 C_1^7}{C_2^{12}} = \frac{5 X 7}{66} = .53$

4.10. The total number of outcomes in the sample space, $N =$

$C_4^{16} = \dfrac{16!}{4!(16-4)!} = 1,820$.

The number of ways to select 2 A's from the 10 available,

$C_2^{10} = \dfrac{10!}{2!(10-2)!} = 45$.

The number of ways to select 2 B's from the 6 available,

$C_2^6 = \dfrac{6!}{2!(6-2)!} = 15$.

The number of outcomes that satisfy the condition of 2A's and 2B's is 45 X 15 = 675. Therefore, the probability that a randomly selected set of 4 will include 2A's and 2B's is $P_A = \dfrac{N_A}{N} = \dfrac{C_2^{10} C_2^6}{C_4^{16}} = \dfrac{45 X 15}{1,820} = .3709$

4.12. $\dfrac{C_2^{20,000}}{C_2^{180,000}} = \dfrac{n_A}{n} = \dfrac{20,000}{180,000} = .1111$. The probability of a random sample of

2 people from the city will contain 2 Norwegians is (.1111)(.1111) = .0123

4.14   a. $P(A) = P(10\% \text{ to } 20\% \cup \text{ more than } 20\%) = .33 + .21 = .54$
       b. $P(B) = P(\text{less than } -10\% \cup -10\% \text{ to } 0\%) = .04 + .14 = .18$
       c. A complement is the event that the rate of return is not more than 10%
       d. $P(\overline{A}) = .04 + .14 + .28 = .46$
       e. The intersection between more than 10% and return will be negative is the null or empty set.
       f. $P(A \cap B) = 0$
       g. The union of A and B is the event that are the rates of return of; less than -10%, -10% to 0%, 0% to 10%, 10% to 20% and more than 20%.
       h. $P(A \cup B) = P(A) + P(B) - P(A \cap B) = .54 + .18 - 0 = .72$
       i. A and B are mutually exclusive because their intersection is the null set
       j. A and B are not collectively exhaustive because their union does not equal 1

4.16. A and $\overline{A}$ of exercise 4-1. are not mutually exclusive. Since P(A) = .68 and P($\overline{A}$) = .75, check if P(A $\cup$ $\overline{A}$) = P(A) + P($\overline{A}$) = .68 + .75 = 1.41 > 1. Therefore, if two events are not mutually exclusive, the probability of their union cannot equal the sum of their individual probabilities

4.18. a. $P(X<3) = .29 + .36 + .22 = .87$
       b. $P(X>1) = .22 + .10 + .03 = .35$
       c. By the third probability postulate, the sum of the probabilities of all outcomes in the sample space must sum to one.

4.20. $P(A) = .40$, $P(B) = .45$, $P(A \cup B) = .85$
By the Addition Rule, $P(A \cup B) = P(A) + P(B) - P(A \cap B)$. Therefore, $.85 = .40 + .45 - P(A \cap B)$. $P(A \cap B) = .40 + .45 - .85 = 0$

4.22. $P(A) = .60$, $P(B) = .45$, $P(A \cap B) = .30$
By the Addition Rule, $P(A \cup B) = P(A) + P(B) - P(A \cap B)$. Therefore, $P(A \cup B) = .60 + .45 - .30 = .75$

4.24. $P(A) = .80$, $P(B) = .10$, $P(A \cap B) = .08$
$$P(A \mid B) = \frac{P(A \cap B)}{P(B)} = \frac{.08}{.10} = .80$$
A and B are independent since the $P(A|B)$ of .80 equals the $P(A)$ of .80

4.26. $P(A) = .70$, $P(B) = .80$, $P(A \cap B) = .50$
$$P(A \mid B) = \frac{P(A \cap B)}{P(B)} = \frac{.50}{.80} = .625$$
A and B are not independent since the $P(A|B)$ of .625 does not equal the $P(A)$ of .70

4.28. a. $7! = 5,040$
b. $1 / 5,040 = 0.0001984$

4.30. $P_3^6 = 6!/3! = 120$. Therefore, the probability of selecting, in the correct order the three best performing stocks by chance is $1/120 = .00833$

4.32. $P_3^5 = 5!/2! = 60$. Therefore, the probability of making the correct prediction by chance is $1/60 = .0167$

4.34. $C_2^8 = 8!/2!6! = 28$

4.36. a. $C_2^5 = 5!/2!3! = 10$, $C_4^6 = 6!/4!2! = 15$. Since the selections are independent, then there are $(10)(15) = 150$ possible combinations.
b. P(select a brother who is a craftsman) $= C_1^4 /10 = [4!/1!3!]/10 = 4/10$. Because there are only 5 craftsmen, once a brother has been selected as a craftsman there are only four ways to fill the second craftsman spot on the work crew. P(select a brother who is a laborer) $= C_3^5 /15 = [5!/2!3!]/10 = 10/15$. Multiply the two probabilities together to find their intersection: $(4/10)(10/15) = .2667$

   c. The probability of the complements is 1 minus the probability of the event. Therefore, P(not selecting a brother who is a craftsman = $1 - 4/10 = 6/10$. P(not selecting a brother who is a laborer) $= 1-10/15 = 5/15$. Multiply the two probabilities together to find their intersection: $(6/10)(5/15) = .20$

4.38. Let A – employment concern, B – grade concerns, $A \cap B$ – both. Then
$P(A \cup B) = P(A) + P(B) - P(A \cap B) = .30 + .25 - .20 = .35$

4.40. a. No, the two events are not mutually exclusive because $P(A \cap B) \neq 0$.
    b. No, the two events are not collectively exhaustive because $P(A \cup B) \neq 1$
    c. No, the two events are not statistically independent because $P(A \cap B)$
      $= .15 \neq .6 = P(A)P(B)$

4.42. $P(A \cup B \cup C) = P(A) + P(B) + P(C) - P(A \cap B) - P(A \cap C) - P(B \cap C) = .02 + .01 + .04 - .0002 - .0008 - .000 = .069$

4.44. Let A – watch a TV program oriented to business and financial issues, B – read a publication, then the $P(A) = .18$, $P(B) = .12$ and $P(A \cap B) = .10$
    a.   Find $P(B|A) = P(A \cap B) / P(A) = .10/.18 = .5556$
    b.   Find $P(A|B) = P(A \cap B) / P(B) = .10/.12 = .8333$

4.46. The number of ways of randomly choosing 2 stocks in order out of 4 is:
$P_2^4 = 4!/2! = 12$, the number of ways of randomly choosing 2 bonds in order from 5: $P_2^5 = 5!/3! = 20$. Then the probability of choosing either the stocks in order or the bonds in order is the union between the two events which is equal to the sum of the individual probabilities minus the probability of the intersection. $= 1/12 + 1/20 - 1/240 = .1292$

4.48. Let event A—portfolio management was attended, B – Chartism attended, C – random walk attended, then $P(A) = .4$, $P(B) = .5$, $P(C) = .80$.
    a. Find $P(A \cup B) = .4 + .5 - 0 = .90$
    b. Find $P(A \cup C)$ if A and C are independent events $= .4 + .8 - .32 = .88$
    c. If the $P(C|B) = .75$, then $P(B \cap C) = P(C|B)P(B) = (.75)(.5) = .375$.
      $P(C \cap B) = P(C) + P(B) - P(C \cap B) = .8 + .5 - .375 = .925$

4.50. Let A – work related problem occurs on Monday and B – work related problem occrs in the last hour of the day's shift, then $P(A) = .3$, $P(B) = .2$ and $P(A \cap B) = .04$, $P(A \cap \bar{B}) = P(A) - P(A \cap B) = .3 - .04 = .26$
    a. $P(\bar{B}|A) = P(A \cap \bar{B})/P(A) = .26/.3 = .867$
    b. Check if $P(A \cap B) = P(A)P(B)$ Since $.04 \neq .06$, the two events are not independent events

4.52.   Let A – new customer, B – call to a rival service customer, then $P(A) = .15$, $P(B) = .6$ and $P(B|A) = .8$. $P(A|B) = P(A \cap B / P(B)$ where $P(A \cap B) = P(B|A)P(A)$. $[(.8)(.15)]/.6 = .2$

4.54. P(High Income $\cap$ Never) $= .05$

4.56. P(Middle Income $\cap$ Never) $= .05$

4.58. P(High Income|Never) $= \dfrac{P(High\ Income \cap Never)}{P(Never)} = \dfrac{.05}{.30} = .1667$

4.60. P(Regular|High Income) $= \dfrac{P(Re\ gular \cap High)}{P(High)} = \dfrac{.10}{.25} = .40$

4.62.   Odds $= \dfrac{.5}{1-.5} = 1$ to 1 odds

4.64. P(High scores|>25 hours) $= .40$, P(Low scores|>25) $= .20$, $\dfrac{.4}{.2} = 2.00$.

Studying increases the probability of achieving high scores.

4.66.   Let F – frequent, I – Infrequent, O – Often, S – Sometimes and N- Never.
   a. $P(F \cap O) = .12$
   b. $P(F|N) = P(F \cap N)/P(N) = .19 / .27 = .7037$
   c.   Check if $P(F \cap N) = P(F)P(N)$. Since $.19 \neq .2133$, the two events are not independent
   d. $P(O|I) = P(I \cap O) / P(I) = .07/.21 = .3333$
   e.   Check if $P(I \cap O) = P(I)P(O)$. Since $.07 \neq .0399$, the two events are not independent
   f. $P(F) = .79$
   g. $P(N) = .27$
   h. $P(F \cup N) = P(F) + P(N) - P(F \cap N) = .79 + .27 - .19 = .87$

4.68.   Let A – Regularly read business section, B – Occasionally, C – Never, TS – Traded stock
   a. $P(C) = .25$
   b. $P(TS) = .32$
   c. $P(TS|C) = P(TS \cap C)/P(C) = .04/.25 = .16$
   d. $PC|TS) = P(TS \cap C / P(TS) = .04/.32 = .125$
   e. $P(TS| \overline{A}) = P(TS \cap (B \cup C)/PB \cup C) = (.10 + .04)/(.41 + .25) = .2121$

4.70.   Let Y – problems were worked, N – Problems not worked
   a. $P(Y) = .32$
   b. $P(A) = .25$
   c. $P(A|Y) = P(A \cap Y)/P(Y) = .12/.32 = .375$

d. $P(Y|A) = P(A \cap Y)/P(A) = .12/.25 = .48$

e. $P(C \cup \text{belowC}|Y) = P(C \cup \text{below } C \cap Y)/P(Y) = (.12 + .02)/.32 = .4375$

f. No, since $P(A \cap Y)$ which is .12 $\neq P(A)P(Y)$ which is .08

4.72. Let R – Readers, V – voted in the last election

a. $P(V) = .76$

b. $P(R) = .77$

c. $P(\overline{V} \mid \overline{R}) = P(\overline{V} \cap \overline{R})/P(\overline{R}) = .1/.23 = .4348$

4.74. $P(G|H) = .1, P(G|L) = .8, P(G|S) = .5, P(H) = .25, P(L) = .15, P(S) = .6$

a. $P(G \cap H) = P(G|H)P(H) = (.1)(.25) = .025$

b. $P(G) = P(G \cap H) + P(G \cap L) + P(G \cap S) = .025 + (.8)(.15) + (.5)(.6)$
   $= .445$

c. $P(L|G) = P(G \cap L) / P(G) = (.8)(.15)/.445 = .2697$

4.76. $P(10\%|T) = .7, P(10\%|M) = .5, P(10\%|B) = .2$

a. $P(10\%) = P(10\% \cap T) + P(10\% \cap M) + P(10\% \cap B) = (.7)(.25) +$
   $(.5)(.5) + (.2)(.25) = .475$

b. $P(T|10\%) = P(10\% \cap T)/P(10\%) = (.7)(.25)/.475 = .3684$

c. $P(\overline{T} \mid \overline{10\%}) = P(\overline{10\%} \cap \overline{T})/P(\overline{10\%}) = P(\overline{10\% \cup T}) / P(\overline{10\%}) =$
   $[1 - P(10\% \cup T)]/P(\overline{10\%}) = [1 - (.475 + .25 - (.7)(.25))] / .525 =$
   $.8571$

4.78. Let M – faulty machine, I – impurity

$P(M) = .4, P(I|M) = .1, P(I) = P(I \cap M) + P(I \cap \overline{M}) = (.4)(.1) + 0 = .04$

$P(M|\overline{I}) = P(\overline{I} \cap M) / P(\overline{I}) = [P(M) - P(I \overline{I} M)] / P(\overline{I}) = (.4 - .04)/.96 = .375$

4.80. $P(A_1) = .4, P(B_1|A_1) = .6, P(B_1|A_2) = .7$

Complements: $P(A_2) = .6, P(B_2|A_1) = .4, P(B_2|A_2) = .3$

$$P(A_1 \mid B_1) = \frac{P(B_1 \mid A_1)P(A_1)}{P(B_1 \mid A_1)P(A_1) + P(B_1 \mid A_2)P(A_2)} = \frac{.6(.4)}{.6(.4) + .7(.6)} = .3636$$

4.82. $P(A_1) = .5, P(B_1|A_1) = .4, P(B_1|A_2) = .7$

Complements: $P(A_2) = .5, P(B_2|A_1) = .6, P(B_2|A_2) = .3$

$$P(A_1 \mid B_2) = \frac{P(B_2 \mid A_1)P(A_1)}{P(B_2 \mid A_1)P(A_1) + P(B_2 \mid A_2)P(A_2)} = \frac{.6(.5)}{.6(.5) + .3(.5)} = .6667$$

4.84. $P(A_1) = .6, P(B_1|A_1)=.6, P(B_1|A_2) = .4$
Complements: $P(A_2) = .4, P(B_2|A_1)=.4, P(B_2|A_2) = .6$

$$P(A_1 | B_1) = \frac{P(B_1 | A_1)P(A_1)}{P(B_1 | A_1)P(A_1) + P(B_1 | A_2)P(A_2)} = \frac{.6(.6)}{.6(.6) + .4(.4)} = .6923$$

4.86. E_1 = Stock performs much better than the market average
E_2 = Stock performs same as the market average
E_3 = Stock performs worse than the market average
A = Stock is rated a 'Buy'
Given that $P(E_1) = .25, P(E_2) = .5, P(E_3) = .25, P(A| E_1) = .4, P(A| E_2) =$
$.2, P(A| E_3) = .1$

Then, $P(E_1 \cap A) = P(A| E_1)P(E_1) = (.4)(.25) = .10$
$\qquad P(E_2 \cap A) = P(A| E_2)P(E_2) = (.2)(.5) = .10$
$\qquad P(E_3 \cap A) = P(A| E_3)P(E_3) = (.1)(.25) = .025$

$$P(E_1 | A) = \frac{P(A | E_1)P(E_1)}{P(A | E_1)P(E_1) + P(A | E_2)P(E_2) + P(A | E_3)P(E_3)}$$

$$= \frac{(.40)(.25)}{(.4)(.25) + (.2)(.5) + (.1)(.25)} = .444$$

4.88. a. True by definition

b. False, only the sum of the probabilities of mutually exclusive events which are collectively exhaustive sum to 1.

c. True, $C_x^n = \dfrac{n!}{x!(n-x)!} = C_{n-x}^n = \dfrac{n!}{(n-x)!(n-(n-x))!} = \dfrac{n!}{(n-x)!x!}$

d. True, $P(A | B) = \dfrac{P(A \cap B)}{P(B)} = \dfrac{P(A \cap B)}{P(A)} = P(B | A)$ for $P(A) = P(B)$

e. True, $P(A) = 1 - P(A) \rightarrow 2P(A) = 1 \rightarrow P(A) = .5$

f. True, $P(\overline{A} \cap \overline{B}) = P(\overline{A}) - P(\overline{A} \cap B)$
$\qquad = 1 - P(A) - [P(B) - P(A \cap B)]$
$\qquad = 1 - P(A) - P(B) + P(A \cap B)$
$\qquad = 1 - P(A) - P(B) + P(A)P(B)$
$\qquad = [1 - P(A)][1 - P(B)] = P(\overline{A})P(\overline{B})$

g. False, $P(\overline{A} \cap \overline{B}) = P(\overline{A \cup B})$

$= 1 - P(A \cup B)$

$= 1 - P(A) - P(B)$ $[P(A \cap B) = 0]$

$= P(\overline{A}) + P(\overline{B}) - 1$

$= 0$ which holds if and only if $P(\overline{A}) + P(\overline{B}) = 1$

4.90. Bayes' theorem is a summary of the relationship between a specific event that has occurred and the effect on a subsequent event. The occurrence of the specific event is the prior information or 'prior probability' that is known. This prior knowledge can be analyzed to understand the effect on the probability of a subsequent event. The subsequent event is the 'posterior probability'.

4.92. By definition, *Joint Probability* is the probability that two events will occur together, e.g., P(female and Liberal Arts major)
Marginal probability is defined as the probability of an individual event, e.g., P(female)
Conditional probability is the probability of occurrence of one event given that another event has occurred, e.g., P(female given Liberal Arts major)

4.94. $P(A \cup B) = P(A) + P(B) - P(A \cap B) = P(A) + P(B) - [P(A|B)P(B)]$
$= P(A) + P(B)[1 - P(A|B)]$

4.96. Solve the following for P(thick) and P(thin):
$.8 = P(\text{thick}) + P(\text{thin})[1 - P(\text{thick/thin})] = P(\text{thick}) + .6\, P(\text{thin})$
$.8 = P(\text{thin}) + P(\text{thick})[1 - P(\text{thin/thick})] = P(\text{thin}) + .4\, P(\text{thick})$
Solving, $P(\text{thin}) = .6316$

a. $P(\text{thick}) = .8 - .6\, P(\text{thin}) = .8 - (.6)(.6316) = .4211$
b. $P(\text{thin}) = .6316$
c. $P(\text{thick} \cap \text{thin}) = P(\text{thick}|\text{thin})\, P(\text{thin}) = (.4)(.6316) = .2526$

4.98. Let HM – customer orders a hot meal, S – customer is a student. $P(\text{HM}) = .35$, $P(S) = .5$, $P(\text{HM}|S) = .25$
a. $P(\text{HM} \cap S) = P(\text{HM}|S)P(S) = (.25)(.5) = .125$
b. $P(S|\text{HM}) = P(\text{HM} \cap S)/P(\text{HM}) = .125/.35 = .3571$
c. $P(\overline{\text{HM} \cup S}) = 1 - P(\text{HM} \cap S) = 1 - .125 = .875$
d. No, since $P(\text{HM} \cap S)$ which is $.125 \neq .175$ which is $P(\text{HM})P(S)$
e. No, their intersection is not zero, hence the two events cannot be mutually exclusive. $P(\text{HM} \cap S) = .125 \neq 0$
f. No, the probability of their union does not equal 1. $P(\text{HM} \cup S) = P(\text{HM}) + P(S) - P(\text{HM} \cap S) = .35 + .5 - .125 = .725$ which is less than 1.

4.100. Let M—men, F – women, G – graduate training, UG—undergraduate training, HS – High School training. $P(M) = .8$, $P(F) = .2$, $P(HS|M) = .6$, $P(UG|M) = .3$, $P(G|M) = .1$. $P(G|F) = .15$, $P(UG|F) = .4$, $P(HS|F) = .45$

   a. $P(M \cap HS) = P(HS|M)P(M) = (.6)(.8) = .48$

   b. $P(G) = P(M \cap G) + P(F \cap G) = P(G|M)P(M) + P(G|F)P(F) = (.10)(.8) + (.15)(.2) = .11$

   c. $P(M|G) = P(M \cap G)/P(G) = .08/.11 = .7273$

   d. No, check if $P(M \cap G)$ which is $.8 \neq .088$ which is $P(M)P(G)$

   e. $P(F|\overline{G}) = P(F \cap \overline{G})/P(\overline{G}) = [P(F) - P(F \cap G)]/P(\overline{G}) = (.2 - (.15)(.2))/.89 = .191$

4.102. a. $C_{12}^{16} = 16!/ 4!12! = 1{,}820$

   b. $P(\text{number of men} \geq 7) = [C_5^8 + C_4^8 + C_2^8 + 8]/1820 = 162/1820 = .089$

4.104. Let T – treatment , C – patient was cured. $P(C) = .5$, $P(C|T) = .75$

   a. $P(C \cap T) = P(C|T)P(T) = (.75)(.1) = .075$

   b. $P(T|C) = P(C \cap T)/P(C) = .075/.525 = .1429$

   c. The probability will be $1 / [C_{10}^{100} = 1/ 100!/10!90! = 10!90!/100!$

4.106. $P(D|P) = P(P \cap D)/P(P) = P(P|D)P(D)/[P(P|D)P(D) + P(P|\overline{D})P(\overline{D})] = (.8)(.08)/[(.8)(.08) + (.2)(.92)] = .2581$

4.108. $P(Af|Am) = P(Af \cap Am)/P(Am) = P(Am|Af)P(Af)/[P(Am|Af)P(Af) + P(Am|\overline{A}f)P(\overline{A}f) = (.7)(.2)/[(.7)(.2) + (.1)(.8)] = .6364$

4.110. a. $P(G \cap F) = P(G|F)P(F) = (.62)(.73) = .4526$

   b. $P(G) = P(G|F)P(F) + P(G|JC)P(JC) = .4526 + (.78)(.27) = .6632$

   c. $P(G \cup F) = P(G) + P(F) - P(G \cap F) = .6632 + .73 - .4526 = .9406$

   d. No, since $P(G \cap JC)$ which is $(.78)(.27) = .2106 \neq .1791$ which is $P(G)P(JC) = (.6632)(.27)$

4.112. Let W – customer orders Wine, WD – customer is Well Dressed, MD – customer is Moderately Dressed, PD – customer is Poorly Dressed

   a. $P(W) = P(W|WD)P(WD) + P(W|MD)P(MD) + P(W|PD)P(PD) = (.7)(.5) + (.5)(.4) + (.3)(.1) = .58$

   b. $P(WD|W) = P(WD \cap W)/P(W) = .35/.58 = .6034$

   c. $P(\overline{WD}|W) = P(MD \cup PD|W) = [P(MD \cap W) + P(PD \cap W)]/P(W) = (.2 + .03)/.58 = .3966$

4.114. The sample space is the number of combinations from $C_5^{16} = 16!/ 5!11! = 4{,}368$. To obtain all five F's for women:

$[C_5^8 = 8!/ 5!3!][C_0^8 = 8!/ 0!8!] = [56][1] = 56$. Probability $= 56/4368 = .0128$.

4.116. Let F–failure (from any source), D–disk error. $P(F) =$ (.5)(.6)+(.3)(.7)+(.2)(.4)=.59

$$P(D|F) = \frac{P(D \cap F)}{P(F)} = \frac{(.5)(.6)}{(.5)(.6)+(.3)(.7)+(.2)(.4)} = \frac{.3}{.59} = .5085$$

Chapter 5:

Discrete Random Variables and Probability Distributions

5.2. The number of defective parts produced in daily production is a discrete random variable that can take on no more than a countable number of values.

5.4. Discrete random variable – number of plays is countable

5.6. Total sales, advertising expenditures, sales of competitors

5.8. Discrete – the number of purchases is a countable number of values

5.10 Probability distribution of number of heads in one toss

X-number of heads	P(x)
0	.5
1	.5

5.12 Various answers

X –# of times missing class	P(x)	F(x)
0	.65	.65
1	.15	.80
2	.10	.90
3	.09	.99
4	.01	1.00

5.14   a. Cumulative probability function:

X	0	1	2	3	4	5	6	7	8	9
P(x)	.10	.08	.07	.15	.12	.08	.10	.12	.08	.10
F(x)	.10	.18	.25	.40	.52	.60	.70	.82	.90	1.00

b. $P(x \geq 5) = .08 + .10 + .12 + .08 + .10 = .48$
c. $P(3 \leq x \leq 7) = .15 + .12 + .08 + .10 + .12 = .57$

5.16   a. Probability distribution function

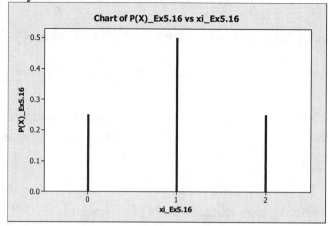

b. Cumulative probability function

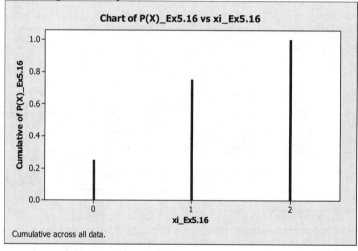

c. Find the mean

X	P(x)	XP(x)
0	.25	0
1	.50	.50
2	.25	.50
		1.00

$$\mu_x = E(X) = \sum xP(x) = 1.00$$

d. Find the variance of X

X	P(x)	XP(x)	(x-mu)^2	(x-mu)^2P(x)
0	.25	0	1.0	.25
1	.50	.50	0	0
2	.25	.50	1	.25
		1.00		.50

$$\sigma^2{}_x = E[(X - \mu_x)^2] = \sum (x - \mu_x)^2 P(x) = .50$$

5.18   a. Probability function:

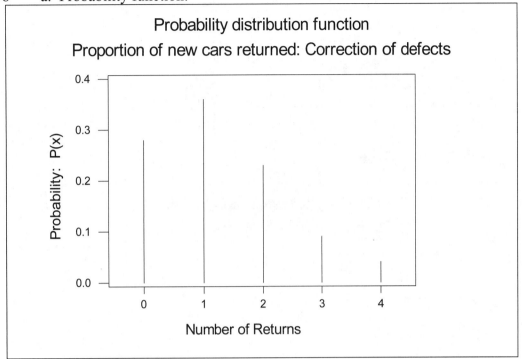

b. Cumulative probability function:

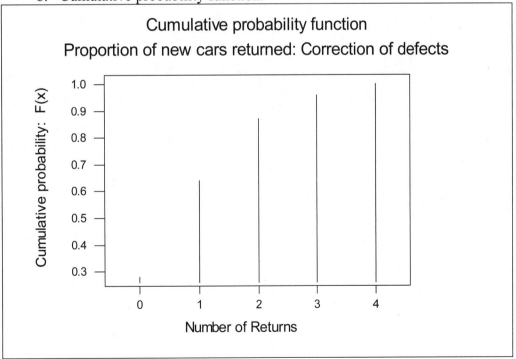

c. $\mu = 0 + .36 + 2(.23) + 3(.09) + 4(.04) = 1.25$ defects

d. $\sigma^2 = \sum x^2 Px(x) - \mu^2{}_x = 1.1675$

Excel output:

Returns	P(x)	F(x)	Mean	Variance
0	0.28	0.28	0	0.4375
1	0.36	0.64	0.36	0.0225
2	0.23	0.87	0.46	0.129375
3	0.09	0.96	0.27	0.275625
4	0.04	1.00	0.16	0.3025
	1.00		1.25	1.1675
			S.D.	1.080509

5.20   a. Probability function

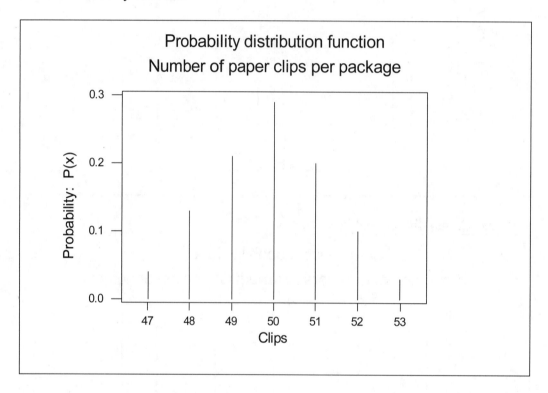

b. Cumulative probability function

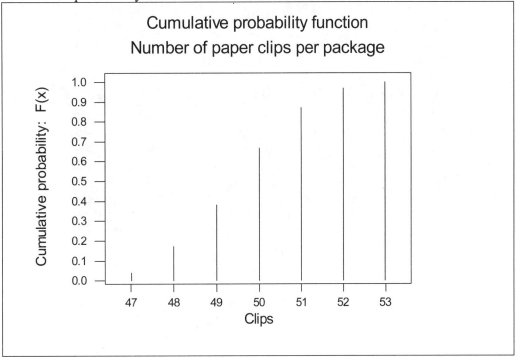

c. $P(49 \leq x \leq 51) = .70$
d. $1 - [P(x < 50)]^2 = 1 - .1444 = .8556$
e. $\mu_x = 47(.04) + 48(.13) + 49(.21) + 50(.29) + 51(.20) + 52(.10) + 53(.03) = 49.9$ clips

   $\sigma^2_x = 1.95$ $\sigma_x = 1.3964$ clips

Excel output:

	M	N	O	P	Q
1	Clips	P(x)	F(x)	Mean	Variance
2	47	0.04	0.04	1.88	0.3364
3	48	0.13	0.17	6.24	0.4693
4	49	0.21	0.38	10.29	0.1701
5	50	0.29	0.67	14.5	0.0029
6	51	0.20	0.87	10.2	0.242
7	52	0.10	0.97	5.2	0.441
8	53	0.03	1.00	1.59	0.2883
9		1.00		49.9	1.95
10					

f. Mean and standard deviation of profit per package:

	S	T	U	V	W
1	ProfitPerPackage	P(x)	F(x)	Mean	Variance
2	0.4	0.04	0.04	0.016	0.00013456
3	0.38	0.13	0.17	0.0494	0.00018772
4	0.36	0.21	0.38	0.0756	0.00006804
5	0.34	0.29	0.67	0.0986	0.00000116
6	0.32	0.20	0.87	0.064	0.00009680
7	0.3	0.10	0.97	0.03	0.00017640
8	0.28	0.03	1.00	0.0084	0.00011532
9		1.00		0.342	0.00078000
10					

$\pi = 1.5 - (.16 + .02X)$

$\mu = E(\pi) = 1.5 - (.16 + (.02)(49.9)) = \$.342$

$\sigma_{\pi} = |.02|(1.3964) = \$.0279$

5.22   a. Probability function

X	0	1	2
P(x)	0.81	0.18	.01

$P_x(0) = (.90)(.90) = .81$

$P_x(1) = (.90)(.10) + (.10)(.90) = .18$

$P_x(2) = (.10)(.10) = .01$

b. $P(Y = 0) = 18/20 \times 17/19 = 153/190$

$P(Y=1) = (2/20 \times 18/19) + (18/20 \times 2/19) = 36/190$

$P(Y=2) = 2/20 \times 1/19 = 1/190$

The answer in part b. is different from part a. because in part b. the probability of picking a defective part on the second draw depends upon the result of the first draw.

c. $\mu = 0(.81) + .18 + 2(.01) = 0.2$ defects

$\sigma^2_x = .22 - (.20)^2 = .18$

d. $\mu = 0(153/190) + (36/190) + 2(1/190) = 38/190 = 0.2$ defects

$\sigma^2_y = 40/190 - (.20)^2 = .1705$

Microsoft Excel - Book1

File Edit View Insert Format Tools OIC Data Window Help

Arial

AJ6

	AE	AF	AG	AH	AI
1	Defects	P(x)	F(x)	Mean	Variance
2	0	0.81	0.81	0	0.03240000
3	1	0.18	0.99	0.18	0.11520000
4	2	0.01	1.00	0.02	0.03240000
5		1.00		0.2	0.18000000
6					

5.24   "One and one" $E(X) = 1(.75)(.25) + 2(.75)^2 = 1.3125$
"Two-shot foul" $E(X) = 1((.75)(.25) + (.25)(.75)) + 2(.75)^2 = 1.50$
The "two-shot foul" has a higher expected value

5.26 $\mu = 3.29$ $\sigma^2 = 1.3259$ $\sigma = 1.1515$

Rating	P(x)	F(x)	Mean	Variance
1	0.07	0.07	0.07	0.367087
2	0.19	0.26	0.38	0.316179
3	0.28	0.54	0.84	0.023548
4	0.30	0.84	1.20	0.15123
5	0.16	1.00	0.80	0.467856
	1.00		3.29	1.3259
			S.D.	1.151477

5.28   a. $\mu = 1.82$ breakdowns $\sigma^2 = 1.0276$ $\sigma = 1.0137$ breakdowns

Breakdowns	P(x)	F(x)	Mean	Variance		Cost	P(x)	F(x)	Mean	Variance
0	0.1	0.10	0	0.33124		0	0.1	0.10	0	745290
1	0.26	0.36	0.26	0.174824		1500	0.26	0.36	390	393354
2	0.42	0.78	0.84	0.013608		3000	0.42	0.78	1260	30618
3	0.16	0.94	0.48	0.222784		4500	0.16	0.94	720	501264
4	0.06	1.00	0.24	0.285144		6000	0.06	1.00	360	641574
	1.00		1.82	1.0276			1.00		2730	2312100
			S.D.	1.013706					S.D.	1520.559

b. Cost: $C = 1500X$
$E(C) = 1500(1.82) = \mu = \$2,730$
$\sigma = |1500|(1.0137) = \$1,520.559$

5.30   Mean and variance of a Bernoulli random variable with P=.5
$\mu_x = E(X) = \sum xP(x) = (0)(1-P) + (1)P = P = .5$
$\sigma^2_x = P(1-P) = .5(1-.5) = .25$

5.32   Probability of a binomial random variable with P=.3 and n = 14, x=7 and x less than 6

Cumulative Distribution Function
```
Binomial with n = 14 and p = 0.3
x   P( X <= x )
0      0.006782
1      0.047476
2      0.160836
3      0.355167
4      0.584201
5      0.780516
6      0.906718
7      0.968531
8      0.991711
```
$P(x=7) = .968531 - .906718 = .06181$
$P(x<6) = .7805$

5.34   Probability of a binomial random variable with P=.7 and n=18, x=12 and x less than 6

Cumulative Distribution Function
```
Binomial with n = 18 and p = 0.7
 x   P( X <= x )
 0      0.000000
 1      0.000000
 2      0.000000
 3      0.000004
 4      0.000039
 5      0.000269
 6      0.001430
 7      0.006073
 8      0.020968
 9      0.059586
10      0.140683
11      0.278304
12      0.465620
13      0.667345
```
$P(x=12) = .465620 - .278304 = .1873$
$P(x<6) = .000269$

5.36

Cumulative Distribution Function
```
Binomial with n = 5 and p = 0.250000
      x     P( X <= x )
     0.00      0.2373
     1.00      0.6328
     2.00      0.8965
     3.00      0.9844
     4.00      0.9990
     5.00      1.0000
```

a. $P(x \geq 1) = 1 - Px(0) = 1 - .2373 = .7627$

b. $P(x \geq 3) = 1 - P(x \leq 2) = 1 - .8965 = .1035$

5.38

Cumulative Distribution Function
```
Binomial with n = 7 and p = 0.500000
        x     P( X <= x )
      0.00         0.0078
      1.00         0.0625
      2.00         0.2266
      3.00         0.5000
      4.00         0.7734
      5.00         0.9375
      6.00         0.9922
      7.00         1.0000
```

$$P(x \geq 4) = 1 - P(x \leq 3) = 1 - .5 = .5$$

5.40

Cumulative Distribution Function
```
Binomial with n = 5 and p = 0.400000
        x     P( X <= x )
      0.00         0.0778
      1.00         0.3370
      2.00         0.6826
      3.00         0.9130
      4.00         0.9898
      5.00         1.0000
```

a. $P(x = 5) = P(x \leq 5) - Px \leq 4) = 1.00 - .9898 = .0102$

b. $P(x \geq 3) = P(x \leq 5) - P(x \leq 2) = 1.000 - .6826 = .3174$

Cumulative Distribution Function
```
Binomial with n = 4 and p = 0.400000
        x     P( X <= x )
      0.00         0.1296
      1.00         0.4752
      2.00         0.8208
      3.00         0.9744
      4.00         1.0000
```

c. $P(x \geq 2) = .5248$

d. $E(X) = np = 5(.4) = 2$ games. Unless of course you are a Cubs fan and then you would hope the Cubs would win all of the games but you would expect them to win none of the games.

e. $E(X) = \mu = 1 + np = 1 + 4(.4) = 2.6$ games

5.42

Cumulative Distribution Function
```
Binomial with n = 4 and p = 0.400000
        x     P( X <= x )
      0.00         0.1296
      1.00         0.4752
      2.00         0.8208
      3.00         0.9744
      4.00         1.0000
```

a. $P(x \geq 2) = P(X \leq 4) - P(X \leq 1) = 1.000 - .4752 = .5248$

b. $E(X) = np = 4(.4) = 1.6 \quad \sigma_x = \sqrt{4(.4)(.6)} = .9798$

5.44   a. $E(X) = 2000(.032) = 64$

$$\sigma_x = \sqrt{2000(.032)(.968)} = 7.871$$

b. Let $Z = 10X$

$E(Z) = 10(64) = \$640$

$\sigma_z = |10|(7.871) = \$78.71$

5.46   a. $E(X) = \mu_x = np = 620(.78) = 483.6, \quad \sigma_x = \sqrt{620(.78)(.22)} = 10.3146$

b. Let $Z = 2X$

$E(Z) = 2(483.6) = \$967.20$

$\sigma_z = |2|(10.314) = \$20.6292$

5.48   The acceptance rules have the following probabilities:

(i)   Rule 1: $P(X=0) = (.8)^{10} = .1074$

(ii)   Rule 2: $P(X \le 1) = (.8)^{20} + 20(.2)(.8)^{19} = .0692$

Therefore, the acceptance rule with the smaller probability of accepting a shipment containing 20% defectives will be the second acceptance rule

5.50

Probability Density Function
Hypergeometric with N = 50, M = 25, and n = 12

```
x    P( X = x )
0      0.000043
1      0.000918
2      0.008078
3      0.038706
4      0.112702
5      0.210376
```
$P(x=5) = .210376$

5.52

Probability Density Function
Hypergeometric with N = 80, M = 42, and n = 20

```
x    P( X = x )
0      0.000000
1      0.000000
2      0.000008
3      0.000093
4      0.000704
5      0.003723
6      0.014348
7      0.041322
8      0.090392
9      0.151769
```
$P(x=9) = .151769$

5.54

Probability Density Function
Hypergeometric with N = 400, M = 200, and n = 15

```
x  P( X = x )
0   0.000023
1   0.000375
2   0.002792
3   0.012743
4   0.039848
5   0.090434
6   0.153879
7   0.199906
8   0.199906
```

$P(x=8) = .1999$

5.56

Cumulative Distribution Function
Hypergeometric with N = 16, X = 8, and n = 8

```
     x     P( X <= x )
   1.00      0.0051
   2.00      0.0660
   3.00      0.3096
   4.00      0.6904
   5.00      0.9340
   6.00      0.9949
   7.00      0.9999
```

$P(x = 4) = P(x \leq 4) - P(x \leq 3) = .6904 - .3096 = .3808$

5.58

Cumulative Distribution Function
Hypergeometric with N = 10, X = 5, and n = 6

```
     x     P( X <= x )
   0.00      0.0000
   1.00      0.0238
   2.00      0.2619
   3.00      0.7381
   4.00      0.9762
   5.00      1.0000
```

$P(x \leq 2) = .2619$

5.60

Probability Density Function
Poisson with mean = 2.5

```
x  P( X = x )
0   0.082085
1   0.205212
2   0.256516
3   0.213763
4   0.133602
```

$P(x=4) = .1336$

5.62

Cumulative Distribution Function

Poisson with mean = 3.5

x	P(X <= x)
0	0.030197
1	0.135888
2	0.320847
3	0.536633
4	0.725445
5	0.857614
6	0.934712

$P(x<6) = .857614$

5.64

Cumulative Distribution Function

Poisson with mu = 3.00000

x	P(X <= x)
0.00	0.0498
1.00	0.1991
2.00	0.4232
3.00	0.6472
4.00	0.8153
5.00	0.9161
6.00	0.9665
7.00	0.9881
8.00	0.9962
9.00	0.9989
10.00	0.9997

$P(x \le 2) = .4232$

5.66

Cumulative Distribution Function

Poisson with mu = 4.20000

x	P(X <= x)
0.00	0.0150
1.00	0.0780
2.00	0.2102
3.00	0.3954
4.00	0.5898
5.00	0.7531
6.00	0.8675
7.00	0.9361
8.00	0.9721
9.00	0.9889
10.00	0.9959

$P(x \ge 3) = 1 - P(x \le 2) = 1 - .2102 = .7898$

5.68

Cumulative Distribution Function
```
Poisson with mu = 5.50000
         x       P( X <= x )
      0.00        0.0041
      1.00        0.0266
      2.00        0.0884
      3.00        0.2017
      4.00        0.3575
      5.00        0.5289
      6.00        0.6860
      7.00        0.8095
      8.00        0.8944
      9.00        0.9462
     10.00        0.9747
```
$P(x \le 2) = .0884$

5.70

Cumulative Distribution Function
```
Poisson with mu = 6.00000
         x       P( X <= x )
      0.00        0.0025
      1.00        0.0174
      2.00        0.0620
      3.00        0.1512
      4.00        0.2851
      5.00        0.4457
      6.00        0.6063
      7.00        0.7440
      8.00        0.8472
      9.00        0.9161
     10.00        0.9574
```
$P(x \ge 3) = 1 - P(x \le 2) = 1 - .0620 = .9380$

5.72   Two models are possible – the poisson distribution is appropriate when the warehouse is serviced by many thousands of independent truckers where the mean number of 'successes' is relatively small. However, under the assumption of a small fleet of 10 trucks with a probability of any truck arriving during a given hour is .1, then the binomial distribution is the more appropriate model. Both models yield similar, although not identical, probabilities.

Cumulative Distribution Function
```
Poisson with mean = 1

    x   P( X <= x )
    0     0.36788
    1     0.73576
    2     0.91970
    3     0.98101
    4     0.99634
    5     0.99941
    6     0.99992
    7     0.99999
    8     1.00000
    9     1.00000
   10     1.00000
```

Cumulative Distribution Function
```
Binomial with n = 10 and p = 0.1

   x  P( X <= x )
   0     0.34868
   1     0.73610
   2     0.92981
   3     0.98720
   4     0.99837
   5     0.99985
   6     0.99999
   7     1.00000
   8     1.00000
   9     1.00000
  10     1.00000
```

5.74   a. Compute marginal probability distributions for X and Y

Exercise_5.74		X_5.74						
Y_5.74		1	2	P(y)	Mean of Y	Var of Y	StDev of Y
	0	0.2	0.25	0.45	0	0.136125	
	1	0.3	0.25	0.55	0.55	0.111375	
P(x)		0.5	0.5	1	0.55	0.2475	0.497494
Mean of X		0.5	1	1.5			
Var of X		0.125	0.125	0.25			
StDev of X				0.5			
xyP(x)		0.3	0.5	0.8			
Cov(x,y) =							
sum xyP(x)-muxmuy		-0.025					

b. Compute the covariance and correlation for X and Y

$$Cov(X,Y) = \sum_x \sum_y xyP(x,y) - \mu_x\mu_y = .80 - (1.5)(.55) = -.025$$

$$\rho = Corr(X,Y) = \frac{Cov(X,Y)}{\sigma_x\sigma_y} = -.025/(.5)(.497494) = -.1005$$

5.76   a. Compute marginal probability distributions for X and Y

Exercise_5.76		X_5.76					
Y_5.76		1	2	P(y)	Mean of Y	Var of Y	StDev of Y
	0	0.3	0.2	0.5	0	0.125	
	1	0.25	0.25	0.5	0.5	0.125	
P(x)		0.55	0.45	1	0.5	0.25	0.5
Mean of X		0.55	0.9	1.45			
Var of X		0.55	1.8	2.35			
StDev of X				1.532971			
xyP(x)		0.25	0.5	0.75			
Cov(x,y) =							
sum xyP(x)-muxmuy		0.025					

b. Compute the covariance and correlation for X and Y

$$Cov(X,Y) = \sum_x \sum_y xyP(x,y) - \mu_x\mu_y = .75 - (1.45)(.5) = 0.025$$

$$\rho = Corr(X,Y) = \frac{Cov(X,Y)}{\sigma_x\sigma_y} = 0.025/(1.53297)(.5) = 0.0326$$

c. Compute the mean and variance for the linear function $W = 2X + Y$

$$\mu_W = a\mu_x + b\mu_y = (2)1.45 + (1).5 = 3.4$$

$$\sigma^2_W = a^2\sigma^2_X + b^2\sigma^2_Y + 2abCov(X,Y) = 2^2(2.35) + 1^2(.25) + 2(2)(1)(0.025) = 9.75$$

5.78   a. Compute the marginal probability distributions for X and Y

		1	2	P(y)	Mean of Y	Var of Y	StDev of Y
	0	0.25	0.25	0.5	0	0.125	
	1	0.25	0.25	0.5	0.5	0.125	
P(x)		0.5	0.5	1	0.5	0.25	0.5

Mean of X	0.5	1	1.5
Var of X	0.125	0.125	0.25
StDev of X			0.5

xyP(x)	0.25	0.5	0.75
Cov(x,y) =			
sum xyP(x)-muxmuy	0		

b. Compute the covariance and correlation for X and Y

$$Cov(X,Y) = \sum_x \sum_y xyP(x,y) - \mu_x\mu_y = .75 - (1.5)(.5) = 0.0$$

$$\rho = Corr(X,Y) = \frac{Cov(X,Y)}{\sigma_x\sigma_y} = 0.0/(.5)(.5) = 0.0$$

Note that when covariance between X and Y is equal to zero, it follows that the correlation between X and Y is also zero.

c. Compute the mean and variance for the linear function $W = X - Y$

$$\mu_W = a\mu_x + b\mu_y = (1)1.5 + (-1).5 = 1.0$$

$$\sigma^2_W = a^2\sigma^2_X + b^2\sigma^2_Y + 2abCov(X,Y) = 1^2(.25) + 1^2(.25) + 2(1)(-1)(0.0) = .5$$

5.80   a. Compute the marginal probability distributions for X and Y.

Exercise_5.80		X_5.80					
Y_5.80		1	2	P(y)	Mean of Y	Var of Y	StDev of Y
	0	0	0.6	0.6	0	0.096	
	1	0.4	0	0.4	0.4	0.144	
P(x)		0.4	0.6	1	0.4	0.24	0.489898
Mean of X		0.4	1.2	1.6			
Var of X		0.144	0.096	0.24			
StDev of X			0.489898				
xyP(x)		0.4	0	0.4			
Cov(x,y) =							
sum xyP(x)-muxmuy		-0.24					

b. Compute the covariance and correlation for X and Y

$$Cov(X,Y) = \sum_x \sum_y xyP(x,y) - \mu_x\mu_y = .40 - (1.6)(.4) = -0.24$$

$$\rho = Corr(X,Y) = \frac{Cov(X,Y)}{\sigma_x\sigma_y} = -0.24/(.489898)(.489898) = -1.00$$

c. Compute the mean and variance for the linear function W = 2X - 4Y

$$\mu_W = a\mu_x + b\mu_y = (2)1.6 + (-4).4 = 1.6$$

$$\sigma^2_W = a^2\sigma^2_X + b^2\sigma^2_Y + 2abCov(X,Y) = 2^2(.24) + (-4)^2(.24) + 2(2)(-4)(-.24) = 8.64$$

5.82   a. Px(0) = .07 + .07 + .06 + .02 = .22
           Px(1) = .09 + .06 + .07 + .04 = .26
           Px(2) = .06 + .07 + .14 + .16 = .43
           Px(3) = .01 + .01 + .03 + .04 = .09
           μ_x = 0 + .26 + 2(.43) + 3(.09) = 1.39
        b. Py(0) = .07 + .09 + .06 + .01 = .23
           Py(1) = .07 + .06 + .07 + .01 = .21
           Py(2) = .06 + .07 + .14 + .03 = .30
           Py(3) = .02 + .04 + .16 + .40 = .26
           μ_y = 0 + .21 + 2(.3) + 3(.26) = 1.59
        c. $P_{Y|X}(0|3)$ = .01/.09 = .1111
           $P_{Y|X}(1|3)$ = .01/.09 = .1111
           $P_{Y|X}(2|3)$ = .03/.09 = .3333
           $P_{Y|X}(3|3)$ = .04/.09 = .4444

d. $Cov(X,Y) = E(XY) - \mu_x\mu_y$

$E(XY) = 0 + 1(1)(.06) + 1(2)(.07) + 1(3)(.04) + 2(1)(.07) + 2(2)(.14)$
$\qquad + 2(3)(.16) + 3(1)(.01) + 3(2)(.03) + 3(3)(.04) = 2.55$
$Cov(X,Y) = 2.55 - (1.39)(1.59) = .3399$

e. No, because $Cov(X,Y) \neq 0$

5.84   a. Py(0) = .08 + .03 + .01 = .12
$\qquad$ Py(1) = .13 + .08 + .03 = .24
$\qquad$ Py(2) = .09 + .08 + .06 = .23
$\qquad$ Py(3) = .06 + .09 + .08 = .23
$\qquad$ Py(4) = .03 + .07 + .08 = .18

b. $P_{Y|X}(y|3)$ = 1/26; 3/26; 6/26; 8/26; 8/26

c. No, because Px,y(3,4) = .08 $\neq$ .0468 = Px(3)Py(4)

5.86   a.

Y/X	0	1	Total
0	.704	.168	.872
1	.096	.032	.128
Total	.80	.20	1.00

b. $P_{Y|X}(y|0)$ = .88; .12

c. Px(0) = .80
$\qquad$ Px(1) = .20
$\qquad$ Py(0) = .872
$\qquad$ Py(1) = .128

d. E(XY) = .032;
$\qquad \mu_x = 0 + 1(.20) = .20$, $\quad \mu_y = 0 + 1(.128) = .128$

$Cov(X,Y) = .032 - (.20)(.128) = .0064$

The covariance indicates that there is a positive association between X and Y, professors are more likely to be away from the office on Friday than during the other days.

5.88. Number of total complaints (food complaints + service complaints) has a mean of (1.36 + 1.64) = 3.00. If the two types of complaints are independent, then the variance of total complaints is equal to the sum of the variance of the two types of complaints because the covariance would be zero. (.8104 + .7904) = 1.6008. The standard deviation will be the square root of the variance = 1.26523.

If the number of food and service complaints are not independent of each other, then the covariance would no longer be zero. The mean would remain the same; however, the standard deviation would change. The variance of the sum of the two types of complaints becomes the variance of one plus the variance of the other plus two times the covariance.

5.90 a. No, not necessarily. There is a probability distribution associated with the rates
        of return in the mutual fund and not all rates of return will equal the expected
        value.
     b. Which fund to invest in will depend not only on the expected value of the return
        but also on the riskiness of each fund and how risk averse the client is.

5.92

Cars	P(x)	F(x)	Mean	Variance
0	0.1	0.10	0	0.48841
1	0.2	0.30	0.2	0.29282
2	0.35	0.65	0.7	0.015435
3	0.16	0.81	0.48	0.099856
4	0.12	0.93	0.48	0.384492
5	0.07	1.00	0.35	0.544887
Ex 5.57	1.00		2.21	1.8259
			S.D.	1.351259

a. E(X) = 2.21 cars sold
b. Standard deviation = 1.3513 cars
c. Mean Salary = $250 + $300 (2.21) = $913. Standard deviation of salary =
    $300(1.3513) = $405.39
d. To earn a salary of $1,000 or more, the salesperson must sell at least 3 cars.
    $P(X \geq 3) = .16 + .12 + .07 = .35$

5.94   a. Positive covariance: Consumption expenditures & Disposable income
      b. Negative covariance: Price of cars and the number of cars sold
      c. Zero covariance: Dow Jones stock market average & rainfall in Brazil

5.96

				X Years				Mean of Y	Var of Y	StDev of Y
Y Visits		1	2	3	4	P(y)				
	0	0.07	0.05	0.03	0.02	0.17	0	0.2057	
	1	0.13	0.11	0.17	0.15	0.56	0.56	0.0056	
	2	0.04	0.04	0.09	0.1	0.27	0.54	0.2187	
P(x)		0.24	0.2	0.29	0.27	1	1.1	0.43	0.6557439
Mean of X		0.24	0.4	0.87	1.08	2.59			
Var of X		0.606744	0.0696	0.048749	0.5368	1.2619			
StDev of X						1.12334			
xyP(x)		0.21	0.38	1.05	1.4	3.04			
sum xyP(x)*muxmuy		0.191							

    a. $Py(0) = .07 + .05 + .03 + .02 = .17$

    b. $E(X) = \mu_x = .24 + 2(.2) + 3(.29) + 4(.27) = 2.59$

        $E(Y) = \mu_y = .56 + 2(.27) = 1.1$

    c. $E(XY) = 3.04$, $Cov(X,Y) = 3.04 - (2.59)(1.1) = .191$. This implies that there is a positive relationship between the number of years in school and the number of visits to a museum in the last year.

5.98   a. $P(x=3) = \binom{5}{3}.55^3 .45^2 = .3369$

       b. $P(x \geq 3) = P(3) + P(4) + P(5) = .3369 + (5)(.55)^4(.45) + (1)(.55)^5(1) = .5931$

       c. $\mu = np = (80)(.55) = 44$ will graduate in 4 years. The proportion is 44/80 = .55. $\sigma = \sqrt{80(.55)(.45)} = 4.4497$. The proportion is 4.4497/80 = .05562

5.100   To evaluate the effectiveness of the analyst's ability, find the probability that x is greater than or equal to 3 at random. $P(x \geq 3) =$

$$\frac{\binom{5}{3}\binom{10}{2}}{\binom{15}{5}} + \frac{\binom{5}{4}\binom{10}{1}}{\binom{15}{5}} + \frac{\binom{5}{5}\binom{10}{0}}{\binom{15}{5}} = .16683$$

5.102   a. $P(0) = e^{-2.4} = .09072$

        b. $P(x > 3) = 1 - e^{-2.4} - e^{-2.4}(2.4) - e^{-2.4}(2.4)^2/2! - e^{-2.4}(2.4)^3/3! = .2213$

5.104 $P(x=0) = e^{-2.4} = .0907$

      Let Y be the number of stalls for both lines.

      Find the $P(Y \geq 1) = 1 - P(Y=0) = 1 - (.0907)^2 = .99177$

5.106   Compute the mean and variance

Exercise_5.106		X_5.106						
Y_5.106		3	4	5	P(y)	Mean of Y	Var of Y	StDev of Y
	4	0.1	0.15	0.05	0.3	1.2		1.2
	6	0.1	0.2	0.1	0.4	2.4	3.15544E-31	
	8	0.05	0.15	0.1	0.3	2.4		1.2
P(x)		0.25	0.5	0.25	1	6		2.4 1.549193
Mean of X		0.75	2	1.25	4			
Var of X		0.25	0	0.25	0.5			
StDev of X					0.707107			
xyP(x)		6	16.8	11	33.8			
cov(x,y) =								
sum xyP(x)-muxmuy		9.8						

$$\mu_W = a\mu_x + b\mu_y = (1)4 + (1)6 = 10$$

$$\sigma^2{}_W = a^2\sigma^2{}_X + b^2\sigma^2{}_Y + 2abCov(X,Y) = 1^2(.5) + 1^2(2.4) + 2(1)(1)(9.8) = 22.5$$

Chapter 6:

Continuous Random Variables
and Probability Distributions

6.2 $P(1.0 < X < 1.9) = F(1.9) - F(1.0) = (.5)(1.9) - (.5)(1.0) = 0.45$

6.4. $P(X > 1.3) = F(1.3) = (.5)(2.0) - (.5)(1.3) = 0.35$

6.6 a.

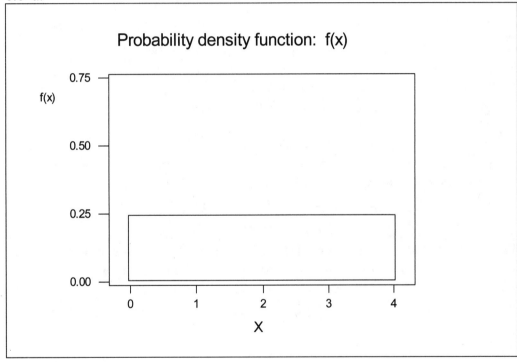

b.

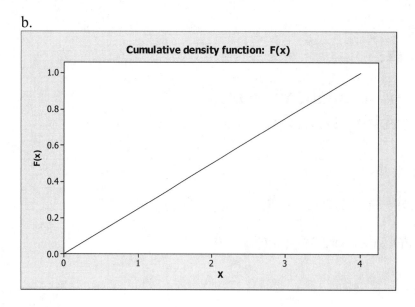

c. $P(x < 1) = .25$

d. $P(X < .5) + P(X > 3.5) = P(X < .5) + 1 - P(X < 3.5) = .25$

6.8.   a. $P(380 < X < 460) = P(X < 460) - P(X < 380) = .6 - .4 = .2$

b. $P(X < 380) < (PX < 400) < P(X < 460); .4 < P(X < 400) < .6$

6.10. $W = a + bX$. If Available Funds = 1000 - 2X where X = number of units produced, find the mean and variance of the profit if the mean and variance for the number of units produced are 50 and 90 respectively. $\mu_w = a + b\mu_x$
= 1000 - 2(50) = 900. $\sigma^2_w = b^2\sigma^2_x = (-2)^2(90) = 360$.

6.12. $W = a + bX$. If Available Funds = 6000 - 3X where X = number of units produced, find the mean and variance of the profit if the mean and variance for the number of units produced are 1000 and 900 respectively.
$\mu_w = a + b\mu_x = 6000 - 2(1000) = 4,000$. $\sigma^2_w = b^2\sigma^2_x = (-3)^2(900) = 8,100$

6.14. $\mu_Y = 20 + \mu_X = 20 + 4 = \$24$ million
Bid = $1.1 \mu_Y = 1.1(24) = \$26.4$ million, $\sigma_\pi = \$1$ million

6.16. $\mu_Y = 6,000 + .08 \mu_X = 6,000 + 48,000 = \$54,000$
$\sigma_Y = |.08| \sigma_X = .08(180,000) = \$14,400$

6.18.   a.   Find Z_0 such that $P(Z < Z_0) = .7$, closest value of $Z_0 = .52$

b.   Find Z_0 such that $P(Z < Z_0) = .25$, closest value of $Z_0 = -.67$

c.   Find Z_0 such that $P(Z > Z_0) = .2$, closest value of $Z_0 = .84$

d.   Find Z_0 such that $P(Z > Z_0) = .6$, closest value of $Z_0 = -.25$

6.20. X follows a normal distribution with $\mu = 80$ and $\sigma^2 = 100$

    a. Find P(X > 60). $P(Z > \dfrac{60-80}{10}) = P(Z > -2.00) = .5 + .4772 = .9772$

    b. Find P(72 < X < 82). $P(\dfrac{72-80}{10} < Z < \dfrac{82-80}{10}) = P(-.80 < Z < .20) =$

       .2881 + .0793 = .3674

    c. Find P(X < 55). $P(Z < \dfrac{55-80}{10}) = P(Z < -2.50) = .5 - .4938 = .0062$

    d. Probability is .1 that X is greater than what number? Z = 1.28.

       $1.28 = \dfrac{X-80}{10}$ X = 92.8

    e. Probability is .08 that X is in the symmetric interval about the mean

       between? Z = +/- .10. $\pm.10 = \dfrac{X-80}{10}$. X = 79 and 81.

6.22. a. $P(Z < \dfrac{400-380}{50}) = P(Z < .4) = .6554$

    b. $P(Z > \dfrac{360-380}{50}) = P(Z > -.4) = F_Z(.4) = .6554$

    c. The graph should show the property of symmetry – the area in the tails equidistant from the mean will be equal.

    d. $P(\dfrac{300-380}{50} < Z < \dfrac{400-380}{50}) = P(-1.6 < Z < .4) = F_Z(.4) - [1-$
       $F_Z(1.6)] = .6554 - .0548 = .6006$

    e. The area under the normal curve is equal to .8 for an infinite number of ranges – merely start at a point that is marginally higher. The shortest range will be the one that is centered on the z of zero. The z that corresponds to an area of .8 centered on the mean is a Z of ±1.28. This yields an interval of the mean plus and minus $64: [$316, $444]

6.24. a. $P(Z > \dfrac{38-35}{4}) = P(Z > .75) = 1 - F_Z(.75) = .2266$

    b. $P(Z < \dfrac{32-35}{4}) = P(Z < -.75) = 1 - F_Z(.75) = .2266$

    c. $P(\dfrac{32-35}{4} < Z < \dfrac{38-35}{4}) = P(-.75 < Z < .75) = 2F_Z(.75) - 1 =$
       $2(.7734) - 1 = .5468$

    d. (i) The graph should show the property of symmetry – the area in the tails equidistant from the mean will be equal.
       (ii) The answers to a, b, c sum to one because the events cover the entire area under the normal curve which by definition, must sum to 1.

6.26.   a. $P(Z < \dfrac{10-12.2}{2.8}) = P(Z < -.79) = 1 - F_z(.79) = .2148$

b. $P(Z > \dfrac{15-12.2}{2.8}) = P(Z > 1) = 1 - F_z(1) = .1587$

c. $P(\dfrac{12-12.2}{2.8} < Z < \dfrac{15-12.2}{2.8}) = P(-.07 < Z < 1) = F_z(1) - [1 - F_z(.07)]$
    $= .8413 - .4721 = .3692$

d. The answer to a. will be larger because 10 grams is closer to the mean than is 15 grams. Thus, there would be a greater area remaining less than 10 grams than will be the area above 15 grams.

6.28. $P(Z > 1.5) = 1 - F_z(1.5) = .0668$

6.30. $P(Z > .67) = .25$, $.67\sigma = 17.8 - \mu$. $P(Z > 1.03) = .15$, $1.04\sigma = 19.2 - \mu$
        Solving for μ, σ: $\mu = 15.265$, $\sigma^2 = (3.7838)^2 = 14.317$

6.32. For Investment A, the probability of a return higher than 10%:
        $P(Z > \dfrac{10-10.4}{1.2}) = P(Z > -.33) = F_Z(.33) = .6293$

        For Investment B, the probability of a return higher than 10%
        $P(Z > \dfrac{10-11.0}{4}) = P(Z > -.25) = F_Z(.25) = .5987$. Investment A is a better

        choice

6.34.   a. $P(Z > -1.28) = .9$, $-1.28 = \dfrac{Xi - 150}{40}$, $Xi = 98.8$

b. $P(Z < .84) = .8$, $.84 = \dfrac{Xi - 150}{40}$, $Xi = 183.6$

c. $P(X \geq 1) = 1 - P(X = 0) = 1 - [P(Z < \dfrac{120-150}{40})]^2 = 1 - [P(Z < -.75)]^2 =$
    $1 - (.2266)^2 = .9487$

6.36.   a. $P(\dfrac{400-420}{80} < Z < \dfrac{480-420}{80}) = P(-.25 < Z < .75) = F_z(.75) - [1 - F_z$
        $(.25)] = .7734 - .4013 = .3721$

b. $P(Z > 1.28) = .1$, $1.28 = \dfrac{Xi - 420}{80}$, $Xi = 522.4$

c. $400 - 439$
d. $520 - 559$

e. $P(X \geq 1) = 1 - P(X = 0) = 1 - [P(Z < \dfrac{500-420}{80})]^2 = 1 - (.8413)^2 =$
    $.2922$

6.38. $P(Z < 1.5) = .9332$, $1.5 = \dfrac{85-70}{\sigma}$, $\sigma = 10$. $P(Z > \dfrac{80-70}{10}) = P(Z > 1) =$

.1587

$P(X \geq 1) = 1 - P(X=0) = 1 - [F_Z(1)]^4 = 1 - (.8413)^4 = .4990$

6.40. n = 1600 from a binomial probability distribution with P = .40

    a.   Find $P(X > 1650)$. $E[X] = \mu = 1600(.4) = 640$, $\sigma = \sqrt{(1600)(.4)(.6)} =$

        19.5959

$$P(Z > \dfrac{1650-1600}{19.5959}) = P(Z > 2.55) = 1 - F_Z(2.55) = .0054$$

    b.   Find $P(X < 1530)$. $P(Z < \dfrac{1530-1600}{19.5959}) = P(Z < -3.57)$

        $= 1 - F_Z(3.57) = .0002$

    c. $P(\dfrac{1550-1600}{19.5959} < Z < \dfrac{1650-1600}{19.5959}) = P(-2.55 < Z < 2.55)$

        $= (2)F_z(2.55) = (2).4946 = .9892$

    d.   Probability is .09 that the number of successes is less than how many?

        $Z = -1.34$. $-1.34 = \dfrac{X-1600}{19.5959}$ $X = 1573.741 \approx 1{,}574$ successes

    e.   Probability is .20 the number of successes is greater than? $Z = .84$.

        $.84 = \dfrac{X-1600}{19.5959}$. $X = 1616.46 \approx 1{,}616$ successes

6.42. n = 1600 from a binomial probability distribution with P = .40

    a.   Find $P(P > .45)$. $E[P] = \mu = P = .40$, $\sigma = \sqrt{\dfrac{P(1-P)}{n}} = \sqrt{\dfrac{.4(1-.4)}{1600}} = .01225$

        $P(Z > \dfrac{.45-.40}{.01225}) = P(Z > 4.082) = 1 - F_Z(4.082) = .0000$

    b.   Find $P(P < .36)$. $P(Z < \dfrac{.36-.40}{.01225}) = P(Z < -3.27) = 1 - F_Z(3.27) = .0005$

    c. $P(\dfrac{.44-.40}{.01225} < Z < \dfrac{.37-.40}{.01225}) = P(3.27 < Z < -2.45) = 1 - [1-F_z(3.27)] + [1-$

        $F_z(2.45)] = 1 - [1-.9995] + [1-.9929] = 1 - [.0005] + [.0071] = .9924$

    d.   Probability is .20 that the percentage of successes is less than what percent?

        $Z = -.84$. $-.84 = \dfrac{X-.40}{.01225}$ $P = 38.971\%$

e.   Probability is .09 the percentage of successes is greater than? $Z = 1.34$.

$1.34 = \dfrac{X - .40}{.01225}$. $P = 41.642\%$

6.44. a. $E[X] = \mu = 900(.2) = 180$, $\sigma = \sqrt{(900)(.2)(.8)} = 12$

$P(Z > \dfrac{200 - 180}{12}) = P(Z > 1.67) = 1 - F_Z(1.67) = .0475$

b. $P(Z < \dfrac{175 - 180}{12}) = P(Z < -.42) = 1 - F_Z(.42) = .3372$

6.46. $E[X] = (100)(.6) = 60$, $\sigma = \sqrt{(100)(.6)(.4)} = 4.899$

$P(Z < \dfrac{50 - 60}{4.899}) = P(Z < -2.04) = 1 - F_Z(2.04) = 1 - .9793 = .0207$

6.48. $P(Z > \dfrac{38 - 35}{4}) = P(Z > .75) = 1 - F_Z(.75) = 1 - .7734 = .2266$

$E[X] = 100(.2266) = 22.66$, $\sigma = \sqrt{(100)(.2266)(.7734)} = 4.1863$

$P(Z > \dfrac{25 - 22.66}{4.1863}) = P(Z > .56) = 1 - F_Z(.56) = 1 - .7123 = .2877$

6.50. $\lambda = 1.0$, what is the probability that an arrival occurs in the first t=2 time units?

Cumulative Distribution Function
```
Exponential with mean = 1
x   P( X <= x )
0      0.000000
1      0.632121
2      0.864665
3      0.950213
4      0.981684
5      0.993262
```

$P(T < 2) = .864665$

6.52. $\lambda = 5.0$, what is the probability that an arrival occurs after t=7 time units?

Cumulative Distribution Function
```
Exponential with mean = 5
x   P( X <= x )
0       0.000000
1       0.181269
2       0.329680
3       0.451188
4       0.550671
5       0.632121
6       0.698806
7       0.753403
8       0.798103
```
P(T>7) = 1-[P(T $\leq$ 8)] = 1 - .7981 = .2019

6.54. $\lambda = 3.0$, what is the probability that an arrival occurs after t=2 time units?
Cumulative Distribution Function
```
Exponential with mean = 3
x   P( X <= x )
0       0.000000
1       0.283469
2       0.486583
3       0.632121
```

P(T<2) = .4866

6.56. $P(X > 18) = e^{-(18/15)} = .3012$

6.58.   a. $P(X > 3) = 1 - [1 - e^{-(3/\mu)}] = e^{-3\lambda}$ since $\lambda = 1 / \mu$

b. $P(X > 6) = 1 - [1 - e^{-(6/\mu)}] = e^{-(6/\mu)} = e^{-6\lambda}$
c. $P(X>6|X>3) = P(X > 6)/P(X > 3) = e^{-6\lambda} / e^{-3\lambda}] = e^{-3\lambda}$
The probability of an occurrence within a specified time in the future is not related to how much time has passed since the most recent occurrence.

6.60.   Find the mean and variance of the random variable: W = 5X + 4Y with correlation = -.5
$\mu_W = a\mu_x + b\mu_y = 5(100) + 4(200) = 1,300$
$\sigma^2_W = a^2\sigma^2_X + b^2\sigma^2_Y + 2abCorr(X,Y)\sigma_X\sigma_Y$
$= 5^2(100) + 4^2(400) + 2(5)(4)(-.5)(10)(20) = 4,900$

6.62.   Find the mean and variance of the random variable: W = 5X – 4Y with correlation = .5. $\mu_W = a\mu_x - b\mu_y = 5(500) - 4(200) = 1,700$
$\sigma^2_W = a^2\sigma^2_X + b^2\sigma^2_Y - 2abCorr(X,Y)\sigma_X\sigma_Y$
$= 5^2(100) + 4^2(400) - 2(5)(4)(.5)(10)(20) = 4,900$

6.64. $\mu_Z = 100,000(.1) + 100,000(.18)$. $\mu_x = 10,000 + 18,000 = 28,000$

$\sigma_Z = 0$. Note that the first investment yields a certain profit of 10% which is a zero standard deviation. $\sigma_x = 100,000(.06) = 6,000$

6.66 $\mu_Z = \mu_1 + \mu_2 + \mu_3 = 50,000 + 72,000 + 40,000 = 162,000$

$\sigma_Z = \sqrt{\sigma_1^2 + \sigma_2^2 + \sigma_3^2} = \sqrt{(10,000)^2 + (12,000)^2 + (9,000)^2} = 18,027.76$

6.68   The calculation of the mean is correct, but the standard deviations of two random variables cannot be summed. To get the correct standard deviation, add the variances together and take the square root. The standard deviation: $\sigma = \sqrt{5(16)^2} = 35.7771$

6.70   a. Compute the mean and variance of the portfolio with correlation of +.5

$\mu_W = a\mu_x + b\mu_y = 50(25) + 40(40) = 2,850$

$\sigma^2_W = a^2\sigma^2_X + b^2\sigma^2_Y + 2abCorr(X,Y)\sigma_X\sigma_Y$
$= 50^2(121) + 40^2(225) + 2(50)(40)(.5)(11)(15) = 992,500$

b. Recompute with correlation of -.5

$\mu_W = a\mu_x + b\mu_y = 50(25) + 40(40) = 2,850$

$\sigma^2_W = a^2\sigma^2_X + b^2\sigma^2_Y + 2abCorr(X,Y)\sigma_X\sigma_Y$
$= 50^2(121) + 40^2(225) + 2(50)(40)(-.5)(11)(15) = 332,500$

6.72   a. $W = aX - bY = 10X - 10Y$. $\mu_W = a\mu_x - b\mu_y = 10(100) - 10(90) = 100$

$\sigma^2_W = a^2\sigma^2_X + b^2\sigma^2_Y - 2abCorr(X,Y)\sigma_X\sigma_Y$
$= 10^2(100) + 10^2(400) - 2(10)(10)(-.4)(10)(20) = 66,000$
$\sigma_W = \sqrt{66,000} = 256.90465$

b. $P(Z < \dfrac{0-100}{256.90465}) = P(Z < -.39) = 1 - F_Z(.39) = 1 - .6517 = .3483$

6.74   a. $W = aX - bY = 1X - 1Y$

$\mu_W = a\mu_x - b\mu_y = 1(100) - 1(105) = -5$

$\sigma^2_W = a^2\sigma^2_X + b^2\sigma^2_Y - 2abCorr(X,Y)\sigma_X\sigma_Y$
$= 1^2(900) + 1^2(625) - 2(1)(1)(.7)(30)(25) = 475$ $\sigma_W = \sqrt{475} = 21.79449$

b. $P(Z > \dfrac{0-(-5)}{21.79449}) = P(Z > .23) = 1 - F_Z(.23) = 1 - .5910 = .4090$

6.76.   a.

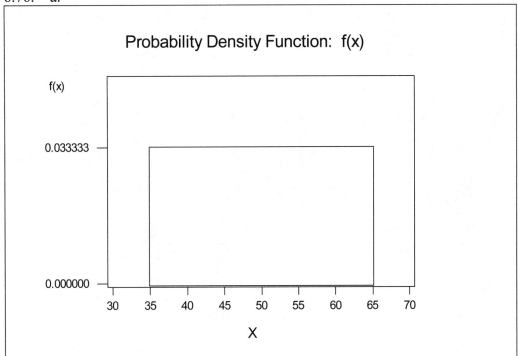

b.   Cumulative density function

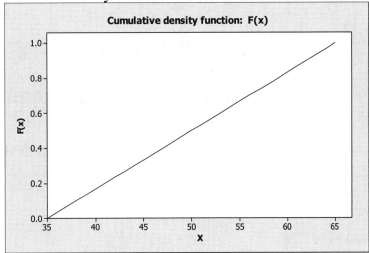

c.   P(40 < X < 50) = (50/30) – (40/30) = 10/30

d. $E[X] = \dfrac{65+35}{2} = 50$

6.78   a. $\mu_Y = 2000(1.1) + 1000(1+ \mu_x) = 2{,}200 + 1{,}160 = 3{,}360$

b. $\sigma_Y = |1000| \, \sigma_x = 1000(.08) = 80$

6.80   Given that the variance of both predicted earnings and forecast error are both positive and given that the variance of actual earnings is equal to the sum of the variances of predicted earnings and forecast error, then the Variance of predicted earnings must be less than the variance of actual earnings

6.82.   a. $P(Z > \dfrac{3-2.6}{.5}) = P(Z > .8) = 1 - F_Z(.8) = .2119$

   b. $P(\dfrac{2.25-2.6}{.5} < Z < \dfrac{2.75-2.6}{.5}) = P(-.7 < Z < .3) = F_z(.3) - [1 - F_Z(.3)] = .3759$

   c. $P(Z > 1.28) = .1$, $1.28 = \dfrac{Xi - 2.6}{.5}$, $Xi = 3.24$

   d. $P(Xi > 3) = .2119$ (from part a)

   $E[X] = 400(.2119) = 84.76$, $\sigma_x = \sqrt{(400)(.2119)(.7881)} = 8.173$

   $P(Z > \dfrac{80 - 84.76}{8.173}) = P(Z > -.58) = F_Z(.58) = .7190$

   e. $P(X \geq 1) = 1 - P(X = 0) = 1 - (.7881)^2 = .3789$

6.84.   a. $P(Z < \dfrac{85 - 100}{30}) = P(Z < -.5) = .3085$

   b. $P(\dfrac{70 - 100}{30} < Z < \dfrac{130 - 100}{30}) = P(-1 < Z < 1) = 2 F_z(1) - 1 = .6826$

   c. $P(Z > 1.645) = .05$, $1.645 = \dfrac{Xi - 100}{30}$, $Xi = 149.35$

   d. $P(Z > \dfrac{60 - 100}{30}) = P(Z > -1.33) = F_Z(1.33) = .9032$

   $P(X \geq 1) = 1 - P(X = 0) = 1 - (.0918)^2 = .9916$

   e. Use the binomial formula: $P(X = 2) = C_2^4 (.9082)^2 (.0918)^2 = 0.0417$

   f. 90 – 109

   g. 130 - 149

6.86. $P(Z > 1.28) = .1$, $1.28 = \dfrac{130 - 100}{\sigma}$, $\sigma = 23.4375$

   $P(Z > \dfrac{140 - 100}{23.4375}) = P(Z > 1.71) = 1 - F_Z(1.71) = .0436$

6.88. $E[X] = 1000(.4) = 400$, $\sigma_x = \sqrt{(1000)(.4)(.6)} = 15.4919$

   $P(Z < \dfrac{500 - 400}{15.4919}) = P(Z < 6.45) \approx 1.0000$

6.90. $P(Z < \dfrac{50 - 70}{\sqrt{70}}) = P(Z < -2.39) = 1 - F_Z(2.39) = .0084$

6.92.   a. $E[X] = 600(.4) = 240$, $\sigma_x = \sqrt{(600)(.4)(.6)} = 12$

$$P(Z > \frac{260-240}{12}) = P(Z > 1.67) = 1 - F_Z(1.67) = .0475$$

b. $P(Z > -.254) = .6$, $-.254 = \frac{Xi-240}{12}$, $Xi = 236.95$ (237 listeners)

6.94. $P(Z>1.28)=.1$, $1.28=\frac{3.5-2.4}{\sigma}$, $\sigma=.8594$. Probability that 1 exec spends

3+ hours on task: $P(Z > \frac{3-2.4}{.8594}) = P(Z > .7) = 1 - F_Z(.7) = .242$. $E[X] =$

$400(.242) = 96.8$, $\sigma_x = \sqrt{(400)(.242)(.758)} = 8.566$.

$$P(Z > \frac{80-96.8}{8.566}) = P(Z>-1.96) = F_Z(1.96)=.975$$

6.96 Portfolio consists of 10 shares of stock A and 8 shares of stock B
   a. Find the mean and variance of the portfolio value: W = 10X + 8Y with
       correlation of .3.

$$\mu_W = a\mu_x + b\mu_y = 10(12) + 8(10) = 200$$
$$\sigma^2_W = a^2\sigma^2_X + b^2\sigma^2_Y + 2abCorr(X,Y)\sigma_X\sigma_Y$$
$$= 10^2(14) + 8^2(12) + 2(10)(8)(.5)(3.74166)(3.4641) = 3,204.919$$

   b. Option 1: Stock 1 with mean of 12, variance of 25, correlation of -.2.

$$\sigma^2_W = a^2\sigma^2_X + b^2\sigma^2_Y + 2abCorr(X,Y)\sigma_X\sigma_Y$$
$$= 12^2(25) + 8^2(12) + 2(10)(8)(-.2)(5)(3.4641) = 3,813.744$$

Option 2: Stock 2 with mean of 10, variance of 9, correlation of .6.
$$= 10^2(9) + 8^2(12) + 2(10)(8)(.6)(3)(3.4641) = 2,665.66$$
To reduce the variance of the porfolio, select Option 2

6.98 a. $\mu_W = a\mu_x + b\mu_y = 1(40) + 1(35) = 75$

$$\sigma^2_W = a^2\sigma^2_X + b^2\sigma^2_Y + 2abCorr(X,Y)\sigma_X\sigma_Y$$
$$= 1^2(100) + 1^2(144) + 2(1)(1)(.6)(10)(12) = 388$$
$$\sigma_W = \sqrt{388} = 19.69772$$

Probability that all seats are filled:
$$\frac{100-75}{19.69772} = 1.27 \ \ Fz = .8980. \ \ 1 - .8980 = .1020$$

   b. Probability that between 75 and 90 seats will be filled:
$$\frac{90-75}{19.69772} = .76 \ \ .5 - Fz(.76) = .2764$$

Chapter 7:

Sampling and Sampling Distributions

7.2   a. Binomial random variable with n = 2, p = .5

Probability Density Function
```
Binomial with n = 2 and p = 0.5
 x   P( X = x )
 0        0.25
 1        0.50
 2        0.25
```

b. Binomial random variable with n = 4, p = .5

Probability Density Function
```
Binomial with n = 4 and p = 0.5
 x   P( X = x )
 0      0.0625
 1      0.2500
 2      0.3750
 3      0.2500
 4      0.0625
```

c. Binomial random variable with n = 10, p = .5

Probability Density Function
```
Binomial with n = 10 and p = 0.5
  x   P( X = x )
  0    0.000977
  1    0.009766
  2    0.043945
  3    0.117188
  4    0.205078
  5    0.246094
  6    0.205078
  7    0.117188
  8    0.043945
  9    0.009766
 10    0.000977
```

7.4 The response should note that there will be errors in taking a census of the entire population as well as errors in taking a sample. Improved accuracy can be achieved via sampling methods versus taking a complete census (see reference to Hogan, 90). By using sample information, we can make valid inferences about the entire population without the time and expense involved in taking a census.

7.6   a. mean and variance of the sampling distribution for the sample mean

$$\mu_{\bar{x}} = \mu = 100$$

$$\sigma^2_{\bar{x}} = \sigma^2 / n = 900 / 30 = 30 \quad \sigma_{\bar{x}} = \sqrt{\sigma_{\bar{x}}^2} = \sqrt{30}$$

b. Probability that $\bar{x} > 109$ $z_{\bar{x}} = \dfrac{109 - 100}{\sqrt{30}} = 1.64 \quad 1 - Fz(1.64) = .0505$

c. Probability that $96 \leq \overline{x} \leq 110$ $z_{\overline{x}} = \dfrac{96-100}{\sqrt{30}} = -.73$ $1 - Fz(.73) = .2327$

$z_{\overline{x}} = \dfrac{110-100}{\sqrt{30}} = 1.83$ $Fz = .9664$. $.9664 - .2327 = .7337$

d. Probability that $\overline{x} \leq 107$ $z_{\overline{x}} = \dfrac{107-100}{\sqrt{30}} = 1.28$ $Fz = .8997$

7.8 a. mean and variance of the sampling distribution for the sample mean

$\mu_{\overline{x}} = \mu = 400$

$\sigma^2_{\overline{x}} = \sigma^2 / n = 1600 / 35 = 45.7143$ $\sigma_{\overline{x}} = \sqrt{\sigma^2_{\overline{x}}} = \sqrt{45.7143}$

b. Probability that $\overline{x} > 412$ $z_{\overline{x}} = \dfrac{412-400}{\sqrt{45.7143}} = 1.77$ $1 - Fz(1.77) = .0384$

c. Probability that $393 \leq \overline{x} \leq 407$ $z_{\overline{x}} = \dfrac{407-400}{\sqrt{45.7143}}$

$= 1.04$ $Fz(1.04) = .8508$

$z_{\overline{x}} = \dfrac{393-400}{\sqrt{45.7143}} = -1.04$ $1 - Fz(1.04) = .1492$. $.8508 - .1492 = .7016$

d. Probability that $\overline{x} \leq 389$ $z_{\overline{x}} = \dfrac{389-400}{\sqrt{45.7143}}$

$= -1.63$ $1 - Fz(1.63) = 1 - .9484 = .0516$

7.10 a. $E(\overline{X}) = \mu_{\overline{x}} = 1,200$

b. $\sigma^2_{\overline{x}} = \dfrac{\sigma^2}{n} = \dfrac{(400)^2}{9} = 17,778$

c. $\sigma_{\overline{x}} = \dfrac{\sigma}{\sqrt{n}} = \dfrac{400}{3} = 133.33$

d. $P(Z < \dfrac{1,050-1,200}{133.33}) = P(Z < -1.13) = .1292$

7.12 a. $P(Z > \dfrac{110-115}{25 / \sqrt{100}}) = P(Z < -2) = .9772$

b. $P(\dfrac{113-115}{25 / \sqrt{100}} < Z < \dfrac{117-115}{25 / \sqrt{100}}) = P(-.8 < Z < .8) = .5762$

c. $P(\dfrac{114-115}{25 / \sqrt{100}} < Z < \dfrac{116-115}{25 / \sqrt{100}}) = P(-.4 < Z < .4) = .3108$

d. $114,000 - $116,000

e. Even with non-normal populations, the sampling distribution of the sample means will be normal for sufficient sample n. Since n is ≥ 30, the sampling distribution of the sample means can assumed to be a normal distribution.

7.14   a. $\sigma_{\bar{x}} = \dfrac{22}{\sqrt{16}} = 5.5$

b. $P(Z < \dfrac{100-87}{5.5}) = P(Z < 2.36) = .9909$

c. $P(Z > \dfrac{80-87}{5.5}) = P(Z > -1.27) = .8980$

d. $P(\dfrac{85-87}{5.5} > Z > \dfrac{95-87}{5.5}) = P(-.36 > Z > 1.45) = .4329$

e. Higher, higher, lower. The graph will show that the standard error of the sample means will decrease with an increased sample size.

7.16   a. $\sigma_{\bar{x}} = \dfrac{40}{\sqrt{100}} = 4$

b. $P(Z > 5/4) = P(Z > 1.25) = .1056$

c. $P(Z < -4/4) = P(Z < -1) = .1587$

d. $P(-3/4 > Z > 3/4) = P(-.75 > Z > .75) = .4532$

7.18   a. $\sigma_{\bar{x}} = \dfrac{1.6}{\sqrt{100}} = .16$, $P(Z > 1.645) = .05$, 1.645

$= \dfrac{Difference}{.16}$, Difference $= \pm.2632$

b. $P(Z < -1.28) = .1$, $-1.28 = \dfrac{Difference}{.16}$, Difference $= -.2048$

c. $P(Z > 1.44) = .075$, $1.44 = \dfrac{Difference}{.16}$, Difference $= \pm.2304$

7.20   a. $P(Z > 1.96) = .025$, $1.96 = \dfrac{2}{8.4/\sqrt{n}}$, $n = 67.766$, take $n = 68$

b. smaller

c. larger

7.22   a. $N = 20$, correction factor $= \dfrac{0}{19}$, $N = 40$, correction factor $= \dfrac{20}{39}$

$N = 100$, correction factor $= \dfrac{80}{99}$, $N = 1,000$, correction factor $= \dfrac{980}{999}$

$N = 10,000$, correction factor $= \dfrac{9,980}{9,999}$

b. When the population size (N) equals the sample size (n), then there is no variation away from the population mean and the standard error will be zero. As the sample size becomes relatively small compared to the population size, the correction factor tends towards 1 and the correction factor becomes less significant in the calculation of the standard error

c. The correction factor tends toward a value of 1 and becomes progressively less important as a modifying factor when the sample size decreases relative to the population size

7.24 $\sigma_{\bar{x}} = \dfrac{30}{\sqrt{50}}\sqrt{\dfrac{200}{249}} = 3.8023$

    a. $P(Z > \dfrac{2.5}{3.8023}) = P(Z > .66) = .2546$

    b. $P(Z < \dfrac{-5}{3.8023}) = P(Z < -1.31) = .0951$

    c. $P(\dfrac{-10}{3.8023} < Z < \dfrac{10}{3.8023}) = P(-2.63 < Z < 2.63) = 1 - .9914 = .0086$

7.26 $E(\hat{p}) = .4$ $\sigma_{\hat{p}} = \sqrt{\dfrac{(.4)(.6)}{100}} = .04899$

    a. Probability that the sample proportion is greater than .45

       $z = \dfrac{.45 - .4}{.04899} = P(Z > 1.02) = .1539$

    b. Probability that the sample proportion is less than .29

       $z = \dfrac{.29 - .4}{.04899} = P(Z < -2.25) = .0122$

    c. Probability that the sample proportion is between .35 and .51

    d. $P(\dfrac{.35 - .4}{.04899} < Z < \dfrac{.51 - .4}{.04899}) = P(-1.02 < Z < 2.25) = .8339$

7.28 $E(\hat{p}) = .60$ $\sigma_{\hat{p}} = \sqrt{\dfrac{(.6)(.4)}{100}} = .04899$

    a. Probability that the sample proportion is greater than .66

       $z = \dfrac{.66 - .6}{.04899} = P(Z > 1.22) = .1112$

    b. Probability that the sample proportion is less than .48

       $z = \dfrac{.48 - .6}{.04899} = P(Z < -2.45) = .0071$

    c. Probability that the sample proportion is between .52 and .66

       $P(z = \dfrac{.52 - .6}{.04899} < Z < z = \dfrac{.66 - .6}{.04899}) = P(-1.63 < Z < 1.22) = .8372$

7.30 a. $E(\hat{p}) = .424$

    b. $\sigma_{\hat{p}}^{2} = \dfrac{(.424)(.576)}{100} = .00244$

    c. $\sigma_{\hat{p}} = .0494$

    d. $P(Z > \dfrac{.5 - .424}{.0494}) = P(Z > 1.54) = .0618$

7.32   a. $E(\hat{p}) = .20$

      b. $\sigma_{\hat{p}}^2 = \dfrac{(.2)(.8)}{180} = .000889$

      c. $\sigma_{\hat{p}} = .0298$

      d. $P(Z < \dfrac{.15 - .2}{.0298}) = P(Z < -1.68) = .0465$

7.34 $\sigma_{\hat{p}} = \sqrt{\dfrac{(.4)(.6)}{120}} = .0447$. $P(\dfrac{.35 - .4}{.0447} < Z < \dfrac{.45 - .4}{.0447})$
      $= P(-1.12 < Z < 1.12) = .7372$

7.36   a. $\sigma_{\hat{p}} = \sqrt{\dfrac{(.2)(.8)}{130}} = .0351$

      b. $P(Z > \dfrac{.15 - .2}{.0351}) = P(Z > -1.42) = .9222$

      c. $P(\dfrac{.18 - .2}{.0351} < Z < \dfrac{.22 - .2}{.0351}) = P(-.57 < Z < .57) = .4314$

      d.   Higher, higher

7.38   The largest value for $\sigma_{\hat{p}}$ is when p = .5.   In this case, $\sigma_{\hat{p}} = \sqrt{\dfrac{(.5)(.5)}{100}} = .05$

7.40   a. $\sigma_{\hat{p}} = \sqrt{\dfrac{(.25)(.75)}{120}} = .0395$

      b. $P(Z > 1.28)$, $1.28 = \dfrac{Difference}{.0395}$,   Difference $= .0506$

      c. $P(Z < -1.645)$, $-1.645 = \dfrac{Difference}{.0395}$,   Difference $= .065$

      d. $P(Z > 1.036)$, $1.036 = \dfrac{Difference}{.0395}$,   Difference $= .0409$

7.42 $\sigma_{\hat{p}} = \sqrt{\dfrac{(.5)(.5)}{250}} = .03162$, $P(Z > \dfrac{.58 - .5}{.03162}) = P(Z > 2.53) = .0057$

7.44   a. $\hat{p} = \dfrac{211}{528} = .3996$

        $\sigma_{\hat{p}} = \sqrt{\dfrac{(.3996)(.6004)}{120}} \sqrt{\dfrac{408}{527}} = .03934$

      b. $P(Z < \dfrac{.33 - .3996}{.03934}) = P(Z < -1.77) = .0384$

c. $P(\dfrac{.5-.3996}{.03934} < Z < \dfrac{.6-.3996}{.03934}) = P(2.55 < Z < 5.09)$

$= .5000 - .4946 = .0054$

7.46 $P(Z < \dfrac{.1-.122}{.036} = P(Z < -.61) = .2709,\ \sigma_{\hat{p}} = \sqrt{\dfrac{(.2709)(.7291)}{81}} = .04969$

$P(Z > \dfrac{.5-.2709}{.04969}) = P(Z > 4.61) \approx .0000$

7.48 a. Probability that the sample mean is > 200.

Probability that $\bar{x} > 200$ $z_{\bar{x}} = \dfrac{200-198}{10/\sqrt{25}} = 1.00\ \ 1 - Fz(1.00) = .1587$

b. 5% of the sample variances would be less than this value

$P(s^2 > k) = P\left[\dfrac{(n-1)s^2}{\sigma^2}\right]\ \ \chi^2_{24,.95} = 13.85\ \ \dfrac{24s^2}{100} < 13.85\ \ s^2 < 57.702$

c. 5% of the samples variances would be greater than this value

$P(s^2 > k) = P\left[\dfrac{(n-1)s^2}{\sigma^2}\right]\ \ \chi^2_{24,.05} = 36.42\ \ \dfrac{24s^2}{100} > 36.42\ \ s^2 > 151.879$

7.50 $P(\dfrac{(n-1)s^2}{\sigma^2} > \dfrac{19(3.1)}{1.75}) = P(\chi^2_{(19)} > 33.66)$

$=$ between .01 and .025 (.0201 exactly)

7.52 a. $P(\dfrac{(n-1)s^2}{\sigma^2} > \dfrac{15(3,000)^2}{(2,500)^2}) = P(\chi^2_{(15)} > 21.6)$

$=$ greater than .1 (.1187 exactly)

b. $P(\dfrac{(n-1)s^2}{\sigma^2} < \dfrac{15(1,500)^2}{(2,500)^2}) = P(\chi^2_{(15)} < 5.4)$

$=$ between .01 and .025 (.0118 exactly)

7.54 a. $P(\dfrac{(n-1)s^2}{\sigma^2} < \dfrac{24(75)^2}{(100)^2}) = P(\chi^2_{(24)} < 13.5)$

$=$ between .025 and .05 (.0428 exactly)

b. $P(\dfrac{(n-1)s^2}{\sigma^2} > \dfrac{24(150)^2}{(100)^2}) = P(\chi^2_{(24)} > 54)$

$=$ less than .005 (.0004 exactly)

7.56

Descriptive Statistics: C20, C21, C22, C23, C24, C25, C26, C27, ...

Variable	Mean	Variance
C20	3.00	2.00
C21	4.00	8.00
C22	4.00	8.00
C23	4.50	12.50
C24	5.00	18.00
C25	5.00	2.00
C26	5.00	2.00
C27	6.00	8.00
C28	6.0000	0.000000000
C29	6.500	0.500
C30	7.00	2.00
C31	6.500	0.500
C32	7.00	2.00
C33	7.500	0.500
C34	5.50	4.50

Descriptive Statistics: Variance

Variable	Mean	StDev	Variance	Sum
Variance	4.72	5.26	27.62	70.80

$$\bar{x} = \frac{70.8}{15} = 4.72 \quad E(s^2) = \frac{15(3.91667)}{(14)} = 4.1964$$

which is not $= \sigma^2 = 47/12 = 3.91667$

7.58   a. $P(\chi^2_{(9)} > 14.68) = .10$, $14.68 = 9(\text{Difference})$,
Difference $= 1.6311$ (163.11%)

b. $P(\chi^2_{(9)} < 2.7) = .025$, $P(\chi^2_{(9)} > 19.02) = .025$,
$2.7 = 9a$, $a = .3$, $19.02 = 9b$, $b = 2.1133$
The probability is .95 that the sample variance is between 30% and 211.33% of the population variance

c. The interval in part b. will be smaller

7.59   a. $P(\chi^2_{(11)} > 4.57) = .95$, $4.57 = 11\text{Difference}$,
Difference $= .4155$ (41.55%)

b. $P(\chi^2_{(11)} > 5.58) = .90$, $5.58 = 11\text{Difference}$,
Difference $= .5073$ (50.73%)

c. $P(\chi^2_{(11)} < 3.82) = .025$, $P(\chi^2_{(11)} > 21.92) = .025$,
$3.82 = 11a$, $a = .34727$, $21.92 = 11b$, $b = 1.9927$
The probability is .95 that the sample variance is between 34.727% and 199.27% of the population variance

7.62 $P(\frac{(n-1)s^2}{\sigma^2} < \frac{24(12.2)}{15.4}) = P(\chi^2_{(24)} < 19.01)$ = less than .90 (.5438 exactly)

7.64   a. $C_2^6 = \frac{6!}{2!4!} = 15$ possible samples

b. (41, 39), (41, 35), (41, 35), (41, 33), (41, 38), (39, 35), (39, 35), (39, 33), (39, 38), (35, 35), (35, 33), (35, 38), (35, 33), (35, 38), (33, 38)

c. $34P_{\bar{X}}(34) = 34\dfrac{2}{15} = 4.5333$, $35P_{\bar{X}}(35) = \dfrac{35}{15} = 2.3333$

$35.5P_{\bar{X}}(35.5) = \dfrac{35.5}{15} = 2.3667$, $36P_{\bar{X}}(36) = \dfrac{36}{15} = 2.4$

$36.5P_{\bar{X}}(36.5) = 36.5\dfrac{2}{15} = 4.8667$, $37P_{\bar{X}}(37) = 37\dfrac{3}{15} = 7.4$

$38P_{\bar{X}}(38) = 38\dfrac{2}{15} = 5.0667$, $38.5P_{\bar{X}}(38.5) = \dfrac{38.5}{15} = 2.5667$

$39.5P_{\bar{X}}(39.5) = \dfrac{39.5}{15} = 2.6333$, $40P_{\bar{X}}(40) = \dfrac{40}{15} = 2.6667$

d. The mean of the sampling distribution of the sample mean is
$\sum \bar{x}P_{\bar{X}}(\bar{x}) = 36.8333$ which is exactly equal to the population mean:

$\dfrac{1}{N}\sum x_i = 36.8333$. This is the result expected from the Central Limit
Theorem.

7.66 a. $P\left(Z > \dfrac{450 - 420}{100/\sqrt{25}}\right) = P(Z > 1.5) = .0668$

b. $P\left(\dfrac{400 - 420}{100/\sqrt{25}} < Z < \dfrac{450 - 420}{100/\sqrt{25}}\right) = P(-1 < Z < 1.5) = .7745$

c. $P(Z > 1.28) = .1$, $1.28 = \dfrac{\bar{x} - 420}{100/\sqrt{25}}$, $\bar{x} = 445.6$

d. $P(Z < -1.28) = .1$, $-1.28 = \dfrac{\bar{x} - 420}{100/\sqrt{25}}$, $\bar{x} = 394.4$

e. $P(\chi^2_{(24)} > 36.42) = .05$, $36.42 = \dfrac{24s^2}{(100)^2}$, $s = 123.1868$

f. $P(\chi^2_{(24)} < 13.85) = .05$, $13.85 = \dfrac{24s^2}{(100)^2}$, $s = 75.966$

g. Smaller. A larger sample size would lead to a smaller standard error
and the graph of the normal distribution would be tighter with less area
in the tails.

7.68 a. $P\left(Z > \dfrac{19 - 14.8}{6.3/\sqrt{9}}\right) = P(Z > 2) = .0228$

b. $P\left(\dfrac{10.6 - 14.8}{6.3/\sqrt{9}} < Z < \dfrac{19 - 14.8}{6.3/\sqrt{9}}\right) = P(-2 < Z < 2) = .9544$

c. $P(Z < -.675) = .25$, $-.675 = \dfrac{X_i - 14.8}{6.3/\sqrt{9}}$, $X_i = 13.3825$

d. $P(\chi^2_{(8)} > 13.36) = .1$, $13.36 = \dfrac{8s^2}{(6.3)^2}$, $s = 8.1414$

e. Smaller

7.70 Let n = N, then $\bar{X} = \mu_x$:

$$E[\sum_{i=1}^{N}(X_i - \bar{X})^2] = n\sigma^2_x - n\frac{\sigma^2_x}{n}\frac{N-n}{N-1} = n\sigma^2_x - \frac{N-n}{N-1}\sigma^2_x =$$

$$\frac{\sigma^2_x}{N-1}(nN - n - N + n) = \frac{N\sigma^2_x}{N-1}(n-1)$$

Therefore, $E[\frac{1}{n-1}\sum(X_i - \bar{X})^2] = \frac{1}{n-1}E[\sum(X_i - \bar{X})^2] = \frac{N\sigma^2_x}{N-1}$

7.72   a. $P(Z < \dfrac{.7 - .8}{\sqrt{(.8)(.2)/60}}) = P(Z < -1.94) = .0262$

b. Use the binomial formula: $6(.7) = 4.2$, $P(X \le 4) = 1 - P(X > 4) = 1 - 6(.8)^5(.2) - (.8)^6 = .3446$

c. $P(Z > \dfrac{30,000 - 29,000}{4,000/\sqrt{6}}) = P(Z > .61) = .2709$

d. $(.8)P(Z > \dfrac{30,000 - 29,000}{4,000}) = (.8)P(Z > .25) = (.8)(.4013) = .3210$

7.74 $P(\dfrac{(n-1)s^2}{\sigma^2} > 20(2)) = P(\chi^2_{(20)} > 40) = .005$

7.76 $10 < \mu_{\bar{x}} < \bar{X} + 10$, $-10 < \bar{X} - \mu_{\bar{x}} < 10$

$P(\dfrac{-10}{40/\sqrt{16}} < Z < \dfrac{10}{40/\sqrt{16}}) = P(-1 < Z < 1) = .6826$

7.78   a. $\sigma_{\bar{x}} = \sqrt{\dfrac{(.4)(.6)}{250}} = .03098$

$P(Z > -.843) = .8$, $-.843 = \dfrac{p - .4}{.03098}$, $p = .3739$

b. $P(Z < 1.28) = .9$, $1.28 = \dfrac{p - .4}{.03098}$, $p = .4397$

c. $P(Z > 1.04) = .35$, $1.04 = \dfrac{Difference}{.03098}$, Difference $= \pm.0322$

7.80   a. $P(\dfrac{(n-1)s^2}{\sigma^2} > \dfrac{24(4,000)^2}{(6,600)^2}) = P(\chi^2_{(24)} > 8.82)$

   $=$ more than .99 (.9979 exactly)

  b. $P(\dfrac{(n-1)s^2}{\sigma^2} < \dfrac{24(8,000)^2}{(6,600)^2}) = P(\chi^2_{(24)} < 35.62)$

   $=$ between .9 and .95 (.9354 exactly)

Chapter 8:

Estimation: Single Population

8.2 a. Evidence of non-normality?

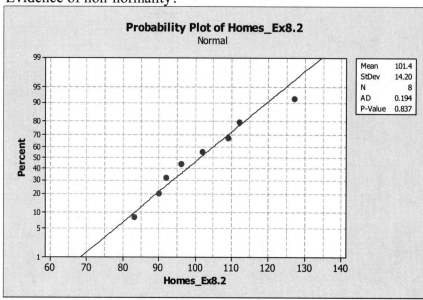

No evidence of non-normality.

b. The minimum variance unbiased point estimator of the population mean is the sample mean: $\bar{X} = \dfrac{\sum X_i}{n} = \dfrac{560}{8} = 101.375$

c. The unbiased point estimate of the variance of the sample mean:
$s^2 = 201.6964$

$$Var(\bar{X}) = \frac{\sigma^2}{n}; \quad V\hat{a}r(\bar{X}) = \frac{s^2}{n} = \frac{201.6964}{8} = 25.2121$$

d. $\hat{p} = \dfrac{x}{n} = \dfrac{3}{8} = .375$

8.4 n = 12 employees. Number of hours of overtime worked in the last month:

a. Unbiased point estimator of the population mean is the sample mean:

$$\bar{X} = \frac{\sum X_i}{n} = 24.42$$

b. The unbiased point estimate of the population variance: $s^2 = 85.72$

c. Unbiased point estimate of the variance of the sample mean

$$Var(\bar{X}) = \frac{s^2}{n} = \frac{85.72}{12} = 7.1433$$

d. Unbiased estimate of the population proportion: $\hat{p} = \dfrac{x}{n} = \dfrac{3}{12} = .25$

e. Unbiased estimate of the variance of the sample proportion:

$$Var(\hat{p}) = \frac{\hat{p}(1-\hat{p})}{n} = \frac{.25(1-.25)}{12} = .015625$$

8.6   a. $E(\bar{X}) = \dfrac{1}{2}E(X_1) + \dfrac{1}{2}E(X_2) = \dfrac{\mu}{2} + \dfrac{\mu}{2} = \mu$

$E(Y) = \dfrac{1}{4}E(X_1) + \dfrac{3}{4}E(X_2) = \dfrac{\mu}{4} + \dfrac{3\mu}{4} = \mu$

$E(Z) = \dfrac{1}{3}E(X_1) + \dfrac{2}{3}E(X_2) = \dfrac{\mu}{3} + \dfrac{2\mu}{3} = \mu$

b. $Var(\bar{X}) = \dfrac{\sigma^2}{n} = \dfrac{1}{4}Var(X_1) + \dfrac{1}{4}Var(X_2) = \dfrac{1}{2}\dfrac{\sigma^2}{8} = \dfrac{\sigma^2}{4}$

$Var(Y) = \dfrac{1}{16}Var(X_1) + \dfrac{9}{16}Var(X_2) = \dfrac{5\sigma^2}{8}$

$Var(Z) = \dfrac{1}{9}Var(X_1) + \dfrac{4}{9}Var(X_2) = \dfrac{5\sigma^2}{9}$

$\bar{X}$ is most efficient since $Var(\bar{X}) < Var(Y) < Var(Z)$

c. Relative efficiency between Y and $\bar{X}$: $\dfrac{Var(Y)}{Var(\bar{X})} = \dfrac{5}{2} = 2.5$

Relative efficiency between Z and $\bar{X}$: $\dfrac{Var(Z)}{Var(\bar{X})} = \dfrac{20}{9} = 2.222$

8.8   a. Evidence of non-normality?
No evidence of the data distribution coming from a non-normal population

b. The minimum variance unbiased point estimator of the population mean is the sample mean: $\bar{X} = \dfrac{\sum X_i}{n} = 3.8079$

Descriptive Statistics: Volumes

Variable	N	Mean	Median	TrMean	StDev	SE Mean
Volumes	75	3.8079	3.7900	3.8054	0.1024	0.0118

Variable	Minimum	Maximum	Q1	Q3
Volumes	3.5700	4.1100	3.7400	3.8700

c. Minimum variance unbiased point estimate of the population variance is the sample variance $s^2 = .0105$

8.10 Calculate the margin of error to estimate the population mean

a. 98% confidence level; n = 64, variance = 144

$$ME = z_{\alpha/2} \; \sigma/\sqrt{n} = 2.33 \left(12/\sqrt{64} \right) = 3.495$$

b. 99% confidence interval, n=120; standard deviation = 100

$$ME = z_{\alpha/2} \; \sigma/\sqrt{n} = 2.58 \left(100/\sqrt{120} \right) = 23.552$$

8.12 Calculate the LCL and UCL

a. $\bar{x} \pm z_{\alpha/2} \; \sigma/\sqrt{n} = 50 \pm 1.96 \left(40/\sqrt{64} \right) = 40.2 \text{ to } 59.8$

b. $\bar{x} \pm z_{\alpha/2} \; \sigma/\sqrt{n} = 85 \pm 2.58 \left(20/\sqrt{225} \right) = 81.56 \text{ to } 88.44$

c. $\bar{x} \pm z_{\alpha/2} \; \sigma/\sqrt{n} = 510 \pm 1.645 \left(50/\sqrt{485} \right) = 506.2652 \text{ to } 513.73478$

8.14 a. Find the reliability factor for 92% confidence level: $z_{\alpha/2} = +/- 1.75$

b. Calculate the standard error of the mean. $\sigma/\sqrt{n} = 6/\sqrt{90} = .63246$

c. Calculate the width of the 92% confidence interval for the population mean

$$\text{width} = 2ME = 2 \left[z_{\alpha/2} \; \sigma/\sqrt{n} \right] = 2 \left[1.75 \left(6/\sqrt{90} \right) \right] = 2.2136$$

8.16 a. $n = 16, \quad \bar{x} = 4.07, \quad \sigma = .12, \quad z_{.005} = 2.58 . \quad 4.07 \pm 2.58(.12/4) = 3.9926$ up to 4.1474

b. narrower since the z score for a 95% confidence interval is smaller than the z score for the 99% confidence interval

c. narrower due to the smaller standard error

d. wider due to the larger standard error

8.18 Find the ME

a. n = 20, 90% confidence level, s = 36

$$ME = t_{\alpha/2} \; s/\sqrt{n} = ME = 1.729 \left(36/\sqrt{120} \right) = 13.9182$$

b. n = 7, 98% confidence level, s = 16

$$ME = t_{\alpha/2} \; s/\sqrt{n} = ME = 3.143 \left(16/\sqrt{7} \right) = 19.007$$

c. n = 16, 95% confidence level, $s^2 = 43$

$$ME = t_{\alpha/2} \; s/\sqrt{n} = ME = 2.131 \left(6.5574/\sqrt{16} \right) = 3.493$$

d. 99% confidence level; $x_1 = 15, x_2 = 17, x_3 = 13, x_4 = 11, x_5 = 14$

$$\bar{x} = 14, \quad s = 2.58199 \quad ME = 5.841 \left(2.58199/\sqrt{4} \right) = 7.5407$$

8.20 Find the LCL and UCL for each of the following:

a. alpha = .05, n = 25, sample mean = 560, s = 45

$$\bar{x} \pm t_{\alpha/2}\left(\frac{s}{\sqrt{n}}\right) = 560 \pm 2.064\left(\frac{45}{\sqrt{25}}\right) = 541.424 \text{ to } 578.576$$

b. alpha/2 = .05, n = 9, sample mean = 160, sample variance = 36

$$\bar{x} \pm t_{\alpha/2}\left(\frac{s}{\sqrt{n}}\right) = 160 \pm 1.860\left(\frac{6}{\sqrt{9}}\right) = 156.28 \text{ to } 163.72$$

c. $1 - \alpha = .98$, n = 22, sample mean = 58, s = 15

$$\bar{x} \pm t_{\alpha/2}\left(\frac{s}{\sqrt{n}}\right) = 58 \pm 2.518\left(\frac{15}{\sqrt{22}}\right) = 49.9474 \text{ to } 66.0526$$

8.22 Calculate the width for each of the following:

a. alpha = 0.05, n = 6, s = 40

$$w = 2ME = 2t_{\alpha/2}\frac{s}{\sqrt{n}} = 2 \cdot 2.571\left(\frac{40}{\sqrt{6}}\right) = 2(41.98425) = 83.9685$$

b. alpha = 0.01, n = 22, sample variance = 400

$$w = 2ME = 2t_{\alpha/2}\frac{s}{\sqrt{n}} = 2 \cdot 2.831\left(\frac{20}{\sqrt{22}}\right) = 2(12.07142) = 24.1428$$

c. alpha = 0.10, n = 25, s = 50

$$w = 2ME = 2t_{\alpha/2}\frac{s}{\sqrt{n}} = 2 \cdot 1.711\left(\frac{50}{\sqrt{25}}\right) = 2(17.11) = 34.22$$

8.24   a.

Results for: Sugar.xls
Descriptive Statistics: Weights

Variable	N	Mean	Median	TrMean	StDev	SE Mean
Weights	100	520.95	518.75	520.52	9.45	0.95

Variable	Minimum	Maximum	Q1	Q3
Weights	504.70	544.80	513.80	527.28

90% confidence interval:

Results for: Sugar.xls
One-Sample T: Weights

Variable	N	Mean	StDev	SE Mean	90.0% CI
Weights	100	520.948	9.451	0.945	(519.379, 522.517)

b. narrower since a smaller value of z will be used in generating the 80% confidence interval.

8.26 $n = 7,$ $\bar{x} = 74.7143,$ $s = 6.3957,$ $t_{6,.025} = 2.447$

margin of error: $\pm\; 2.447(6.3957/\sqrt{7}) = \pm\, 5.9152$

8.28 $n = 25,$ $\bar{x} = 42,740,$ $s = 4,780,$ $t_{24,.05} = 1.711$

$42,740 \pm 1.711(4780/5) = \$41,104.28$ up to $\$44,375.72$

8.30 Find the standard error of the proportion for

a. $n = 250,$ $\hat{p} = 0.3$ $\sqrt{\dfrac{\hat{p}(1-\hat{p})}{n}} = \sqrt{\dfrac{.3(.7)}{250}} = .02898$

b. $n = 175,$ $\hat{p} = 0.45$ $\sqrt{\dfrac{\hat{p}(1-\hat{p})}{n}} = \sqrt{\dfrac{.45(.55)}{175}} = .03761$

c. $n = 400,$ $\hat{p} = 0.05$ $\sqrt{\dfrac{\hat{p}(1-\hat{p})}{n}} = \sqrt{\dfrac{.05(.95)}{400}} = .010897$

8.32 Find the confidence level for estimating the population proportion for
a. 92.5% confidence level; n = 650, $\hat{p} = .10$

$\hat{p} \pm z_{\alpha/2}\sqrt{\dfrac{\hat{p}(1-\hat{p})}{n}} = .10 \pm 1.78\sqrt{\dfrac{.10(1-.10)}{650}} = .079055$ to $.120945$

b. 99% confidence level; n = 140, $\hat{p} = .01$

$\hat{p} \pm z_{\alpha/2}\sqrt{\dfrac{\hat{p}(1-\hat{p})}{n}} = .01 \pm 2.58\sqrt{\dfrac{.01(1-.01)}{140}} = 0.0$ to $.031696$

c. alpha = .09; n = 365, $\hat{p} = .50$

$\hat{p} \pm z_{\alpha/2}\sqrt{\dfrac{\hat{p}(1-\hat{p})}{n}} = .50 \pm 1.70\sqrt{\dfrac{.5(.5)}{650}} = .4555$ to $.5445$

8.34 $n = 95,$ $\hat{p} = 67/95 = .7053,$ $z_{.005} = 2.58$

$\hat{p} \pm z_{\alpha/2}\sqrt{\dfrac{\hat{p}(1-\hat{p})}{n}} = .7053 \pm (2.58)\sqrt{\dfrac{.7053(.2947)}{95}} =$

99% confidence interval: .5846 up to .8260

8.36 $n = 320,$ $\hat{p} = 80/320 = .25,$ $z_{.025} = 1.96$

$\hat{p} \pm z_{\alpha/2}\sqrt{\dfrac{\hat{p}(1-\hat{p})}{n}} = .25 \pm (1.96)\sqrt{.25(.75)/320} =$

95% confidence interval: .2026 up to .2974

8.38 $width = .545 - .445 = .100;\ ME = 0.05\ \hat{p} = 0.495$

$$\sqrt{\frac{\hat{p}(1-\hat{p})}{n}} = \sqrt{\frac{.495(.505)}{198}} = .0355,\ .05 = z_{\alpha/2}\ (.0355),\ z_{\alpha/2} = 1.41$$

$$\alpha = 2[1 - F_z(1.41)] = .0793.\quad 100(1-.1586)\% = 84.14\%$$

8.40 $n = 246,\quad \hat{p} = 40/246 = .1626,\quad z_{.01} = 2.326.\ \hat{p} \pm z_{\alpha/2}\sqrt{\frac{\hat{p}(1-\hat{p})}{n}} = .1626$

$\pm(2.326)\sqrt{.1626(.8374)/246} = 98\%$ confidence interval:
.1079 up to .2173

8.42   a. $n = 10,\quad \overline{x} = 257,\quad s = 37.2,\quad t_{9,.05} = 1.833$

$$\overline{x} \pm t_{\alpha/2}\left(\frac{s}{\sqrt{n}}\right) = 257 \pm 1.833(37.2/\sqrt{10}) = 235.4318 \text{ up to } 278.5628$$

assume that the population is normally distributed

b. 95% and 98% confidence intervals:

$$[95\%]:\ \overline{x} \pm t_{\alpha/2}\left(\frac{s}{\sqrt{n}}\right) = 257 \pm 2.262(37.2/\sqrt{10})$$

$= 230.39$ up to 283.61

$$[98\%]:\ \overline{x} \pm t_{\alpha/2}\left(\frac{s}{\sqrt{n}}\right) = 257 \pm 2.821(37.2/\sqrt{10}) = 223.815 \text{ up to}$$

290.185

8.44 $n = 50,\quad \overline{x} = 30,\quad s = 4.2,\quad z_{.05} = 1.645$

$= 30 \pm 1.645(4.2/\sqrt{50}) = 29.0229$ up to 30.9771

8.46   a. Use a 5% risk. Incorrect labels $= 8/48 = 0.1667$

$$0.1667 \pm 1.96\sqrt{\frac{0.1667(0.8333)}{48}} = 0.1667 \pm 0.1054$$

$= 0.0613$ up to 0.2721

b. For a 90% confidence interval,

$$0.1667 \pm 1.645\sqrt{\frac{0.1667(0.8333)}{48}} = 0.1667 \pm 0.0885$$

$= 0.0782$ up to 0.2552

8.48 $3.69 - 3.59 = 0.10 = z_{\alpha/2}(1.045/\sqrt{457}),\quad z_{\alpha/2} = 2.05$

$\alpha = 2[1 - F_z(2.05)] = .0404$
$100(1-.0404)\% = 95.96\%$

8.50 $n = 33$ accounting students who recorded study time

a. An unbiased, consistent, and efficient estimator of the population
mean is the sample mean $\overline{x} = 8.545$

b. Find the sampling error for a 95% confidence interval; Using degrees of freedom = 30, $ME = 2.042\left(\dfrac{3.817}{\sqrt{33}}\right) = 1.3568$

8.52 n = 250, x = 100

a. Find the standard error to estimate population proportion of first timers

$\sqrt{\dfrac{\hat{p}(1-\hat{p})}{n}} = \sqrt{\dfrac{.4(1-.4)}{250}} = .03098$

b. Find the sampling error. Since no confidence level is specified, we find the sampling error (Margin of Error) for a 95% confidence interval.

$ME = 1.96\,(0.03098) = 0.0607$

c. For a 92% confidence interval,

$ME = 1.75\,(0.03098) = 0.05422$

$0.40 \pm .05422$ giving 0.3457 up to 0.4542

8.54 a. Find a 95% confidence interval estimate for the population proportion of students who would like supplements in their smoothies.

Tally for Discrete Variables: Supplements, Health Consciousness

Supplements		Count	Percent	Health Consciousness		Count	Percent
No	0	42	37.17	Very	1	29	25.66
Yes	1	71	62.83	Moderately	2	55	48.67
	N=	113		Slight	3	20	17.70
				Not Very	4	9	7.96
					N=	113	

$n = 113, \quad \hat{p} = 71/113 = .62832, \quad z_{.05} = 1.96$

$\hat{p} \pm z_{\alpha/2}\sqrt{\dfrac{\hat{p}(1-\hat{p})}{n}} = .62832 \pm 1.96\sqrt{\dfrac{.62832(1-.62832)}{113}}$

$= 0.62832 \pm 0.0891 = 0.5392$ up to 0.71742.

b. $\hat{p} = 29/113 = 0.2566$ For 98% confidence level,

$\hat{p} \pm 2.33\sqrt{\dfrac{(0.2566)(1-0.2566)}{113}} = 0.2566 \pm 0.09573$

or 0.1609 up to 0.3523

c. $\hat{p} = 77/113 = 0.6814$

$0.6814 \pm 1.645\sqrt{\dfrac{(0.6814)(1-0.6814)}{113}} = 0.6814 \pm 0.0721$

or 0.6093 up to 0.7535

8.56   a. Estimate the average age of the store's customers by the sample mean

$$\bar{x} = \frac{\sum x_i}{n} = \frac{6310}{125} = 50.48$$

To find a confidence interval estimate we will assume a 95% confidence level:

$$50.48 \pm 1.96 \frac{13.06}{\sqrt{125}} = 50.48 \pm 2.29; \ 48.19 \text{ up to } 52.77 \text{ years}$$

b. Estimate the population proportion of customers dissatisfied with the delivery system

Tally for Discrete Variables: Dissatisfied with Delivery
```
Dissatisfied
With Delivery   Count   Percent
            1       9      7.20
            2     116     92.80
          N=     125
```

$\hat{p} = 9/125 = .072$; Assuming a 95% confidence level, we find:

$$0.072 \pm 1.96 \sqrt{\frac{(0.072)(1 - 0.072)}{125}} = 0.072 \pm 0.0453$$

or 0.0267 up to 0.1173

c. Estimate the population mean amount charged to a Visa credit card

Descriptive Statistics: Cost of Flowers

Variable	Method of Payment	Mean	SE Mean	TrMean	StDev	Median
Cost of Flowers	American Express	52.99	2.23	52.83	10.68	50.55
	Cash	51.34	4.05	51.46	16.19	50.55
	Master Card	54.58	3.11	54.43	15.25	55.49
	Other	53.42	2.99	53.72	14.33	54.85
	Visa	52.65	2.04	52.58	12.71	50.65

The population mean can be estimated by the sample mean amount charged to a Visa credit card = $52.65.

8.58   From the data in 8.57, find the confidence level if the interval extends from 0.34 up to 0.46.

ME = ½ the width of the confidence interval. 0.46 – 0.34 = 0.12 / 2 = 0.06

$$ME = z_{\alpha/2} \sqrt{\frac{\hat{p}(1 - \hat{p})}{n}} \quad \text{or} \quad 0.06 = z_{\alpha/2} \sqrt{\frac{(0.4)(0.6)}{500}}$$

Solving for z: $z_{\alpha/2} = 2.74$

Area from the z-table = .4969 x 2 = .9938. The confidence level is 99.38%

8.60   a. What is the margin of error for a 99% confidence interval

$$\hat{p} = \frac{x}{n} = \frac{250}{350} = .7143 \;, \; ME = z_{\alpha/2}\sqrt{\frac{\hat{p}(1-\hat{p})}{n}} =$$

$$ME = 2.58\sqrt{\frac{.7143(1-.7143)}{350}}$$

ME = .0623

b. Is the margin of error for a 95% confidence larger, smaller or the same as the 99% confidence level? The margin of error will be smaller (more precise) for a lower confidence level. The difference in the equation is the value for z which would drop from 2.58 down to 1.96.

Chapter 9:

Estimation: Additional Topics

9.2 Two normally distributed populations based on dependent samples of n=5 observations

    a. Find the margin of error for 90% confidence level

Paired T-Test and CI: Before_Ex9.2, After_Ex9.2
```
Paired T for Before_Ex9.2 - After_Ex9.2
                N      Mean     StDev   SE Mean
Before_Ex9.2    5    8.4000    2.6077    1.1662
After_Ex9.2     5   10.2000    3.1145    1.3928
Difference      5   -1.80000   0.83666   0.37417
90% CI for mean difference: (-2.59766, -1.00234)
```

$$ME = t_{n-1,\alpha/2} \frac{s_d}{\sqrt{n_d}} \;=\; ME = 2.132 \frac{.83666}{\sqrt{5}} = .79772$$

    b. Find the UCL and LCL for a 90% confidence interval
        UCL = -2.59766, LCL = -1.00234

    c. Find the width of a 95% confidence interval

$$width = 2\left[ME = t_{n-1,\alpha/2} \frac{s_d}{\sqrt{n_d}} \right] = 2\left[2.776 \frac{.83666}{\sqrt{5}} \right] = 2.07737$$

9.4 Let X = Without Passive Solar; Y = With Passive Solar; $d_i = x_i - y_i$

$$n = 10, \quad \sum d_i = 373, \quad \bar{d} = 37.3, \quad t_{9,.05} = 1.833$$

$$s_d = \sqrt{\frac{\sum\left(d_i - \bar{d}\right)^2}{n_d - 1}} = \sqrt{2806.1/9} = 17.6575, \quad 37.3 \pm 1.833(17.6575)/\sqrt{10}$$

$$27.0649 < \mu_x - \mu_y < 47.5351$$

9.6 Let X = machine A and Y = machine B.

$$\bar{x} = 130, \; \sigma_x = 8.4, \; n_x = 40 \quad \bar{y} = 120, \; \sigma_y = 11.3, \; n_y = 36$$

Find the 95% confidence interval for the difference in means

$$(\bar{x} - \bar{y}) \pm z_{\alpha/2} \sqrt{\frac{\sigma^2_x}{n_x} + \frac{\sigma^2_y}{n_y}} = (130 - 120) \pm 1.96 \sqrt{\frac{8.4^2}{40} + \frac{11.3^2}{36}}$$

$$= 10 \pm 4.5169, \; 5.4831 \text{ up to } 14.5169$$

9.8 Compute the pooled sample variance, for parts (a) through (c) of Exercise 9.7

$$s_p^2 = \frac{(n_1-1)s_1^2 - (n_2-1)s_2^2}{n_1 + n_2 - 2}$$

a. $s_p^2 = \dfrac{(12-1)30+(14-1)36}{12+14-2} = 33.25$

b. $s_p^2 = \dfrac{(6-1)30+(7-1)36}{6+7-2} = 33.2727$

c. $s_p^2 = \dfrac{(9-1)16+(12-1)25}{9+12-2} = 21.2105$

9.10 Find the margin of error for a 95% confidence interval, assume equal population variances

a. $ME = t_{n_1+n_2-2,\alpha/2} s_p \sqrt{\dfrac{1}{n_1} + \dfrac{1}{n_2}}$ where $s_p = \sqrt{\dfrac{(n_1-1)s_1^2 + (n_2-1)s_2^2}{n_1 + n_2 - 2}}$

$s_p = \sqrt{\dfrac{(12-1)6+(14-1)10}{12+14-2}} = 2.85774$ $ME = 2.064(2.85774)\sqrt{\dfrac{1}{12} + \dfrac{1}{14}}$

$= 2.3204$

b. $s_p = \sqrt{\dfrac{(6-1)6+(7-1)10}{6+7-2}} = 2.8604$ $ME = 2.201(2.8604)\sqrt{\dfrac{1}{6} + \dfrac{1}{7}}$

$= 3.5026$

c. Doubling the size of both samples will reduce the margin of error; however, it does not reduce it in half.

9.12

Descriptive Statistics: Machine 1, Machine 2

Variable Mean	N	Mean	Median	TrMean	StDev	SE
Machine 0.95	100	520.95	518.75	520.52	9.45	
Machine 0.55	100	513.75	514.05	513.91	5.49	

Variable	Minimum	Maximum	Q1	Q3
Machine	504.70	544.80	513.80	527.28
Machine	496.50	527.00	510.33	517.68

95% confidence level: assuming normal populations and similar variances

$$(520.95-513.75) \pm (1.96)\sqrt{\dfrac{(9.45)^2}{100} + \dfrac{(5.49)^2}{100}} = 5.0579 \text{ up to } 9.3421$$

9.14 $\quad n_1 = 200, \quad \overline{x} = .517, \quad s_1 = .148, \quad z_{.005} = 2.58$

$\quad\quad n_2 = 400, \quad \overline{y} = .489, \quad s_2 = .159$

$$(.517 - .489) \pm (2.58)\sqrt{\frac{(.148)^2}{200} + \frac{(.159)^2}{400}} = -.00591 \text{ up to } .061907$$

9.16 Calculate the margin of error, assuming 95% confidence level

a. $\quad ME = z_{\alpha/2}\sqrt{\frac{\hat{p}_1(1-\hat{p}_1)}{n_1} + \frac{\hat{p}_2(1-\hat{p}_2)}{n_2}} = 1.96\sqrt{\frac{.75(1-.75)}{260} + \frac{.68(1-.68)}{200}}$

$\quad\quad = .083367$

b. $\quad ME = z_{\alpha/2}\sqrt{\frac{\hat{p}_1(1-\hat{p}_1)}{n_1} + \frac{\hat{p}_2(1-\hat{p}_2)}{n_2}} = 1.96\sqrt{\frac{.60(1-.60)}{400} + \frac{.68(1-.68)}{500}}$

$\quad\quad = .063062$

c. $\quad ME = z_{\alpha/2}\sqrt{\frac{\hat{p}_1(1-\hat{p}_1)}{n_1} + \frac{\hat{p}_2(1-\hat{p}_2)}{n_2}} = 1.96\sqrt{\frac{.20(1-.20)}{500} + \frac{.25(1-.25)}{375}}$

$\quad\quad = .056126$

9.18

$\quad n_x = 120, \quad \hat{p}_x = \frac{x}{n} = \frac{85}{120} = .7083, \quad n_y = 163, \quad \hat{p}_y = \frac{y}{n} = \frac{78}{163} = .4785, \quad z_{.01} = 2.33$

$$(\hat{p}_x - \hat{p}_y) \pm z_{\alpha/2}\sqrt{\frac{\hat{p}_x(1-\hat{p}_x)}{n_x} + \frac{\hat{p}_y(1-\hat{p}_y)}{n_y}} =$$

$$(.7083 - .4785) \pm (2.326)\sqrt{\frac{(.7083)(.2917)}{120} + \frac{(.4785)(.5215)}{163}}$$

$$= .2298 \pm .132657 = .0971 \text{ up to } .3625$$

9.20 $\quad \hat{p}_{freshmen} = 80/138 = .5797, \quad \hat{p}_{sophs} = 73/96 = .7604$

$$(.5797 - .7604) \pm (1.96)\sqrt{\frac{(.5797)(.4203)}{138} + \frac{(.7604)(.2396)}{96}} =$$

$$-.1807 \pm .1187 = -.3001 \text{ up to } -.0627$$

9.22 $\quad n_x = 510, \quad \hat{p}_x = .6275, \quad n_y = 332, \quad \hat{p}_y = .6024, \quad z_{.05} = 1.645$

$$(.6275 - .6024) \pm (1.645)\sqrt{\frac{(.6275)(.3725)}{510} + \frac{(.6024)(.3976)}{332}}$$

$$.0251 \pm .0565 = -.0314 \text{ up to } .0816$$

9.24   a. $n = 21$, $s^2 = 16$, *taking* $\alpha = .05$, $\chi^2_{20,.975} = 9.59$, $\chi^2_{20,.025} = 34.17$

$$\frac{(n-1)s^2}{\chi^2_{n-1,\alpha/2}} < \sigma^2 < \frac{(n-1)s^2}{\chi^2_{n-1,1-\alpha/2}} = \frac{21(16)}{34.17} < \sigma^2 < \frac{21(16)}{9.59}$$

$$= 9.8332 < \sigma^2 < 35.036$$

b. $n = 16$, $s = 8$, $\chi^2_{15,.975} = 6.26$, $\chi^2_{15,.025} = 27.49$

$$\frac{(n-1)s^2}{\chi^2_{n-1,\alpha/2}} < \sigma^2 < \frac{(n-1)s^2}{\chi^2_{n-1,1-\alpha/2}} = \frac{15(8)^2}{27.49} < \sigma^2 < \frac{15(8)^2}{6.26}$$

$$= 34.9218 < \sigma^2 < 153.3546$$

c. $n = 28$, $s = 15$, $\chi^2_{27,.995} = 11.81$, $\chi^2_{27,.005} = 49.64$

$$\frac{(n-1)s^2}{\chi^2_{n-1,\alpha/2}} < \sigma^2 < \frac{(n-1)s^2}{\chi^2_{n-1,1-\alpha/2}} = \frac{28(15)^2}{49.64} < \sigma^2 < \frac{28(15)^2}{11.81}$$

$$= 126.9138 < \sigma^2 < 533.446$$

9.26   No evidence of non-nomality

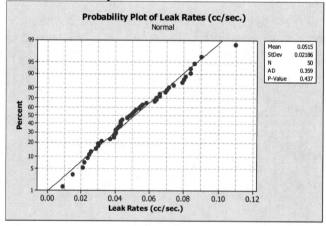

$n = 50$, $s^2 = 0.000478$ Since df = 49 is not in the Chi-Square Table in the Appendix, we will approximate the interval using df = 50.

$$\frac{(n-1)s^2}{\chi^2_{n-1,\alpha/2}} < \sigma^2 < \frac{(n-1)s^2}{\chi^2_{n-1,1-\alpha/2}} \approx \frac{49(0.000478)}{71.42} < \sigma^2 < \frac{49(0.000478)}{32.36}$$

$$= 3.279\text{E-}4 < \sigma^2 < 7.238\text{E-}4$$

9.28 $n = 20, \quad s^2 = 6.62, \quad \chi^2_{19,.025} = 32.85, \quad \chi^2_{19,.975} = 8.91$

$$\frac{(n-1)s^2}{\chi^2_{n-1,\alpha/2}} < \sigma^2 < \frac{(n-1)s^2}{\chi^2_{n-1,1-\alpha/2}} = \frac{19(6.62)}{32.85} < \sigma^2 < \frac{19(6.62)}{8.91}$$

= 3.8289 up to 14.1167.   Assume that the population is normally distributed.

9.30   a. $n = 15, \quad s^2 = (2.36)^2 = 5.5696$

$$\frac{14(5.5696)}{26.12} < \sigma^2 < \frac{14(5.5696)}{5.63} = 2.9852 \text{ up to } 13.8498$$

b.   wider since the chi-square statistic for a 99% confidence interval is larger than for a 95% confidence interval

9.32   How large a sample is needed to estimate the mean of a normally distributed population?

a. $n = \dfrac{\left(z_{\alpha/2}\right)^2 \sigma^2}{ME^2} = \dfrac{2.58^2 40^2}{5^2} = 426.01.$ Take a sample of size n = 427.

b. $n = \dfrac{\left(z_{\alpha/2}\right)^2 \sigma^2}{ME^2} = \dfrac{2.58^2 40^2}{10^2} = 106.502$ Take a sample of size n = 107.

c.   In order to cut the ME in half, the sample size must be quadrupled.

9.34   How large a sample size to estimate the population proportion?

a. $n = \dfrac{.25\left(z_{\alpha/2}\right)^2}{ME^2} = \dfrac{.25(2.58)^2}{.05^2} = 665.64.$ Take a sample of size n = 666.

b. $n = \dfrac{.25\left(z_{\alpha/2}\right)^2}{ME^2} = \dfrac{.25(1.645)^2}{.05^2} = 270.6.$ Take a sample of size n = 271.

c.   In order to increase the confidence level for a given margin of error, the sample size must be increased

9.36 $z_{.005} = 2.58, \quad ME = .05$

$$n = \frac{.25(z_{\alpha/2})^2}{ME^2} = \frac{(.25)(2.58)^2}{(.05)^2} = 665.64 \text{ , take } n = 666$$

9.38   Independent random samples from two normally distributed populations. Assuming equal variances, find the 90% confidence interval

$$(\bar{x} - \bar{y}) \pm t_{n_1 + n_2 - 2, \alpha/2} s_p \sqrt{\frac{1}{n_x} + \frac{1}{n_y}} \quad \text{where} \quad s_p = \sqrt{\frac{(n_x - 1)s^2_x + (n_y - 1)s^2_y}{n_x + n_y - 2}}$$

$$s_p = \sqrt{\frac{(15-1)20^2 + (13-1)25^2}{15+13-2}} = 22.4465$$

$$(400 - 360) \pm 1.706(22.4465)\sqrt{\frac{1}{15} + \frac{1}{13}}$$

$$= 40 \pm 14.5107 = 25.4893 \text{ to } 54.5107$$

9.40   Independent random samples from two normally distributed populations
a. If the unknown population variances are equal, find a 90% confidence interval

$$(\bar{x} - \bar{y}) \pm t_{n_1 + n_2 - 2, \alpha/2} s_p \sqrt{\frac{1}{n_x} + \frac{1}{n_y}} \quad \text{where} \quad s_p = \sqrt{\frac{(n_x - 1)s^2_x + (n_y - 1)s^2_y}{n_x + n_y - 2}}$$

$$s_p = \sqrt{\frac{(10-1)30^2 + (12-1)25^2}{10+12-2}} = 27.3633$$

$$(480 - 520) \pm 1.725(27.3633)\sqrt{\frac{1}{10} + \frac{1}{12}}$$

$$= -40 \pm 20.2106 = -60.21056 \text{ to } -19.7894$$

b. If the unknown population variances are unequal, find a 90% CI

$$(\bar{X} - \bar{Y}) \pm t_{(v, \alpha/2)}\sqrt{\frac{s^2_x}{n_x} + \frac{s^2_y}{n_y}} \quad \text{where} \quad v = \frac{\left[\left(\frac{s^2_x}{n_x}\right) + \left(\frac{s^2_y}{n_y}\right)\right]^2}{\left(\frac{s^2_x}{n_x}\right)^2 / (n_x - 1) + \left(\frac{s^2_y}{n_y}\right)^2 / (n_y - 1)}$$

$$= v = \frac{\left[\left(\frac{30^2}{10}\right) + \left(\frac{25^2}{12}\right)\right]^2}{\left(\frac{30^2}{10}\right)^2 / (10-1) + \left(\frac{25^2}{12}\right)^2 / (12-1)} = 17.606 \approx 18$$

$$(480 - 520) \pm 1.734\sqrt{\frac{30^2}{10} + \frac{25^2}{12}} = -40 \pm 20.669 = -60.669 \text{ to } -19.331$$

9.42 $n_x = 21$, $\bar{x} = 72.1$, $s_x = 11.3$, $t_{37,.10} = 1.303$ (df = 37 does not appear in

Appendix Table 7; we used df = 40 to give an approximate answer)

$n_y = 18$, $\bar{y} = 73.8$, $s_y = 10.6$

$$(\bar{x} - \bar{y}) \pm t_{n_1+n_2-2,\alpha/2} s_p \sqrt{\frac{1}{n_x} + \frac{1}{n_y}} \text{ where } s_p = \sqrt{\frac{(n_x-1)s^2_x + (n_y-1)s^2_y}{n_x + n_y - 2}}$$

$$s_p = \sqrt{\frac{(21-1)11.3^2 + (18-1)10.6^2}{21+18-2}} = 10.9839$$

$$(72.1 - 73.8) \pm 1.303(10.9839)\sqrt{\frac{1}{21} + \frac{1}{18}} = -1.7 \pm 4.5971 = -6.2971 \text{ to } 2.8971$$

9.44 $\hat{p}_x - \hat{p}_y = .6222 - .5714 = .0508$

Minitab results:

CI for Two Proportions
```
Sample       X       N   Sample p
1           140     225   0.622222
2           120     210   0.571429
Estimate for p(1) - p(2):  0.0507937
95% CI for p(1) - p(2):  (-0.0413643, 0.142952)
```

9.46   Assume both populations are distributed normally with equal variances
and a 90% confidence interval.

$n_x = 15$, $\bar{x} = 470$, $s_x = 5$, $t_{25,.05} = 1.708$. $n_y = 12$, $\bar{y} = 460$, $s_y = 7$

$$(470 - 460) \pm (1.708)\sqrt{\frac{(n_x-1)s_x^2 + (n_y-1)s_y^2}{n_x + n_y - 2}}\sqrt{\frac{1}{n_x} + \frac{1}{n_y}}$$

$$(470 - 460) \pm (1.708)\sqrt{\frac{(15-1)5^2 + (12-1)7^2}{15+12-2}}\sqrt{\frac{1}{15} + \frac{1}{12}}$$

$10 \pm (1.708)(5.9632)(.3873) = 10 \pm 3.9447 = 6.055$ up to 13.945
Since both endpoints of the confidence interval are positive, this provides
evidence that the new machine provides a larger mean filling weight than the old

9.48   98% confidence interval for student pair:

Paired T-Test and CI: COURSE, NO COURSE
```
Paired T for COURSE - NO COURSE
              N       Mean     StDev    SE Mean
COURSE        6    70.6667   16.0333     6.5456
NO COURSE     6    66.1667   14.1904     5.7932
Difference    6    4.50000    4.13521    1.68819

98% CI for mean difference:  (-1.18066, 10.18066)
```

9.50   Construct a 95% confidence interval of the difference in population proportions

$$\hat{p}_1 = \frac{x}{n} = \frac{300}{400} = .75, \quad \hat{p}_2 = \frac{x}{n} = \frac{225}{500} = .45$$

$$(\hat{p}_1 - \hat{p}_2) \pm z_{\alpha/2}\sqrt{\frac{\hat{p}_1(1-\hat{p}_1)}{n_1} + \frac{\hat{p}_2(1-\hat{p}_2)}{n_2}} =$$

$$(.75 - .45) \pm 1.96\sqrt{\frac{.75(1-.75)}{400} + \frac{.45(1-.45)}{500}} = .30 \pm .06085$$

$$= .23915 \text{ up to } .36085$$

Chapter 10:

Hypothesis Testing

10.2 H_0: No change in interest rates is warranted

H_1: Reduce interest rates to stimulate the economy

10.4 a. European perspective:

H_0: Genetically modified food stuffs are not safe

H_1: They are safe

b. U.S. farmer perspective:

H_0: Genetically modified food stuffs are safe

H_1: They are not safe

10.6 A random sample is obtained from a population with a variance of 625 and the sample mean is computed. Test the null hypothesis $H_0: \mu = 100$ versus the alternative $H_1: \mu \geq 100$. Compute the critical value $\bar{x}_c$ and state the decision rule

a. n = 25. Reject H_0 if $\bar{x} > \bar{x}_c = \mu_0 + z_\alpha \sigma / \sqrt{n}$

$= 100 + 1.645(25) / \sqrt{25} = 108.225$

b. n = 16. Reject H_0 if $\bar{x} > \bar{x}_c = \mu_0 + z_\alpha \sigma / \sqrt{n}$

$= 100 + 1.645(25) / \sqrt{16} = 110.28125$

c. n = 44. Reject H_0 if $\bar{x} > \bar{x}_c = \mu_0 + z_\alpha \sigma / \sqrt{n}$

$= 100 + 1.645(25) / \sqrt{44} = 106.1998$

d. n = 32 Reject H_0 if $\bar{x} > \bar{x}_c = \mu_0 + z_\alpha \sigma / \sqrt{n}$

$= 100 + 1.645(25) / \sqrt{32} = 107.26994$

10.8 The critical value $\bar{x}_c$ is farther away from the hypothesized value the smaller the sample size n. This is due to the increase in the standard error with a smaller sample size.

The critical value $\bar{x}_c$ is farther away from the hypothesized value the larger the population variance. This is due to the increased standard error with a larger population variance.

10.10 A random sample of n = 25, variance = σ^2 and the sample mean is = 70. Consider the null hypothesis $H_0: \mu = 80$ versus the alternative $H_1: \mu \leq 80$. Compute the p-value.

a. $\sigma^2 = 225$. $z = \dfrac{\bar{x} - \mu_0}{\sigma/\sqrt{n}} = \dfrac{70-80}{15/\sqrt{25}} = -3.33$. $p-value = P(z_p < -3.33) = .0004$

b. $\sigma^2 = 900$. $z = \dfrac{\bar{x} - \mu_0}{\sigma/\sqrt{n}} = \dfrac{70-80}{30/\sqrt{25}} = -1.67$. $p-value = P(z_p < -1.67) = .0475$

c. $\sigma^2 = 400$. $z = \dfrac{\bar{x} - \mu_0}{\sigma/\sqrt{n}} = \dfrac{70-80}{20/\sqrt{25}} = -2.50$. $p-value = P(z_p < -2.50) = .0062$

d. $\sigma^2 = 600$. $z = \dfrac{\bar{x} - \mu_0}{\sigma/\sqrt{n}} = \dfrac{70-80}{24.4949/\sqrt{25}} = -2.04$. $p-value = P(z_p < -2.04) =$ .0207

10.12 $H_0: \mu \geq 50$; $H_1: \mu < 50$; reject H_0 if $Z_{.10} < -1.28$

$Z = \dfrac{48.2 - 50}{3/\sqrt{9}} = -1.80$, therefore, reject H_0 at the 10% level.

10.14 Test $H_0: \mu \leq 100$; $H_1: \mu > 100$, using n = 25 and alpha = .05

a. $\bar{x} = 106, s = 15$. Reject if $\dfrac{\bar{x} - \mu_0}{s/\sqrt{n}} > t_{n-1,\alpha/2}$, $\dfrac{106-100}{15/\sqrt{25}} = 2.00$. Since 2.00 is

greater than the critical value of 1.711, there is sufficient evidence to reject the null hypothesis.

b. $\bar{x} = 104, s = 10$. Reject if $\dfrac{\bar{x} - \mu_0}{s/\sqrt{n}} > t_{n-1,\alpha/2}$, $\dfrac{104-100}{10/\sqrt{25}} = 2.00$. Since 2.00 is

greater than the critical value of 1.711, there is sufficient evidence to reject the null hypothesis.

c. Assuming a one-tailed lower tailed test, $\bar{x} = 95, s = 10$. Reject if

$\dfrac{\bar{x} - \mu_0}{s/\sqrt{n}} > t_{n-1,\alpha/2}$, $\dfrac{95-100}{10/\sqrt{25}} = -2.50$. Since -2.50 is less than the critical value of

-1.711, there is sufficient evidence to reject the null hypothesis.

d. Assuming a one-tailed lower test, $\bar{x} = 92, s = 18$. Reject if $\dfrac{\bar{x} - \mu_0}{s/\sqrt{n}} > t_{n-1,\alpha/2}$,

$\dfrac{92-100}{18/\sqrt{25}} = -2.22$. Since -2.22 is less than the critical value of -1.711, there is

sufficient evidence to reject the null hypothesis.

10.16 $H_0: \mu \geq 3; H_1: \mu < 3;$

$t = \dfrac{2.4 - 3}{1.8 / \sqrt{100}} = -3.33$, p-value is $= .0004$.

Reject H_0 at any common level of alpha.

10.18 $H_0: \mu = 0; H_1: \mu \neq 0;$

$t = \dfrac{.078 - 0}{.201 / \sqrt{76}} = 3.38$, p-value is $= .0008$.

Reject H_0 at any common level of alpha.

10.20 $H_0: \mu = 0; H_1: \mu < 0;$

$t = \dfrac{-2.91 - 0}{11.33 / \sqrt{170}} = -3.35$, p-value is $= .0004$.

Reject H_0 at any common level of alpha.

10.22 a. No, the 95% confidence level provides for 2.5% of the area in either tail. This does not correspond to a one-tailed hypothesis test with an alpha of 5% which has 5% of the area in one of the tails.

b. Yes.

10.24 $H_0: \mu = 20; H_1: \mu \neq 20;$ reject H_0 if $|t_{8, .05/2}| > 2.306$

$t = \dfrac{20.3556 - 20}{.6126 / \sqrt{9}} = 1.741$, therefore, do not reject H_0 at the 5% level

10.26 The population values must be assumed to be normally distributed.

$H_0: \mu \geq 50; H_1: \mu < 50;$ reject H_0 if $t_{19, .05} < -1.729$

$t = \dfrac{41.3 - 50}{12.2 / \sqrt{20}} = -3.189$, therefore, reject H_0 at the 5% level

10.28 A random sample is obtained to test the null hypothesis of the proportion of women who said yes to a new shoe model. $H_0: p \leq .25; H_1: p > .25;$. What value of the sample proportion is required to reject the null hypothesis with alpha $= .03$?

a.   n = 400. Reject H_0 if $\hat{p} > \hat{p}_c = p_0 + z_\alpha \sqrt{p_0(1-p_0)/n} = .25 + 1.88$

$\sqrt{(.25)(1-.25)/400} = .2907$

b.   n = 225. Reject H_0 if $\hat{p} > \hat{p}_c = p_0 + z_\alpha \sqrt{p_0(1-p_0)/n} = .25 + 1.88$

$\sqrt{(.25)(1-.25)/225} = .30427$

c. $n = 625$. Reject H_0 if $\hat{p} > \hat{p}_c = p_0 + z_\alpha \sqrt{p_0(1-p_0)/n} = .25 + 1.88$

$\sqrt{(.25)(1-.25)/625} = .28256$

d. $n = 900$. Reject H_0 if $\hat{p} > \hat{p}_c = p_0 + z_\alpha \sqrt{p_0(1-p_0)/n} = .25 + 1.88$

$\sqrt{(.25)(1-.25)/900} = .2771$

10.30 $H_0: p \le .25; H_1: p > .25;$

$z = \dfrac{.2908 - .25}{\sqrt{(.25)(.75)/361}} = 1.79$, p-value $= 1 - F_Z(1.79) = 1 - .9633 = .0367$

Therefore, reject H_0 at alpha greater than 3.67%

10.32 $H_0: p = .5; H_1: p \ne .5;$

$z = \dfrac{.45 - .5}{\sqrt{(.5)(.5)/160}} = -1.26$, p-value $= 2[1 - F_Z(1.26)] = 2[1 - .8962] = .2076$

The probability of finding a random sample with a sample proportion this far or further from .5 if the null hypothesis is really true is .2076

10.34 $H_0: p = .5; H_1: p > .5;$

$z = \dfrac{.56 - .5}{\sqrt{(.5)(.5)/50}} = .85$, p-value $= 1 - F_Z(.85) = 1 - .8023 = .1977$

Therefore, reject H_0 at alpha levels in excess of 19.77%

10.36 $H_0: p \ge .75; H_1: p < .75;$

$z = \dfrac{.6931 - .75}{\sqrt{(.75)(.25)/202}} = -1.87$, p-value $= 1 - F_Z(1.87) = 1 - .9693 = .0307$

Therefore, reject H_0 at alpha levels in excess of 3.07%

10.38 What is the probability of Type II error if the actual proportion is

a. $P = .52$. $\beta = P(.46 \le \hat{p} \le .54 \mid p = p^*) = P\left[\dfrac{.46 - p^*}{\sqrt{\dfrac{p^*(1-p^*)}{n}}} \le z \le \dfrac{.54 - p^*}{\sqrt{\dfrac{p^*(1-p^*)}{n}}} \right]$

$= P\left[\dfrac{.46 - .52}{\sqrt{\dfrac{.52(1-.52)}{600}}} \le z \le \dfrac{.54 - .52}{\sqrt{\dfrac{.52(1-.52)}{600}}} \right] = P(-2.94 \le z \le .98)$

$= .4984 + .3365 = .8349$

b. $P = .58$. $\beta = P(.46 \leq \hat{p} \leq .54 \mid p = p^*) = P\left[\dfrac{.46 - .58}{\sqrt{\dfrac{.58(1 - .58)}{600}}} \leq z \leq \dfrac{.54 - .58}{\sqrt{\dfrac{.58(1 - .58)}{600}}} \right]$

$= P(-5.96 \leq z \leq -1.99) = .5000 - .4767 = .0233$

c. $P = .53$. $\beta = P(.46 \leq \hat{p} \leq .54 \mid p = p^*) = P\left[\dfrac{.46 - .53}{\sqrt{\dfrac{.53(1 - .53)}{600}}} \leq z \leq \dfrac{.54 - .53}{\sqrt{\dfrac{.53(1 - .53)}{600}}} \right]$

$= P(-3.44 \leq z \leq .49) = .4997 + .1879 = .6876$

d. $P = .48$. $\beta = P(.46 \leq \hat{p} \leq .54 \mid p = p^*) = P\left[\dfrac{.46 - .48}{\sqrt{\dfrac{.48(1 - .48)}{600}}} \leq z \leq \dfrac{.54 - .48}{\sqrt{\dfrac{.48(1 - .48)}{600}}} \right]$

$= P(-.98 \leq z \leq 2.94) = .3365 + .4984 = .8349$

e. $P = .43$. $\beta = P(.46 \leq \hat{p} \leq .54 \mid p = p^*) = P\left[\dfrac{.46 - .43}{\sqrt{\dfrac{.43(1 - .43)}{600}}} \leq z \leq \dfrac{.54 - .43}{\sqrt{\dfrac{.43(1 - .43)}{600}}} \right]$

$= P(1.48 \leq z \leq 5.44) = .5000 - .4306 = .0694$

10.40   a. H_0 is rejected when $\dfrac{\bar{X} - 3}{.4 / \sqrt{64}} > 1.645$ or when $\bar{X} > 3.082$. Since the sample

mean is 3.07% which is less than the critical value, the decision is do not reject the null hypothesis.

b. The $\beta = P(Z < \dfrac{3.082 - 3.1}{.4 / \sqrt{64}}) = 1 - F_Z(.36) = .3594$. Power of the test = $1 - \beta =$

.6406

10.42 H_0 is rejected when $\dfrac{p - .5}{\sqrt{.25 / 802}} < -1.28$ or when $p < .477$

The power of the test = $1 - \beta = 1 - P(Z > \dfrac{.477 - .45}{\sqrt{(.45)(.55) / 802}}) = 1 - P(Z > 1.54) =$

.9382

10.44   a. H_0 is rejected when $-1.645 > \dfrac{p - .5}{\sqrt{.25 / 199}} > 1.645$ or when $.442 > p > .558$.

Since the sample proportion is .5226 which is within the critical values. The decision is that there is insufficient evidence to reject the null hypothesis.

b. $\beta = P(\dfrac{.442-.6}{\sqrt{(.6)(.4)/199}} < Z < \dfrac{.558-.6}{\sqrt{(.6)(.4)/199}}) = 1\text{-}P(\text{-}4.55 < Z < \text{-}1.21) = .1131$

10.46   a. $\alpha = P(Z > \dfrac{.14-.10}{\sqrt{(.1)(.9)/100}}) = P(Z > 1.33) = .0918$

b. $\alpha = P(Z > \dfrac{.14-.10}{\sqrt{(.1)(.9)/400}}) = P(Z > 2.67) = .0038.$ The smaller probability of a

Type I error is due to the larger sample size which lowers the standard error of the mean.

c. $\beta = P(Z < \dfrac{.14-.20}{\sqrt{(.2)(.8)/100}}) = P(Z < \text{-}1.5) = .0668$

d.   i)   lower,   ii)   higher

10.48   The p-value indicates the likelihood of getting the sample result at least as far away from the hypothesized value as the one that was found, assuming that the distribution is really centered on the null hypothesis. The smaller the p-value, the stronger the evidence against the null hypothesis.

10.50   a.   False. The significance level is the probability of making a Type I error – falsely rejecting the null hypothesis when in fact the null is true.
   b.   True
   c.   True
   d.   False. The power of the test is the ability of the test to correctly reject a false null hypothesis.
   e.   False. The rejection region is farther away from the hypothesized value at the 1% level than it is at the 5% level. Therefore, it is still possible to reject at the 5% level but not at the 1% level.
   f.   True
   g.   False. The p-value tells the strength of the evidence against the null hypothesis.

10.52   a. $\alpha = P(Z < \dfrac{776-800}{120/\sqrt{100)}}) = P(Z < \text{-}2) = .0228$

b. $\beta = P(Z > \dfrac{776-740}{120/\sqrt{100}}) = P(Z > 3) = .0014$

c.   i) smaller ii) smaller
d.   i) smaller ii) larger

10.54 $H_0: p = .5; H_1: p \neq .5;$

$$z = \frac{.4808 - .5}{\sqrt{(.5)(.5)/104}} = -.39, \text{ p-value} = 2[1\text{-}F_Z(.39)] = 2[1\text{-}.6517] = .6966$$

Therefore, reject H_0 at levels in excess of 69.66%

10.56 $H_0: p \leq .25; H_1: p > .25;$ reject H_0 if $z_{.05} > 1.645$

$$z = \frac{.3333 - .25}{\sqrt{(.25)(.75)/150}} = 2.356, \text{ therefore, reject } H_0 \text{ at the 5\% level}$$

10.58 Cost Model where W = Total Cost: W = 1,000 + 5X
$\mu_W = 1,000 + 5(400) = 3,000$

$$\sigma^2_W = (5)^2 (625) = 15,625, \quad \sigma_W = 125, \quad \sigma_{\overline{W}} = \frac{125}{\sqrt{25}} = 25$$

$H_0: W \leq 3000; \quad H1: W > 3000;$

Using the test statistic criteria: (3050 – 3000)/25 = 2.00 which yields a p-value of .0228, therefore, reject H_0 at the .05 level.

Using the sample statistic criteria: $\overline{X}_{crit} = 3,000 + (25)(1.645) = 3041.1,$
$\overline{X}_{calc} = 3,050$, since $\overline{X}_{calc} = 3,050 > \overline{X}_{crit} = 3041.1$, therefore, reject H_0 at the .05 level.

10.60 Assume that the population of matched differences are normally distributed
$H_o: \mu_x - \mu_y = 0; H_1: \mu_x - \mu_y \neq 0;$

$$t = \frac{1.3667 - 0}{2.414 / \sqrt{12}} = 1.961. \text{ Reject } H_0 \text{ at the 10\% level since } 1.961$$
$> 1.796 = t_{(11, .05)}$

10.62 $H_0: \mu \leq 40, H_1: \mu > 40; \overline{X} = 49.73 > 42.86$ reject H_0

One-Sample T: Salmon Weight
Test of mu = 40 vs mu > 40

Variable	N	Mean	StDev	SE Mean
Salmon Weigh	39	49.73	10.60	1.70

Variable	95.0% Lower Bound	T	P
Salmon Weigh	46.86	5.73	0.000

At the .05 level of significance we have strong enough evidence to reject Ho that the true mean weight of salmon is no different than 40 in favor of Ha that the true mean weight is significantly greater than 40.

$\overline{X}_{crit} = Ho + t_{crit}(S_{\overline{x}})$: $40 + 1.686(1.70) = 42.8662$

Population mean for $\beta = .50$ (power=.50): tcrit = 0.0: $42.8662 + 0.0(1.70) = 42.8662$

Population mean for $\beta = .25$ (power=.75): tcrit = .681: $42.8662 + .681(1.70) = 44.0239$

Population mean for $\beta = .10$ (power=.90): tcrit = 1.28: $42.8662 + 1.28(1.70) = 45.0422$

Population mean for $\beta = .05$ (power=.95): tcrit = 1.645: $42.8662 + 1.645(1.70) = 45.6627$

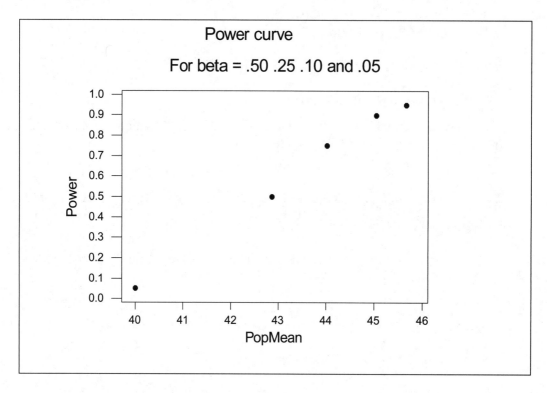

Chapter 11:

Hypothesis Testing II

11.2   n = 25 paired observations with sample means of 50 and 56 for populations 1 and 2. Can you reject the null hypothesis at an alpha of .05 if

a. $s_d = 20$, $H_0: \mu_1 - \mu_2 \geq 0$; $H_1: \mu_1 - \mu_2 < 0$;

$$t = \frac{(-6) - 0}{20/\sqrt{25}} = -1.50,\ \text{p-value} = .073.\ \text{Do not reject } H_0 \text{ at alpha of .05.}$$

Paired T-test and CI

```
              N      Mean     StDev   SE Mean
Difference   25  -6.00000  20.00000   4.00000
95% upper bound for mean difference: 0.84353
T-Test of mean difference = 0 (vs < 0): T-Value = -1.50  P-Value =
0.073
```

b. $s_d = 30$, $H_0: \mu_1 - \mu_2 \geq 0$; $H_1: \mu_1 - \mu_2 < 0$;

$$t = \frac{(-6) - 0}{30/\sqrt{25}} = -1.00,\ \text{p-value} = .164.\ \text{Do not reject } H_0 \text{ at alpha of .05.}$$

Paired T-Test and CI

```
              N      Mean     StDev   SE Mean
Difference   25  -6.00000  30.00000   6.00000
95% upper bound for mean difference: 4.26529
T-Test of mean difference = 0 (vs < 0): T-Value = -1.00  P-Value =
0.164
```

c. $s_d = 15$, $H_0: \mu_1 - \mu_2 \geq 0$; $H_1: \mu_1 - \mu_2 < 0$;

$$t = \frac{(-6) - 0}{15/\sqrt{25}} = -2.00,\ \text{p-value} = .028.\ \text{Reject } H_0 \text{ at alpha of .05.}$$

Paired T-Test and CI

```
              N      Mean     StDev   SE Mean
Difference   25  -6.00000  15.00000   3.00000
95% upper bound for mean difference: -0.86735
T-Test of mean difference = 0 (vs < 0): T-Value = -2.00  P-Value =
0.028
```

d. $s_d = 40$, $H_0: \mu_1 - \mu_2 \geq 0$; $H_1: \mu_1 - \mu_2 < 0$;

$$t = \frac{(-6) - 0}{40/\sqrt{25}} = -.75,\ \text{p-value} = .230.\ \text{Do not reject } H_0 \text{ at alpha of .05.}$$

Paired T-Test and CI
```
                N      Mean     StDev   SE Mean
Difference     25   -6.00000  40.00000  8.00000
95% upper bound for mean difference: 7.68706
T-Test of mean difference = 0 (vs < 0): T-Value = -0.75  P-Value =
0.230
```

11.4 $H_0: \mu_x - \mu_y = 0; H_1: \mu_x - \mu_y > 0;$

$$z = \frac{85.8 - 71.5}{\sqrt{(19.13)^2/151 + (12.2)^2/108}} = 7.334.$$

Reject H_0 at all common levels of alpha.

11.6 $H_0: \mu_x - \mu_y = 0; H_1: \mu_x - \mu_y \neq 0;$

$$z = \frac{2.71 - 2.79}{\sqrt{(.64)^2/114 + (.56)^2/123}} = -1.0207, \text{ p-value} = 2[1 - F_Z(1.02)]$$

$= 2[1 - .8461] = .3078$
Therefore, reject H_0 at levels of alpha in excess of 30.78%.

11.8 Assuming both populations are normal with equal variances:

$$H_0: \mu_x - \mu_y = 0; H_1: \mu_x - \mu_y \neq 0; \quad s^2_p = \frac{69(6.14)^2 + 50(4.29)^2}{70 + 51 - 2} = 29.592247$$

$$t = \frac{\bar{X} - \bar{Y} - D_0}{\sqrt{\frac{s_p^2}{n_x} + \frac{s_p^2}{n_y}}} = \frac{3.97 - 2.86}{\sqrt{\frac{29.592247}{70} + \frac{29.592247}{51}}} = 1.108$$

Therefore, do not reject H_0 at the 10% alpha level since $1.108 < 1.645 = t_{(119,.05)}$

11.10 $H_0: \mu_x - \mu_y = 0; H_1: \mu_x - \mu_y > 0;$

$$t = \frac{1475 - 0}{1862.985/\sqrt{8}} = 2.239, \text{ p-value} = .0301.$$

Reject H_0 at levels in excess of 3%.

Paired T-Test and CI: Male, Female
```
Paired T for Male - Female
               N      Mean     StDev   SE Mean
Male           8   46437.5    2680.1    947.5
Female         8   44962.5    2968.4   1049.5
Difference     8   1475.00    1862.99   658.66
95% lower bound for mean difference: 227.11
T-Test of mean difference = 0 (vs > 0): T-Value = 2.24  P-Value = 0.030
```

11.12 a. $H_0 : P_x - P_y = 0; H_1 : P_x - P_y < 0;$

$$\hat{p}_o = \frac{500(.42) + 600(.50)}{500 + 600} = .4636,$$

$$z = \frac{.42 - .50}{\sqrt{\dfrac{(.4636)(1 - .4636)}{500} + \dfrac{(.4636)(1 - .4636)}{600}}} = -2.65 \text{ p-value} = .004.$$

Therefore, reject H_0 at all common levels of alpha.

b. $H_0 : P_x - P_y = 0; H_1 : P_x - P_y < 0;$

$$\hat{p}_o = \frac{500(.60) + 600(.64)}{500 + 600} = .6218,$$

$$z = \frac{.60 - .64}{\sqrt{\dfrac{(.6218)(1 - .6218)}{500} + \dfrac{(.6218)(1 - .6218)}{600}}} = -1.36$$

p-value = .0869. Therefore, reject H_0 at .10, but do not reject at the .05 level.

c. $H_0 : P_x - P_y = 0; H_1 : P_x - P_y < 0;$

$$\hat{p}_o = \frac{500(.42) + 600(.49)}{500 + 600} = .4582,$$

$$z = \frac{.42 - .49}{\sqrt{\dfrac{(.4582)(1 - .4582)}{500} + \dfrac{(.4582)(1 - .4582)}{600}}} = -2.32$$

p-value = .0102. Therefore, reject H_0 at the .05 level, but do not reject at the .01 level.

d. $H_0 : P_x - P_y = 0; H_1 : P_x - P_y < 0;$

$$\hat{p}_o = \frac{500(.25) + 600(.34)}{500 + 600} = .299,$$

$$z = \frac{.25 - .34}{\sqrt{\dfrac{(.299)(1 - .299)}{500} + \dfrac{(.299)(1 - .299)}{600}}} = -3.25$$

p-value = .0006. Therefore, reject H_0 at all common levels of alpha.

e. $H_0: P_x - P_y = 0; H_1: P_x - P_y < 0;$

$$\hat{p}_o = \frac{500(.39) + 600(.42)}{500 + 600} = .4064,$$

$$z = \frac{.39 - .42}{\sqrt{\dfrac{(.4064)(1 - .4064)}{500} + \dfrac{(.4064)(1 - .4064)}{600}}} = -1.01$$

p-value = .1562. Therefore, do not reject H_0 at any common level of alpha.

11.14 $H_0: P_x - P_y = 0; H_1: P_x - P_y < 0;$

$$\hat{p}_o = \frac{1556(.384) + 1108(.52)}{1556 + 1108} = .44, \quad z = \frac{.384 - .52}{\sqrt{\dfrac{(.44)(.56)}{1556} + \dfrac{(.44)(.56)}{1108}}} = -6.97$$

Reject H_0 at all common levels of alpha.

11.16 $H_0: P_x - P_y = 0; H_1: P_x - P_y \neq 0;$ reject H_0 if $|z_{.025}| > 1.96$

$$\hat{p}_o = \frac{78 + 208}{175 + 604} = .36714$$

$$z = \frac{.446 - .344}{\sqrt{\dfrac{(.36714)(.63286)}{175} + \dfrac{(.36714)(.63286)}{604}}} = 2.465. \quad \text{Reject } H_0 \text{ at the 5\% level.}$$

11.18 $H_0: P_x - P_y = 0; H_1: P_x - P_y > 0;$ reject H_0 if $|z_{.05}| > 1.645$

$$\hat{p}_o = \frac{138 + 128}{240 + 240} = .554$$

$$z = \frac{.575 - .533}{\sqrt{\dfrac{(.554)(.446)}{240} + \dfrac{(.554)(.446)}{240}}} = .926. \quad \text{Do not reject } H_0 \text{ at the 5\% level.}$$

11.20 a. $H_0: \sigma^2 \leq 100; H_1: \sigma^2 > 100; \quad \chi^2 = \dfrac{(n-1)s^2}{\sigma^2} = \dfrac{24(165)}{100} = 39.6,$

$\chi^2_{(24,.025)} = 39.36, \chi^2_{(24,.010)} = 42.98$ Therefore, reject H_0 at the 2.5% level but not at the 1% level of significance.

b. $H_0: \sigma^2 \leq 100; H_1: \sigma^2 > 100; \quad \chi^2 = \dfrac{(n-1)s^2}{\sigma^2} = \dfrac{28(165)}{100} = 46.2,$

$\chi^2_{(28,.025)} = 44.46, \chi^2_{(28,.010)} = 48.28$ Therefore, reject H_0 at the 2.5% level but not at the 1% level of significance.

c. $H_0: \sigma^2 \le 100; H_1: \sigma^2 > 100; \chi^2 = \dfrac{(n-1)s^2}{\sigma^2} = \dfrac{24(159)}{100} = 38.16,$

$\chi^2_{(24,.050)} = 36.42, \chi^2_{(24,.025)} = 39.36$, Therefore, reject H_0 at the 5% level but not at the 2.5% level of significance.

d. $H_0: \sigma^2 \le 100; H_1: \sigma^2 > 100; \chi^2 = \dfrac{(n-1)s^2}{\sigma^2} = \dfrac{37(67)}{100} = 24.79,$

$\chi^2_{(30,.100)} = 40.26, \chi^2_{(40,.100)} = 51.81$, Therefore, do not reject H_0 at any common level of significance.

11.22 a. $s^2 = 5.1556$

b. $H_0: \sigma^2 \le 2.25; H_1: \sigma^2 > 2.25$; reject H_0 if $\chi^2_{(9,.05)} > 16.92$

$\chi^2 = \dfrac{9(5.1556)}{2.25} = 20.6224$. Reject H_0 at the 5% level.

11.24 The hypothesis test assumes that the population values are normally distributed

$H_0: \sigma = 2.0; H_1: \sigma > 2.0$; reject H_0 if $\chi^2_{(19,.05)} > 30.14$

$\chi^2 = \dfrac{19(2.36)^2}{(2)^2} = 26.4556$. Do not reject H_0 at the 5% level.

11.26 a. $H_0: \sigma^2_x = \sigma^2_y; H_1: \sigma^2_x > \sigma^2_y$

   $F = 125/51 = 2.451$. Reject H_0 at the 1% level since $2.451 > 2.11 \approx F_{(44,40,.01)}$

b. $H_0: \sigma^2_x = \sigma^2_y; H_1: \sigma^2_x > \sigma^2_y$

   $F = 235/125 = 1.88$. Reject H_0 at the 5% level since $1.88 > 1.69 \approx F_{(43,44,.05)}$

c. $H_0: \sigma^2_x = \sigma^2_y; H_1: \sigma^2_x > \sigma^2_y$

   $F = 134/51 = 2.627$. Reject H_0 at the 1% level since $2.627 > 2.11 \approx F_{(47,40,.01)}$

d. $H_0: \sigma^2_x = \sigma^2_y; H_1: \sigma^2_x > \sigma^2_y$

   $F = 167/88 = 1.90$. Reject H_0 at the 5% level since $1.90 > 1.79 \approx F_{(24,38,.05)}$

11.28 $H_0: \sigma^2_x = \sigma^2_y; H_1: \sigma^2_x > \sigma^2_y$; reject H_0 if $F_{(3,6,.05)} > 4.76$

$F = 114.09/16.08 = 7.095$. Reject H_0 at the 5% level.

11.30 $H_0: \sigma^2_x = \sigma^2_y; H_1: \sigma^2_x \ne \sigma^2_y$;

$F = (2107)^2/(1681)^2 = 1.57$

Therefore, do not reject H_0 at the 10% level since $1.57 < 3.18 \approx F_{(9,9,.05)}$

11.32 No. The probability of rejecting the null hypothesis given that it is true is 5%.

11.34 a. Assume that the population is normally distributed

One-Sample T: Grams:

```
Test of mu = 5 vs mu not = 5
Variable            N      Mean    StDev    SE Mean
Grams:11-34        12    4.9725   0.0936    0.0270

Variable              95.0% CI              T      P
Grams:11-34     ( 4.9130,  5.0320)      -1.02  0.331
```

$\bar{x} = 4.9725; s = .0936$, $H_0 : \mu = 5; H_1 : \mu \neq 5$;

reject H_0 if $|t_{(11, .025)}| > 2.201$

$t = \dfrac{4.9725 - 5}{.0936 / \sqrt{12}} = -1.018$. Do not reject H_0 at the 5% level

b. Assume that the population is normally distributed

$H_0 : \sigma = .025; H_1 : \sigma > .025$; reject H_0 if $\chi^2_{(11, .05)} > 19.68$

$\chi^2 = \dfrac{11(.0936)^2}{(.025)^2} = 154.19$. Therefore, reject H_0 at the 5% level

11.36 $H_0 : \mu_x - \mu_y = 0; H_1 : \mu_x - \mu_y \neq 0$;

$s_p^{\,2} = \dfrac{(n_x - 1)s_x^{\,2} + (n_y - 1)s_y^{\,2}}{n_x + n_y - 2} = \dfrac{33(2.21)^2 + 85(1.69)^2}{34 + 85 - 2} = 3.4525$

$t = \dfrac{\bar{X} - \bar{Y} - D_0}{\sqrt{\dfrac{s_p^{\,2}}{n_x} + \dfrac{s_p^{\,2}}{n_y}}} = \dfrac{2.21 - 1.47}{\sqrt{\dfrac{3.4525}{34} + \dfrac{3.4525}{86}}} = 1.966$

p-value is between (.025, .010) x 2 = .05 and .02. Reject H_0 at levels in excess
of 5%

11.38 $H_0 : \mu_x - \mu_y = 0; H_1 : \mu_x - \mu_y \neq 0$; reject H_0 if $|t_{.05}| > 1.645$

$s_p^{\,2} = \dfrac{(n_x - 1)s_x^{\,2} + (n_y - 1)s_y^{\,2}}{n_x + n_y - 2} = \dfrac{43(18.20)^2 + 67(18.94)^2}{44 + 68 - 2} = 347.980$

$t = \dfrac{\bar{X} - \bar{Y} - D_0}{\sqrt{\dfrac{s_p^{\,2}}{n_x} + \dfrac{s_p^{\,2}}{n_y}}} = \dfrac{35.02 - 36.34}{\sqrt{\dfrac{347.98}{44} + \dfrac{347.98}{68}}} = -.201$.

Do not reject H_0 at levels in excess of 5%

11.40 Assuming the populations are normally distributed with equal variances and independent random samples:

Magazine A: $\overline{X} = 10.968; s_x = 2.647$, Magazine B: $\overline{Y} = 6.738; s_y = 1.636$

$H_0: \mu_x - \mu_y = 0; H_1: \mu_x - \mu_y > 0$; reject H_0 if $t_{(10,.05)} > 1.812$

$$s_p^2 = \frac{(n_x - 1)s_x^2 + (n_y - 1)s_y^2}{n_x + n_y - 2} = \frac{5(2.647)^2 + 5(1.636)^2}{6 + 6 - 2} = 4.8416$$

$$t = \frac{\overline{X} - \overline{Y} - D_0}{\sqrt{\frac{s_p^2}{n_x} + \frac{s_p^2}{n_y}}} = \frac{10.968 - 6.738}{\sqrt{\frac{4.8416}{6} + \frac{4.8416}{6}}} = 3.330.$$

Reject H_0 at levels in excess of 5%

11.42 $H_0: \mu_x - \mu_y = 0; H_1: \mu_x - \mu_y < 0$; Sample sizes greater than 100, use the z-test.

$$z = \frac{2.83 - 3.0}{\sqrt{\frac{(.89)^2}{202} + \frac{(.67)^2}{291}}} = -2.30, \text{ p-value} = 1 - F_Z(2.3) = 1 - .9893 = .0107$$

Therefore, reject H_0 at levels of alpha in excess of 1.07%

11.44 a. $H_0: P \geq .5; H_1: P < .5$; reject H_0 if $z_{.05} < -1.645$

$$z = \frac{.455 - .5}{\sqrt{(.5)(.5)/178}} = -1.20. \text{ Do not reject } H_0 \text{ at the 5\% level}$$

b. $H_0: P_x - P_y = 0; H_1: P_x - P_y \neq 0$; reject Ho if $|z_{.025}| > 1.96$

$$\hat{p}_o = \frac{75 + 81}{148 + 178} = .478, \quad z = \frac{.5068 - .455}{\sqrt{(.478)(.522)(\frac{1}{148} + \frac{1}{178})}} = .932$$

Therefore, do not reject H_0 at the 5% level

11.46 $H_0: P_x - P_y = 0; H_1: P_x - P_y < 0$; reject Ho if $|z_{.01}| < -2.33$

$$\hat{p}_o = \frac{11 + 27}{67 + 113} = .211, \quad z = \frac{.164 - .239}{\sqrt{(.211)(.789)(\frac{1}{67} + \frac{1}{113})}} = -1.19.$$

Do not reject H_0 at the 1% level

11.48 $H_0 : P_x - P_y = 0; H_1 : P_x - P_y < 0;$

$$\hat{p}_o = \frac{53 + 47}{94 + 68} = .617, \quad z = \frac{.564 - .691}{\sqrt{(.617)(.383)(\frac{1}{94} + \frac{1}{68})}}$$

= -1.653, p-value = 1–F$_Z$(1.65)]=.0495

Therefore, reject H_0 at levels of alpha in excess of 4.95%

11.50 $H_0 : \sigma_x = \sigma_y; H_1 : \sigma_x \neq \sigma_y; \quad s_x = 4.16314, \quad s_y = 4.05421, \quad F = \frac{s^2_x}{s^2_y} =$

$(4.16314)^2/(4.05421)^2 = 1.0545.$ Do not reject H_0 at the 5% level, $1.0545 < 2.85$

$= F_{(11,11,.05)}$. There is insufficient evidence to suggest that the population variances differ between the two forecasting analysts.

11.52 a. $H_0 : P_2 - P_1 = 0; H_1 : P_2 - P_1 \neq 0;$ reject H_0 if $|z_{.015}| > 2.17$

$$\hat{p}_o = \frac{258 + 260}{800 + 700} = .3453, \quad z = \frac{.3714 - .3225}{\sqrt{\frac{(.3453)(.6547)}{800} + \frac{(.3453)(.6547)}{700}}} = 1.987$$

Therefore, reject H_0 at the 5% level, but do not reject at the 3% level

b. $H_0 : P_2 - P_1 = 0; H_1 : P_2 - P_1 > 0;$ reject H_0 if $|z_{.03}| > 1.88$

$$\hat{p}_o = \frac{258 + 260}{800 + 700} = .3453, \quad z = \frac{.3714 - .3225}{\sqrt{\frac{(.3453)(.6547)}{800} + \frac{(.3453)(.6547)}{700}}} = 1.987$$

Therefore, reject H_0 at the 3% level

11.54 a. The box plots of the raw data show similar medians and interquartile ranges for both brands. However, brand 2 is dominated by three outliers that is skewing the brand 2 data to the right:

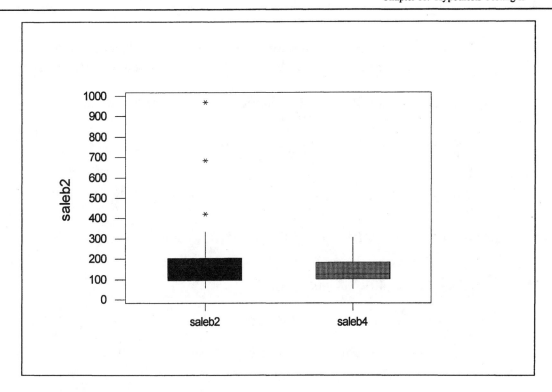

The descriptive statistics shows the effect of the extreme outliers on brand 2 sales – note the sizeable standard deviation of brand 2:

Descriptive Statistics: saleb2, saleb4

Variable	N	Mean	Median	TrMean	StDev	SE Mean
saleb2	52	181.2	127.0	155.7	154.9	21.5
saleb4	52	140.29	125.50	136.80	60.84	8.44

Variable	Minimum	Maximum	Q1	Q3
saleb2	59.0	971.0	94.8	203.3
saleb4	55.00	305.00	101.25	182.75

The matched pairs t-test on the original data shows a significant difference between the weekly sales with brand 2 found to be significantly larger than brand 4 at the .05 level:

Paired T-Test and CI: saleb2, saleb4

Paired T for saleb2 - saleb4

Variable	N	Mean	StDev	SE Mean
saleb2	52	181.2	154.9	21.5
saleb4	52	140.3	60.8	8.4
Difference	52	40.9	169.5	23.5

95% lower bound for mean difference: 1.5
T-Test of mean difference = 0 (vs > 0): T-Value = 1.74 P-Value = 0.044

b. However, with only the largest outlier removed from the data of brand 2, the difference between the two brands becomes insignificant at the .05 level:

Paired T-Test and CI: saleb2_1, saleb4 (with outlier removed)
```
Paired T for saleb2_1 - saleb4
                 N      Mean    StDev   SE Mean
saleb2_1        51     165.7    108.5     15.2
saleb4          51     140.8     61.3      8.6
Difference      51      24.9    125.7     17.6
95% lower bound for mean difference: -4.6
T-Test of mean difference = 0 (vs > 0): T-Value = 1.42   P-Value =
0.081
```

11.56 Flour A: $\mu_A = 8, \sigma^2{}_A = .04$.   Flour B: $\mu_B = 8, \sigma^2{}_B = .06$

Mix $X_M = X_A + X_B$, $\mu_M = 8 + 8 = 16$

$\sigma^2{}_M = .04 + .06 + 2(.40)\sqrt{.04}\sqrt{.06} = .1392$

$\sigma^2{}_{\bar{x}_M} = \dfrac{\sigma^2{}_M}{4} = \dfrac{.1392}{4} = (.186)^2 = .0346, \quad \sigma_{\bar{x}_M} = .186$

$z_{.005} = 2.575$, Acceptance interval: $16 \pm 2.575(.186) = 16 \pm .48$

The control limits will be at 16.48 and 15.52

Chapter 12:

Simple Regression

___

12.2   a. $H_o: \rho = 0, H_1: \rho \neq 0$, $t = \dfrac{r\sqrt{(n-2)}}{\sqrt{(1-r^2)}} = t = \dfrac{.35\sqrt{38}}{\sqrt{(1-.35^2)}} = 2.303$,

       $t_{38,.05} \approx 2.021$, $t_{38,.01} \approx 2.704$. Reject H_0 at the 5% level.
       Insufficient evidence to reject H_0 at the 1% level.

     b. $H_o: \rho = 0, H_1: \rho \neq 0$, $t = \dfrac{r\sqrt{(n-2)}}{\sqrt{(1-r^2)}} = t = \dfrac{.5\sqrt{58}}{\sqrt{(1-.5^2)}} = 4.397$

       $t_{58,.05} \approx 2.000$, $t_{58,.01} \approx 2.660$. Therefore, reject H_0 at the 1% level.

     c. $H_o: \rho = 0, H_1: \rho \neq 0$, $t = \dfrac{r\sqrt{(n-2)}}{\sqrt{(1-r^2)}} = t = \dfrac{.62\sqrt{43}}{\sqrt{(1-.62^2)}} = 5.182$

       $t_{43,.05} \approx 2.021$, $t_{43,.01} \approx 2.704$. Therefore, reject H_0 at the 1% level.

     d. $H_o: \rho = 0, H_1: \rho \neq 0$, $t = \dfrac{r\sqrt{(n-2)}}{\sqrt{(1-r^2)}} = t = \dfrac{.60\sqrt{23}}{\sqrt{(1-.60^2)}} = 3.597$

       $t_{23,.05} \approx 2.069$, $t_{23,.01} \approx 2.807$. Therefore, reject H_0 at the 1% level.

12.4 $H_o: \rho = 0, H_1: \rho > 0$, $t = \dfrac{r\sqrt{(n-2)}}{\sqrt{(1-r^2)}} = t = \dfrac{.75\sqrt{47}}{\sqrt{(1-.75^2)}} = 7.7736$

       $t_{47,.05} \approx 1.684$, $t_{47,.01} \approx 2.423$. Therefore, reject H_0 at all common levels of alpha.

12.6 $H_o: \rho = 0, H_1: \rho > 0$, $t = \dfrac{.51\sqrt{66}}{\sqrt{(1-.51^2)}} = 4.8168$

       Therefore, reject H_0 at the 5% level since $4.8168 > 1.671 \approx t_{66,.05}$

12.8   a.   Let x = Instructor Rating and y = Expected Grade. Using the computer, calculate r.

Correlations: Instructor Rating, Expected Grade
```
Pearson correlation of Instructor Rating and Expected Grade = 0.7217
P-Value = 0.008
```

     b. $H_o: \rho = 0, H_1: \rho > 0$, $t = \dfrac{.7217\sqrt{10}}{\sqrt{1-(.7217)^2}} = 3.2971$

       Reject H_0 at 10% level since $3.2971 > 1.372 = t_{10,.10}$ and p-value of .008 < alpha of .10.

12.10 Given the estimated regression equation $\hat{y} = 100 + 10X$

    a. Y changes by +30

    b. Y changes by -40

    c. $\hat{y} = 100 + 10(12) = 220$

    d. $\hat{y} = 100 + 10(23) = 330$

    e. Regression results do not "prove" that increased values of X "causes" increased values of Y. Theory will help establish conclusions of causation.

12.12 Given the estimated regression equation $\hat{y} = 43 + 10X$

    a. Y changes by +80

    b. Y changes by -60

    c. $\hat{y} = 43 + 10(11) = 153$

    d. $\hat{y} = 43 + 10(29) = 333$

    e. Regression results do not "prove" that increased values of X "causes" increased values of Y. Theory will help establish conclusions of causation.

12.14   A population regression equation consists of the true regression coefficients β_i's and the true model error ε_i. By contrast, the estimated regression model consists of the estimated regression coefficients b_i's and the residual term e_i. The population regression equation is a model that purports to measure the actual value of Y as a function of X while the sample regression equation is an estimate of the predicted value of the dependent variable Y as a function of X.

12.16 The constant represents an adjustment for the estimated model and not the number sold when the price is zero.

12.18   Compute the least squares regression coefficients;

$$b_1 = r_{xy}\frac{s_y}{s_x} \quad b_0 = \bar{y} - b_1\bar{x} \quad \hat{y}_i = b_0 + b_1 x_i$$

    a. $b_1 = .6\frac{75}{25} = 1.80 \quad b_0 = 100 - 1.80(50) = 10 \quad \hat{y}_i = 10 + 1.80x_i$

    b. $b_1 = .7\frac{65}{35} = 1.30 \quad b_0 = 210 - 1.30(60) = 132 \quad \hat{y}_i = 132 + 1.30x_i$

    c. $b_1 = .75\frac{78}{60} = .975 \quad b_0 = 100 - .975(20) = 80.5 \quad \hat{y}_i = 80.5 + .975x_i$

    d. $b_1 = .4\frac{75}{100} = .30 \quad b_0 = 50 - .30(10) = 47 \quad \hat{y}_i = 47 + .30x_i$

    e. $b_1 = .6\frac{70}{80} = .525 \quad b_0 = 200 - .525(90) = 152.75 \quad \hat{y}_i = 152.75 + .525x_i$

12.20 a. $n = 20, \overline{X} = 25.4 / 20 = 1.27, \overline{Y} = 22.6 / 20 = 1.13$

$$b_1 = \frac{150.5 - (20)(1.13)(1.27)}{145.7 - (20)(1.27)^2} = 1.0737, \ b_0 = 1.13 - 1.0737(1.27) = -.2336$$

   b.   For a one unit increase in the rate of return of the S&P 500 index, we estimate that the rate of return of the corporation's stock will increase by 1.07%

   c.   When the percentage rate of return of the S&P 500 index is zero, we estimate that the corporation's rate of return will be -.2336%

12.22 a. $b_1 = 180/350 = .5143, \ b_0 = 16 - .5143(25.5) = 2.8854 \quad \hat{y} = 2.8854 + .5143x$

   b.   For a one unit increase in the average cost of a meal, we would estimate that the number of bottles sold would increase by .5148%

   c.   Yes. 2.8854 bottles are estimated to be sold, regardless of the price paid for a meal.

12.24 a. $\hat{y} = 1.89 + 0.0896x$

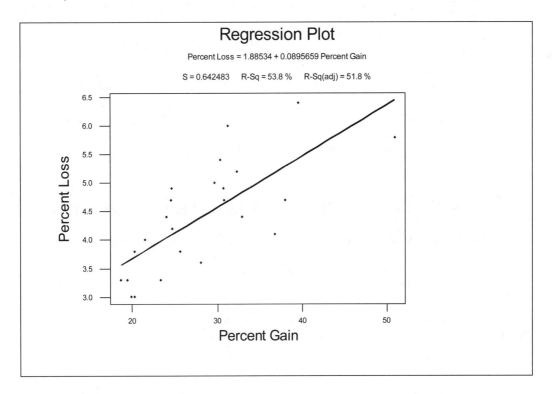

   b.   0.0896%. For a one percent pre-November 13 gain, we would estimate that there would be a loss of .0896% on November 13.

12.26 Compute SSR, SSE, s^2_e and the coefficient of determination.

Note that $R^2 = r^2_{xy}$, $R^2 = \dfrac{SSR}{SST} = 1 - \dfrac{SSE}{SST}$, and $\hat{\sigma}^2 = s_e^2 = \dfrac{SSE}{n-2}$

a. $.5 = \dfrac{SSR}{100,000}$ Solve for SSR. SSR = 50,000. Therefore, given that SST =

SSR + SSE, 100,000 = 50,000 + SSE. Solve for SSE. SSE=50,000.

$\hat{\sigma}^2 = s_e^{\ 2} = \dfrac{50,000}{52-2} = 1,000.$ R^2=.5

b. $.7 = \dfrac{SSR}{90,000}$ Solve for SSR. SSR = 63,000. Therefore, given that SST = SSR

+ SSE, 90,000 = 63,000 + SSE. Solve for SSE. SSE = 27,000.

$\hat{\sigma}^2 = s_e^{\ 2} = \dfrac{27,000}{52-2} = 540.$ R^2=.7

c. $.8 = \dfrac{SSR}{240}$ Solve for SSR. SSR = 192. Therefore, given that SST = SSR +

SSE, 240 = 192 + SSE. Solve for SSE. SSE = 48. $\hat{\sigma}^2 = s_e^{\ 2} = \dfrac{48}{52-2} = .96.$

R^2 = .8

d. $.3 = \dfrac{SSR}{200,000}$ Solve for SSR. SSR = 60,000. Therefore, given that SST =

SSR + SSE, 200,000 = 60,000 + SSE. Solve for SSE. SSE = 140,000.

$\hat{\sigma}^2 = s_e^{\ 2} = \dfrac{140,000}{74-2} = 1,944.444.$ R^2 = .3

e. $.9 = \dfrac{SSR}{60,000}$ Solve for SSR. SSR = 54,000. Therefore, given that SST = SSR

+ SSE, 60,000 = 54,000 + SSE. Solve for SSE. SSE = 6,000.

$\hat{\sigma}^2 = s_e^{\ 2} = \dfrac{6,000}{40-2} = 157.8947.$ R^2 = .9

12.28 a. $R^2 = \dfrac{\sum (\hat{y}_i - \bar{y})^2}{\sum (y_i - \bar{y})^2} = \dfrac{\sum [(b_i(x_i - \bar{x})]^2}{\sum (y_i - \bar{y})^2} = b_i^2 \dfrac{\sum (x_i - \bar{x})^2}{\sum (y_i - \bar{y})^2}$

b. $R^2 = b_i^2 \dfrac{\sum (x_i - \bar{x})^2}{\sum (y_i - \bar{y})^2} = b \dfrac{\sum (x_i - \bar{x})(y_i - \bar{y})}{\sum (y_i - \bar{y})^2} = \dfrac{[\sum (x_i - \bar{x})(y_i - \bar{y})]^2}{\sum (x_i - x)^2 \sum (y_i - y)^2} = r^2$

c. $b_1 b_1^* = \dfrac{\sum (x_i - \bar{x})(y_i - \bar{y})}{\sum (x_i - \bar{x})^2} \dfrac{\sum (x_i - \bar{x})(y_i - \bar{y})}{\sum (y_i - \bar{y})^2} = r^2$

12.30 $n = 13, \bar{x} = .5538, \sum x^2 = 80.06, \bar{y} = 11.8154, \sum y^2 = 3718.76, b = -2.0341$

Based on the result from Exercise 28.a:

$$R^2 = (2.0341)^2 \frac{80.06 - 13(.5538)^2}{3718.76 - 13(11.8154)^2} = .1653$$

From Exercise 12.7: r = -.4066, $r^2 = .1653 = R^2$
Or, from the Minitab output:

Regression Analysis: Dow1Yr versus Dow5day
```
The regression equation is
Dow1Yr = 12.9 - 2.03 Dow5day
Predictor          Coef      SE Coef           T         P
Constant         12.942        3.420        3.78     0.003
Dow5day          -2.034        1.378       -1.48     0.168

S = 12.02         R-Sq = 16.5%       R-Sq(adj) = 8.9%

Analysis of Variance
Source             DF           SS           MS          F         P
Regression          1        314.8        314.8       2.18     0.168
Residual Error     11       1589.2        144.5
Total              12       1903.9
```

The result from Exercise 12.7 of r = -.4066. Squaring the simple correlation coefficient of -.4066 yields the coefficient determination for the corresponding bivariate regression $r^2 = .1653$.

12.32   a. The Minitab output below shows the predicted value (Fit) and the residuals:

Regression: Change in Mean absence illness versus Change in Absentee rate
```
The regression equation is
Change in Mean absence illness = 0.0449 - 0.224 Change in Absentee Rate
Predictor                   Coef   SE Coef      T       P
Constant                 0.04485   0.06347   0.71   0.498
Change in Absentee Rate -0.22426   0.05506  -4.07   0.003
S = 0.207325    R-Sq = 64.8%    R-Sq(adj) = 60.9%
Analysis of Variance
Source          DF       SS       MS       F       P
Regression       1  0.71315  0.71315   16.59   0.003
Residual Error   9  0.38685  0.04298
Total           10  1.10000
```

b. $SST = \sum y^2 - n\bar{y}^2 = 1.1 - 25(0.0)^2 = 1.1$, $SSR = \sum (\hat{y}_i - \bar{y})^2 = .713$,

$SSE = \sum e_i^2 = .387$

$SST = 1.1 = .713 + .387 = SSR + SSE$

c. $R^2 = SSR / SST = .713 / 1.1 = .648$, 64.8% of the variation in the dependent variable mean employee absence rate due to own illness can be explained by the variation in the change in absentee rate.

12.34 $R^2 = r^2 = (.11)^2 = .0121$. 1.21% of the variation in the dependent variable annual raises can be explained by the variation in teaching evaluations.

12.36   For a simple regression problem, test the hypothesis $H_o : \beta_1 = 0 \; vs \; H_1 : \beta_1 \neq 0$

Given that $R^2 = r^2{}_{xy}$, $R^2 = \dfrac{SSR}{SST} = 1 - \dfrac{SSE}{SST}$, and $\hat{\sigma}^2 = s_e{}^2 = \dfrac{SSE}{n-2}$

a.   n=35, SST = 100,000, r = .46

$R^2 = (.46)^2 = .2116$. $.2116 = \dfrac{SSR}{100,000}$ SSR = 21,160. Therefore, given that

SST = SSR + SSE, 100,000 = 21,160 + SSE.   SSE = 78,840.

$\hat{\sigma}^2 = s_e{}^2 = \dfrac{78,840}{35-2} = 2,389.091$

$F = \dfrac{MSR}{MSE} = \dfrac{SSR}{s^2{}_e} = \dfrac{21,160}{2389.091} = 8.857$. $F_{\alpha,1,n-2} = t^2{}_{\alpha/2,n-2} = 2.042^2 = 4.170$

Therefore, at the .05 level, Reject H_0.

b. $R^2 = (.65)^2 = .4225$. $.4225 = \dfrac{SSR}{123,000}$ SSR = 51,967.5. Given that SST =

SSR + SSE, 123,000 = 51,967.5 + SSE.   SSE = 71,032.5.

$\hat{\sigma}^2 = s_e{}^2 = \dfrac{71,032.5}{61-2} = 1,203.941$

$F = \dfrac{MSR}{MSE} = \dfrac{SSR}{s^2{}_e} = \dfrac{51,967.5}{1203.941} = 43.165$. $F_{\alpha,1,n-2} = t^2{}_{\alpha/2,n-2} = 2.000^2 = 4.00$.

Therefore, at the .05 level, Reject H_0.

c. $R^2 = (.69)^2 = .4761$. $.4761 = \dfrac{SSR}{128,000}$ SSR = 60,940.8. Given that SST =

SSR + SSE, 128,000 = 60,940.8 + SSE.   SSE = 67,059.2.

$\hat{\sigma}^2 = s_e{}^2 = \dfrac{67,059.2}{25-2} = 2,915.617$

$F = \dfrac{MSR}{MSE} = \dfrac{SSR}{s^2{}_e} = \dfrac{60,940.8}{2915.617} = 20.902$. $F_{\alpha,1,n-2} = t^2{}_{\alpha/2,n-2} = 2.069^2 = 4.281$

Therefore, at the .05 level, Reject H_0.

12.38   a. n = 8, $n = 8, \bar{X} = 52/8 = 6.5, \sum x^2 = 494$,

$\bar{Y} = 54.4/8 = 6.8, \sum y^2 = 437.36, \sum xy = 437.7$,

$$b_1 = \frac{437.7 - 8(6.5)(6.8)}{494 - 8(6.5)^2} = .5391$$

$b_0 = 6.8 - .5391(6.5) = 3.2958$

b. $\sum e_i^2 = [437.36 - 8(6.8)^2] - (.5391)^2[494 - 8(6.5)^2] = 22.1019$

$s_e^2 = 22.1019/6 = 3.6836$, $s_b^2 = \dfrac{3.6836}{494 - 8(6.5)^2} = .0236$, $t_{6,.05} = 1.943$,

Therefore, the 90% confidence interval is: $.5391 \pm 1.943\sqrt{.0236}$, .2406 up to .8376

Regression Analysis: SalesChg_Ex12.38 versus AdvertChg_Ex12.38

```
The regression equation is
SalesChg_Ex12.38 = 3.30 + 0.539 AdvertChg_Ex12.38
Predictor              Coef   SE Coef       T       P
Constant              3.296     1.208    2.73   0.034
AdvertChg_Ex12.38    0.5391    0.1537    3.51   0.013

S = 1.91927    R-Sq = 67.2%    R-Sq(adj) = 61.8%
Analysis of Variance
Source            DF        SS       MS       F       P
Regression         1    45.339   45.339   12.31   0.013
Residual Error     6    22.101    3.684
Total              7    67.440
```

12.40

Regression Analysis: Dow1Yr versus Dow5day

```
The regression equation is
Dow1Yr = 12.9 - 2.03 Dow5day
Predictor     Coef   SE Coef      T       P
Constant    12.942     3.420    3.78   0.003
Dow5day     -2.034     1.378   -1.48   0.168

S = 12.0195    R-Sq = 16.5%    R-Sq(adj) = 8.9%
Analysis of Variance
Source            DF       SS       MS       F       P
Regression         1    314.8    314.8    2.18   0.168
Residual Error    11   1589.2    144.5
Total             12   1903.9
```

a. $\sum e_i^2 = SSE = 1589.2$

$s_e^2 = SSE/(n-2) = 1589.2/11 = 144.4686$

b. $s_b^2 = (1.378)^2 = 1.899$

c. $t_{11,.025} = 2.201$. Therefore, the 95% confidence interval is: $-2.0341 \pm$ 2.201(1.378), -5.0673 up to .9991

$$H_o : \beta = 0; H_1 : \beta \neq 0;$$

d. $$t = \frac{-2.0341}{1.378} = -1.48$$

Therefore, do not reject H_0 at the 10% level since t = -1.48 > -1.796 = -t $_{11,.05}$

12.42   Given a simple regression: $\hat{y}_{n+1} = 12 + 5(13) = 77$

95% Prediction Interval: $\hat{y}_{n+1} \pm t_{n-2,\alpha/2} \sqrt{\left[1 + \frac{1}{n} + \frac{(x_{n+1} - \overline{x})^2}{\sum (x_i - \overline{x})^2} \right]} (s_e)$

$77 \pm 2.042 \sqrt{\left[1 + \frac{1}{32} + \frac{(13-8)^2}{500} \right]} (9.67) = 77 \pm 20.533, \ (56.467, \ 97.533)$

95% Confidence Interval: $\hat{y}_{n+1} \pm t_{n-2,\alpha/2} \sqrt{\left[\frac{1}{n} + \frac{(x_{n+1} - \overline{x})^2}{\sum (x_i - \overline{x})^2} \right]} (s_e)$

$77 \pm 2.042 \sqrt{\left[\frac{1}{32} + \frac{(13-8)^2}{500} \right]} (9.67) = 77 \pm 5.629, \ (71.371, \ 82.629)$

12.44   Given a simple regression: $\hat{y}_{n+1} = 22 + 8(17) = 158$

95% Prediction Interval: $\hat{y}_{n+1} \pm t_{n-2,\alpha/2} \sqrt{\left[1 + \frac{1}{n} + \frac{(x_{n+1} - \overline{x})^2}{\sum (x_i - \overline{x})^2} \right]} (s_e)$

$158 \pm 2.086 \sqrt{\left[1 + \frac{1}{22} + \frac{(17-11)^2}{400} \right]} (3.45) = 158 \pm 7.669, \ (150.331, \ 165.669)$

95% Confidence Interval: $\hat{y}_{n+1} \pm t_{n-2,\alpha/2} \sqrt{\left[\frac{1}{n} + \frac{(x_{n+1} - \overline{x})^2}{\sum (x_i - \overline{x})^2} \right]} (s_e)$

$158 \pm 2.086 \sqrt{\left[\frac{1}{22} + \frac{(17-11)^2}{400} \right]} (3.45) = 158 \pm 2.649, \ (155.351, \ 160.649)$

12.46 $s_e^{\ 2} = 80.6 / 23 = 3.5043$, $s_b^{\ 2} = \frac{3.5043}{130} = .027$

a. $H_o : \beta = 0; H_1 : \beta < 0;$, $t = \frac{-1.2}{\sqrt{.027}} = -7.303$

Therefore, reject H_0 at the 1% level since t = -7.303 > -2.807 = -t $_{23,.005}$

b. $y_{n+1} = 12.6 - 1.2(4) = 7.8$, $7.8 \pm 1.714 \sqrt{\left[1 + \frac{1}{25} + \frac{(4-6)^2}{130} \right]} (1.872)$

$7.8 \pm 3.3203, \ (4.4798, \ 11.1203)$

12.48   a. $R^2 = 1 - \dfrac{SSE}{SST}, SSE = SST(1-R^2), R^2 = .7662$

$SST = \sum y^2 - n\bar{y}^2 = 196.2 - 20(1.13)^2 = 170.662$,

$SSE = 170.662(1-.7662) = 39.9008$

$s^2{}_e = 39.9008/18 = 2.2167$, $s^2{}_b = \dfrac{2.2167}{145.7 - 20(1.27)^2} = .0195$

$H_o : \beta = 0, H_1 : \beta > 0$, $t = \dfrac{1.0737}{\sqrt{.0195}} = 7.689$,

Therefore, reject H_0 at the 1% level since t = 7.689 > 2.878 = t $_{18,.005}$

   b. $H_o : \beta = 1, H_1 : \beta \neq 1$, $t = \dfrac{1.0737-1}{\sqrt{.0195}} = .5278$

Therefore, do not reject H_0 at the 20% level since t = .5278 < 1.33 = t $_{18,.10}$

12.50 $s^2{}_b = .000299, b = .0896$

$H_o : \beta = 0, H_1 : \beta \neq 0$, $t = \dfrac{.0896}{\sqrt{.000299}} = 5.1817$,

Therefore, reject H_0 at the 1% level since t = 5.1817 > 2.807 = t $_{23,.005}$

12.52

$\sum (y_i - \bar{y})^2 = 250(16) = 4000$

$\sum (x_i - \bar{x})^2 = 350(16) = 5600$

$SSE = 4000 - (.5143)^2(5600) = 2518.7749$, $s^2{}_e = 2518.7749/15 = 167.9183$

$s^2{}_b = 167.9183/5600 = .03$, $H_o : \beta = 0, H_1 : \beta \neq 0$, $t = \dfrac{.5143}{\sqrt{.03}} = 2.969$

Therefore, reject H_0 at the 1% level since t = 2.969 > 2.947 = t $_{15,.005}$

12.54 $H_o : \beta = 0, H_1 : \beta < 0$, $t = \dfrac{-5.903}{\sqrt{.3316}} = -10.251$

Therefore, reject H_0 at the .5% level since t = -10.251 < -3.707 = t $_{6,.005}$

12.56 $\hat{Y}_{n+1} = 12.942 - 2.034(1) = 10.9079$, $t_{11,.05} = 1.796$

The 90% prediction interval for prediction of the actual value:

$10.9079 \pm 1.796 \sqrt{[1 + \dfrac{1}{13} + \dfrac{(1-.5538)^2}{80.06 - 13(.5538)^2}](12.0195)}$

10.9079 ± 22.4291, -11.5212 up to 33.337

The 90% confidence interval for prediction of the expected value:

$10.9079 \pm 1.796 \sqrt{[\dfrac{1}{13} + \dfrac{(1-.5538)^2}{80.06 - 13(.5538)^2}](12.0195)}$

10.9070 ± 6.0882, 4.8197 up to 16.9961

The prediction interval is the estimate of the actual value that results for a single observation of the independent variable. The confidence interval estimates the conditional mean, that is, the average value of the dependent variable when the independent variable is fixed at a specific level.

12.58 $\hat{Y}_{n+1} = -.2336 + 1.0737(1) = .8401$, $t_{18,.05} = 1.734$

The 90% confidence interval for prediction of the expected value:

$$.8401 \pm 1.734 \sqrt{[\frac{1}{20} + \frac{(1-1.27)^2}{145.7 - 20(1.27)^2}]}(1.4889), .8401 \pm .581, .2591 \text{ up to } .14211$$

95% confidence interval for the prediction of the expected value:

$$.8401 \pm 2.101 \sqrt{[\frac{1}{20} + \frac{(1-1.27)^2}{145.7 - 20(1.27)^2}]}(1.4889), .8401 \pm .7039, .1362 \text{ up to } 1.544$$

12.60

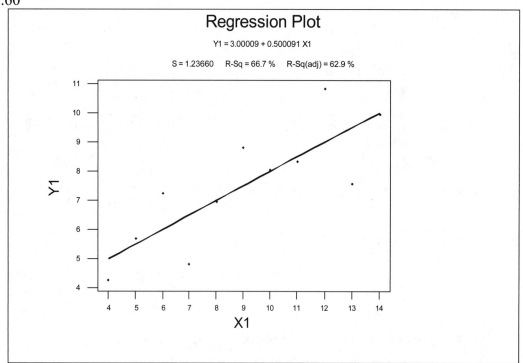

Regression Plot

Y1 = 3.00009 + 0.500091 X1

S = 1.23660   R-Sq = 66.7 %   R-Sq(adj) = 62.9 %

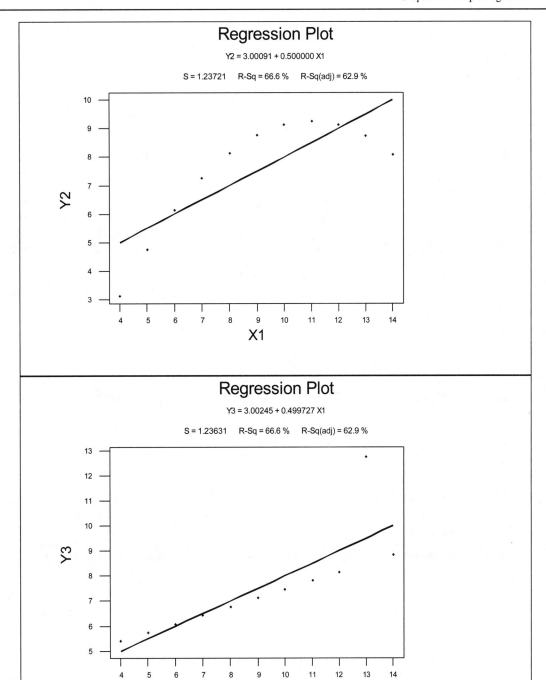

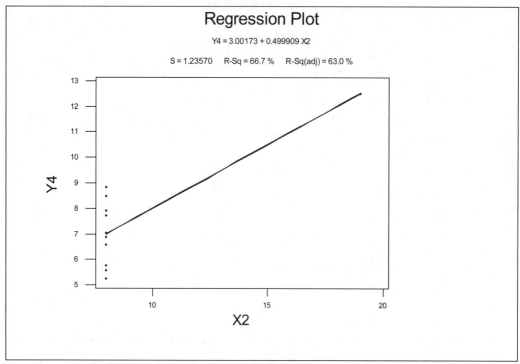

The model of Y1 = f(X1) is a good fit for a linear model
The model of Y2 = f(X1) is a non-linear model
The model of Y3 = f(X1) has a significant outlier at the largest value of X1
The model of Y4 = f(X1) has only two values of the independent variable

12.62   Two random variables are positively correlated if low values of one are associated with low values of the other and high values of one are associated with high values of the other.

a.   Total consumption expenditures are positively correlated with disposable income

b.   Price of a good or service are negatively related with the quantity sold

c.   The price of peanut butter and the sales of wrist watches are uncorrelated

12.64 $H_o : \rho = 0, H_1 : \rho > 0$, $t = \dfrac{r\sqrt{(n-2)}}{\sqrt{(1-r^2)}} = t = \dfrac{.37\sqrt{51}}{\sqrt{(1-.37^2)}} = 2.844$

Therefore, reject H_0 at the .5% level since t = 2.844 > 2.666 ≈ t $_{51,.005}$

12.66 $H_o : \rho = 0, H_1 : \rho > 0$, $t = \dfrac{r\sqrt{(n-2)}}{\sqrt{(1-r^2)}} = t = \dfrac{.293\sqrt{64}}{\sqrt{(1-.293^2)}} = 2.452$

Therefore, reject H_0 at the 1% level since t = 2.452 > 2.39 ≈ t $_{60,.01}$

12.68   To show this, let $x = \bar{x}$ for the regression of y on x, y = b$_0$ + b$_1$x
        $\hat{y} = b_0 + b_1 \bar{x} = \bar{y} - b\bar{x} + b\bar{x} = \bar{y}$

12.70 a. For a one unit change in the inflation rate, we estimate that the actual spot rate will change by .7916 units.

b. $R^2 = 9.7\%$. 9.7% of the variation in the actual spot rate can be explained by the variations in the spot rate predicted by the inflation rate.

c. $H_o : \beta = 0, H_1 : \beta > 0$, $t = \dfrac{.7916}{.2759} = 2.8692$, Reject H_0 at the .5% level since t = 2.8692 > 2.66 = $t_{77, .005}$

d. $H_o : \beta = 0, H_1 : \beta \ne 0$, $t = \dfrac{.7916 - 1}{.2759} = -.7553$,

Do not reject H_0 at any common level

12.72 a. For each unit increase in the diagnostic statistcs test, we estimate that the final student score at the end of the course will increase by .2875 points.

b. 11.58% of the variation in the final student score can be explained by the variation in the diagnostic statistics test

c. The two methods are 1) the test of the significance of the population regression slope coefficient (β) and 2) the test of the significance of the population correlation coefficient (ρ)

1) $H_o : \beta = 0, H_1 : \beta > 0$, $t = \dfrac{.2875}{.04566} = 6.2965$

Therefore, reject H_0 at any common level of alpha

2) $H_o : \rho = 0, H_1 : \rho > 0$, $r = \sqrt{R^2} = \sqrt{.1158} = .3403$

$t = \dfrac{r\sqrt{(n-2)}}{\sqrt{(1-r^2)}}$ = $t = \dfrac{.3403\sqrt{304}}{\sqrt{(1-.3403^2)}} = 6.3098$,

Reject H_0 at any common level

12.74 a. $R^2 = 1 - \dfrac{SSE}{SST} = 1 - \dfrac{204}{268} = .2388$. 23.88% of the variation in the dependent variable can be explained by the variation in the independent variable.

b. $\sum (x_i - \bar{x})^2 = \dfrac{SST(R^2)}{b^2} = \dfrac{268(.2388)}{(1.3)^2} = 37.8689$

$s^2_e = 204 / 23 = 8.8696$ $s^2_b = 8.8696 / 37.8689 = .2342$

$H_o : \beta = 0, H_1 : \beta \ne 0$, $t = \dfrac{1.3}{\sqrt{.2342}} = 2.6863$

Therefore, reject H_0 at the 5% level since t = 2.6863 > 2.069 = $t_{23, .025}$

c. $1.3 \pm 2.069\sqrt{.2342}$, the interval runs from .2987 up to 2.3013

12.76   The linear regression model could still be appropriate if the quantity of fertilizer used were within the range of values that were utilized in estimating the regression equation. To extrapolate out beyond the range of values is where the regression equations may not be as useful in forecasting.

12.78   a. Relationships are shown below in the correlation matrix with graphical plots to follow

Correlations: deaths, vehwt, impcars, lghttrks, carage

	deaths	vehwt	impcars	lghttrks
vehwt	0.244			
	0.091			
impcars	-0.284	-0.943		
	0.048	0.000		
lghttrks	0.726	0.157	-0.175	
	0.000	0.282	0.228	
carage	-0.422	0.123	0.011	-0.329
	0.003	0.400	0.943	0.021

Cell Contents: Pearson correlation
                P-Value

Unusual data points include outliers of .55 crash deaths. This data point is much higher than expected given the levels of the independent variables.

Graphical plots (a) and Regression analyses (b):

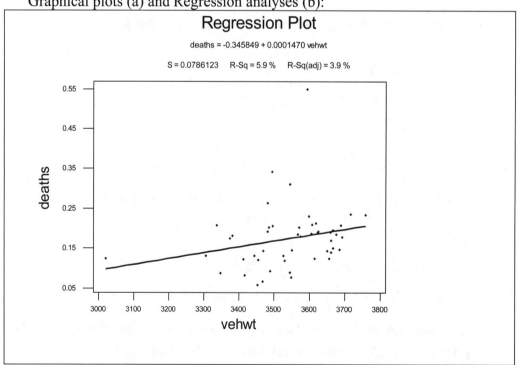

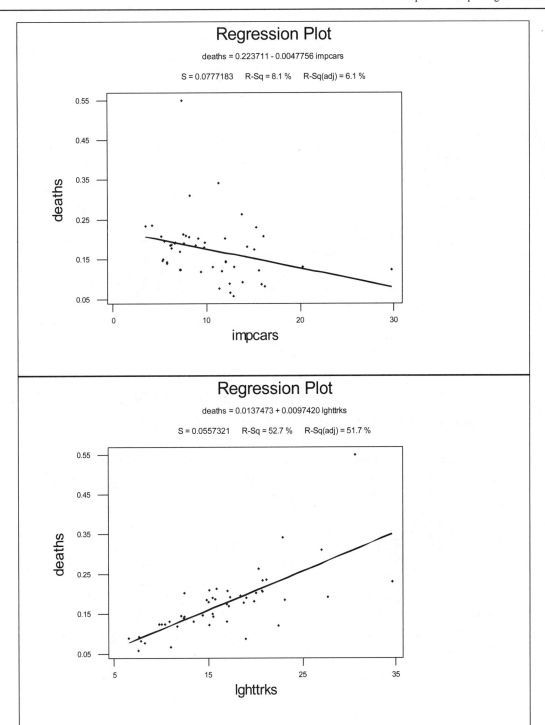

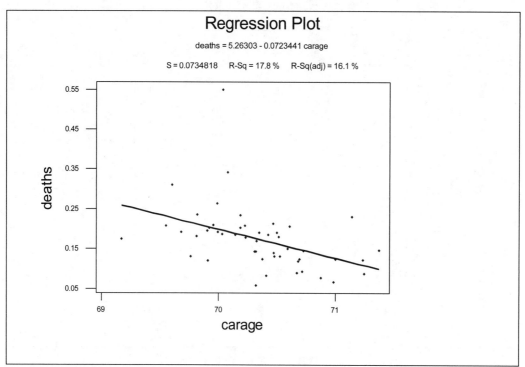

Light trucks has the strongest linear association (52.7%) followed by age (17.8%), then imported cars (8.1%) and then vehicle weight (5.9%).

c. Rank predictor variables in terms of their relationship to crash deaths.
   Independent variables are ranked based on the R-sq of the simple regression.

Variable	R-Sq	Rank
Light trucks	52.7%	1
Car age	17.8%	2
Imported cars	8.1%	3
Vehicle weight	5.9%	4

Crash deaths are positively related to both weight and percent of light trucks. Deaths are negatively related to percent import cars and the age of the vehicle. Light trucks has the strongest association followed by age, imported cars and then vehicle weight.

12.80   a. Citydat file

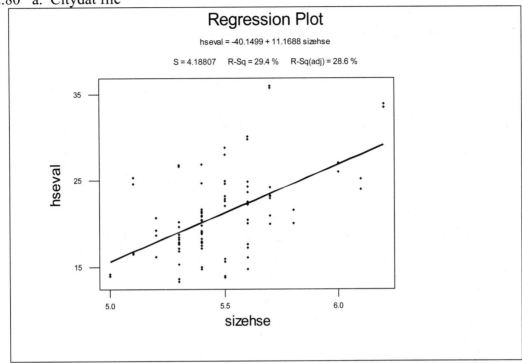

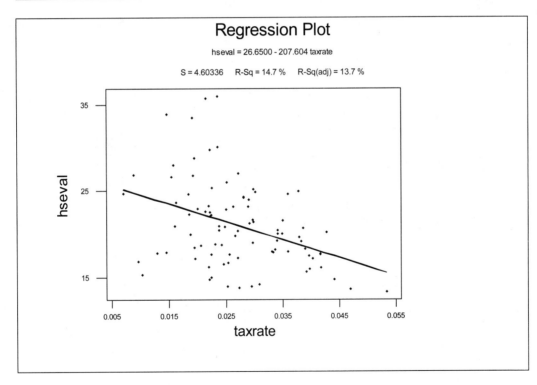

b.

Regression Analysis: hseval versus sizehse

```
The regression equation is
hseval = - 40.1 + 11.2 sizehse
Predictor        Coef      SE Coef           T          P
Constant       -40.15        10.11       -3.97      0.000
sizehse        11.169        1.844        6.06      0.000


S = 4.188       R-Sq = 29.4%      R-Sq(adj) = 28.6%


Analysis of Variance
Source            DF           SS          MS          F          P
Regression         1       643.12      643.12      36.67      0.000
Residual Error    88      1543.51       17.54
Total             89      2186.63
```

Regression Analysis: hseval versus taxrate

```
The regression equation is
hseval = 26.6 - 208 taxrate
Predictor        Coef      SE Coef           T          P
Constant       26.650        1.521       17.52      0.000
taxrate       -207.60        53.27       -3.90      0.000


S = 4.603       R-Sq = 14.7%      R-Sq(adj) = 13.7%
Analysis of Variance
Source            DF           SS          MS          F          P
Regression         1       321.83      321.83      15.19      0.000
Residual Error    88      1864.80       21.19
Total             89      2186.63
```

Size of house is a stronger predictor than is the taxrate.

c. Whether tax rates are lowered or not does not have as large an impact as does the size of the house on the evaluation.

12.82

Fixed Residential Investment vs. Bank Prime Rate:

Regression Analysis: FRH versus FBPR

```
The regression equation is
FRH = 132 + 10.5 FBPR
210 cases used 8 cases contain missing values
Predictor        Coef      SE Coef           T          P
Constant      132.004        9.828       13.43      0.000
FBPR           10.529        1.233        8.54      0.000


S = 64.19       R-Sq = 26.0%      R-Sq(adj) = 25.6%
Analysis of Variance
Source            DF           SS          MS          F          P
Regression         1       300683      300683      72.98      0.000
Residual Error   208       857000        4120
Total            209      1157683
```

Fixed Private Residential Investment vs. Federal funds rate:

Regression Analysis: FRH versus FFED

```
The regression equation is
FRH = 191 + 5.01 FFED
184 cases used 34 cases contain missing values

Predictor         Coef      SE Coef         T         P
Constant        190.67        10.25     18.60     0.000
FFED             5.013        1.480      3.39     0.001

S = 66.41       R-Sq = 5.9%      R-Sq(adj) = 5.4%
Analysis of Variance
Source            DF           SS          MS         F         P
Regression         1        50610       50610     11.48     0.001
Residual Error   182       802687        4410
Total            183       853297
```

b. 95% confidence intervals for the slope coefficient:
   Bank prime rate:

   $$\hat{\beta_1} \pm t_{.025,212}(s_{\hat{\beta_1}}) = 10.529 \pm 1.96(1.233): \quad 10.529 \pm 2.417 = 8.112 \text{ up to}$$

   12.946

   Federal funds rate:

   $$\hat{\beta_1} \pm t_{.025,212}(s_{\hat{\beta_1}}) = 5.013 \pm 1.96(1.48): \quad 5.013 \pm 2.901 = 2.112 \text{ up to } 7.914$$

c. Two point increase in interest rates:
   Bank prime rate: $\hat{Y} = 132.004 + (10.529)(2) = 153.062$
   Federal funds rate: $\hat{Y} = 190.67 + (5.013)(2) = 200.696$

d. 95% confidence intervals given a 2 percentage point increase in interest rates:

Descriptive Statistics: FBPR, FFED

```
Variable             N          N*        Mean      Median      TrMean
StDev
FBPR               210           8       7.118       6.687       6.840
3.602
FFED               184          34       6.086       5.447       5.835
3.317
Variable      SE Mean    Minimum     Maximum          Q1          Q3
FBPR            0.249      1.750      20.323       4.500       8.842
FFED            0.245      0.940      17.780       3.569       8.071
```

Given a 2% increase in each interest rate:
Bank prime rate $x_{n+1} = 9.2467 + 2 = 11.2467$. Fed funds rate
$x_{n+1} = 6.2733 + 2 = 8.2733$

For bank prime rate: the 90% confidence interval for the expected value of Y is $153.062 \pm 1.96\sqrt{\dfrac{1}{210} + \dfrac{(11.2467 - 7.118)^2}{2711.6504}} = 153.062 \pm .2061 = 152.8559$ up to 153.2681

For federal funds rate: the 90% confidence interval for the expected value of Y is $200.696 \pm 1.96\sqrt{\dfrac{1}{184} + \dfrac{(8.2733 - 6.086)^2}{2013.4555}} = 200.696 \pm .1753 = 200.5225$ up to 200.8695

Chapter 13:

Multiple Regression

13.2 Given the following estimated linear model: $\hat{y} = 10 + 5x_1 + 4x_2 + 2x_3$

    a. $\hat{y} = 10 + 5(20) + 4(11) + 2(10) = 174$

    b. $\hat{y} = 10 + 5(15) + 4(14) + 2(20) = 181$

    c. $\hat{y} = 10 + 5(35) + 4(19) + 2(25) = 311$

    d. $\hat{y} = 10 + 5(10) + 4(17) + 2(30) = 188$

13.4 Given the following estimated linear model: $\hat{y} = 10 + 2x_1 + 12x_2 + 8x_3$

    a. $\hat{y}$ increases by 8   b. $\hat{y}$ increases by 8   c. $\hat{y}$ increases by 24

13.6 The estimated regression slope coefficients are interpreted as follows:
$b_1 = .661$: All else equal, an increase in the plane's top speed by one mph will increase the expected number of hours in the design effort by an estimated .661 million or 661 thousand worker-hours.
$b_2 = .065$: All else equal, an increase in the plane's weight by one ton will increase the expected number of hours in the design effort by an estimated .065 million or 65 thousand worker-hours
$b_3 = -.018$: All else equal, an increase in the percentage of parts in common with other models will result in a decrease in the expected number of hours in the design effort by an estimated .018 million or 18 thousand worker-hours

13.8 a. $b_1 = .052$: All else equal, an increase of one hundred dollars in weekly income results in an estimated .052 quarts per week increase in milk consumption. $b_2 = 1.14$: All else equal, an increase in family size by one person will result in an estimated increase in milk consumption by 1.14 quarts per week.

    b. The intercept term b_0 of -.025 is the estimated milk consumption of quarts of milk per week given that the family's weekly income is 0 dollars and there are 0 members in the family. This is likely extrapolating beyond the observed data series and is not a useful interpretation.

13.10 Compute the slope coefficients for the model: $\hat{y}_i = b_0 + b_1 x_{1i} + b_2 x_{2i}$

    Given that $b_1 = \dfrac{s_y (r_{x_1y} - r_{x_1x_2} r_{x_2y})}{s_{x_1}(1 - r^2_{x_1x_2})}$, $b_2 = \dfrac{s_y (r_{x_2y} - r_{x_1x_2} r_{x_1y})}{s_{x_2}(1 - r^2_{x_1x_2})}$

    a. $b_1 = \dfrac{400(.60 - (.50)(.70))}{200(1 - .50^2)} = 2.000$, $b_2 = \dfrac{400(.70 - (.50)(.60))}{200(1 - .50^2)} = 3.200$

b. $b_1 = \dfrac{400(-.60-(-.50)(.70))}{200(1-(-.50)^2)} = -.667,$

$b_2 = \dfrac{400(.70-(-.50)(-.60))}{200(1-(-.50)^2)} = 1.067$

c. $b_1 = \dfrac{400(.40-(.80)(.45))}{200(1-(.80)^2)} = .083,$ $b_2 = \dfrac{400(.45-(.80)(.40))}{200(1-(.80)^2)} = .271$

d. $b_1 = \dfrac{400(.60-(-.60)(-.50))}{200(1-(-.60)^2)} = .9375,$

$b_1 = \dfrac{400(-.50-(-.60)(.60))}{200(1-(-.60)^2)} = -.4375$

13.12   a. Electricity sales as a function of number of customers and price

Regression Analysis: salesmw2 versus priclec2, numcust2
```
The regression equation is
salesmw2 = - 647363 + 19895 priclec2 + 2.35 numcust2
Predictor         Coef      SE Coef          T         P
Constant        -647363       291734      -2.22     0.030
priclec2          19895        22515       0.88     0.380
numcust2         2.3530       0.2233      10.54     0.000

S = 66399      R-Sq = 79.2%     R-Sq(adj) = 78.5%
Analysis of Variance
Source          DF           SS           MS         F         P
Regression       2  1.02480E+12  5.12400E+11    116.22     0.000
Residual Error  61  2.68939E+11   4408828732
Total           63  1.29374E+12
```

All else equal, for every one unit increase in the price of electricity, we estimate that sales will increase by 19895 mwh. Note that this estimated coefficient is not significantly different from zero (p-value = .380).
All else equal, for every additional residential customer who uses electricity in the heating of their home, we estimate that sales will increase by 2.353 mwh.

b. Electricity sales as a function of number of customers

Regression Analysis: salesmw2 versus numcust2
```
The regression equation is
salesmw2 = - 410202 + 2.20 numcust2
Predictor         Coef      SE Coef          T         P
Constant        -410202       114132      -3.59     0.001
numcust2         2.2027       0.1445      15.25     0.000

S = 66282      R-Sq = 78.9%     R-Sq(adj) = 78.6%
Analysis of Variance
Source          DF           SS           MS         F         P
Regression       1  1.02136E+12  1.02136E+12    232.48     0.000
Residual Error  62  2.72381E+11   4393240914
Total           63  1.29374E+12
```

An additional residential customer will add 2.2027 mwh to electricity sales. The two models have roughly equivalent explanatory power; therefore, adding price as a variable does not add a significant amount of explanatory power to the model. There appears to be a problem of high correlation between the independent variables of price and customers.

c.

Regression Analysis: salesmw2 versus priclec2, degrday2

The regression equation is
salesmw2 = 2312260 - 165275 priclec2 + 56.1 degrday2

Predictor	Coef	SE Coef	T	P
Constant	2312260	148794	15.54	0.000
priclec2	-165275	24809	-6.66	0.000
degrday2	56.06	60.37	0.93	0.357

S = 110725   R-Sq = 42.2%   R-Sq(adj) = 40.3%

Analysis of Variance

Source	DF	SS	MS	F	P
Regression	2	5.45875E+11	2.72938E+11	22.26	0.000
Residual Error	61	7.47863E+11	12260053296		
Total	63	1.29374E+12			

All else equal, an increase in the price of electricity will reduce electricity sales by 165,275 mwh.

All else equal, an increase in the degree days (departure from normal weather) by one unit will increase electricity sales by 56.06 mwh.

Note that the coefficient on the price variable is now negative, as expected, and it is significantly different from zero (p-value = .000)

d.

Regression Analysis: salesmw2 versus Yd872, degrday2

The regression equation is
salesmw2 = 293949 + 326 Yd872 + 58.4 degrday2

Predictor	Coef	SE Coef	T	P
Constant	293949	67939	4.33	0.000
Yd872	325.85	21.30	15.29	0.000
degrday2	58.36	35.79	1.63	0.108

S = 66187   R-Sq = 79.3%   R-Sq(adj) = 78.7%

Analysis of Variance

Source	DF	SS	MS	F	P
Regression	2	1.02652E+12	5.13259E+11	117.16	0.000
Residual Error	61	2.67221E+11	4380674677		
Total	63	1.29374E+12			

All else equal, an increase in personal disposable income by one unit will increase electricity sales by 325.85 mwh.

All else equal, an increase in degree days by one unit will increase electricity sales by 58.36 mwh.

13.14   a. Horsepower as a function of weight, cubic inches of displacement

Regression Analysis: horspwr versus weight, displace

```
The regression equation is
horspwr = 23.5 + 0.0154 weight + 0.157 displace
151 cases used 4 cases contain missing values
Predictor        Coef      SE Coef         T         P       VIF
Constant       23.496        7.341      3.20     0.002
weight       0.015432     0.004538      3.40     0.001       6.0
displace      0.15667      0.03746      4.18     0.000       6.0


S = 13.64       R-Sq = 69.2%     R-Sq(adj) = 68.8%
Analysis of Variance
Source           DF           SS           MS         F         P
Regression        2        61929        30964    166.33     0.000
Residual Error  148        27551          186
Total           150        89480
```

All else equal, a 100 pound increase in the weight of the car is associated with a 1.54 increase in horsepower of the auto.

All else equal, a 10 cubic inch increase in the displacement of the engine is associated with a 1.57 increase in the horsepower of the auto.

b. Horsepower as a function of weight, displacement, number of cylinders

Regression Analysis: horspwr versus weight, displace, cylinder

```
The regression equation is
horspwr = 16.7 + 0.0163 weight + 0.105 displace + 2.57 cylinder
151 cases used 4 cases contain missing values
Predictor        Coef      SE Coef         T         P       VIF
Constant       16.703        9.449      1.77     0.079
weight       0.016261     0.004592      3.54     0.001       6.2
displace      0.10527      0.05859      1.80     0.074      14.8
cylinder        2.574        2.258      1.14     0.256       7.8


S = 13.63       R-Sq = 69.5%     R-Sq(adj) = 68.9%
Analysis of Variance
Source           DF           SS           MS         F         P
Regression        3        62170        20723    111.55     0.000
Residual Error  147        27310          186
Total           150        89480
```

All else equal, a 100 pound increase in the weight of the car is associated with a 1.63 increase in horsepower of the auto.

All else equal, a 10 cubic inch increase in the displacement of the engine is associated with a 1.05 increase in the horsepower of the auto.

All else equal, one additional cylinder in the engine is associated with a 2.57 increase in the horsepower of the auto.

Note that adding the independent variable number of cylinders has not added to the explanatory power of the model. R square has increased marginally. Engine displacement is no longer significant at the .05 level (p-value of .074) and the estimated regression slope coefficient on the number of cylinders is not significantly different from zero. This is due to the strong correlation that exists between cubic inches of engine displacement and the number of cylinders.

c. Horsepower as a function of weight, displacement and fuel mileage

Regression Analysis: horspwr versus weight, displace, milpgal

```
The regression equation is
horspwr = 93.6 + 0.00203 weight + 0.165 displace - 1.24 milpgal
150 cases used 5 cases contain missing values
```

Predictor	Coef	SE Coef	T	P	VIF
Constant	93.57	15.33	6.11	0.000	
weight	0.002031	0.004879	0.42	0.678	8.3
displace	0.16475	0.03475	4.74	0.000	6.1
milpgal	-1.2392	0.2474	-5.01	0.000	3.1

```
S = 12.55      R-Sq = 74.2%     R-Sq(adj) = 73.6%
Analysis of Variance
```

Source	DF	SS	MS	F	P
Regression	3	66042	22014	139.77	0.000
Residual Error	146	22994	157		
Total	149	89036			

All else equal, a 100 pound increase in the weight of the car is associated with a .203 increase in horsepower of the auto.

All else equal, a 10 cubic inch increase in the displacement of the engine is associated with a 1.6475 increase in the horsepower of the auto.

All else equal, an increase in the fuel mileage of the vehicle by 1 mile per gallon is associated with a reduction in horsepower of 1.2392.

Note that the negative coefficient on fuel mileage indicates the trade-off that is expected between horsepower and fuel mileage. The displacement variable is significantly positive, as expected, however, the weight variable is no longer significant. Again, one would expect high correlation among the independent variables.

d. Horsepower as a function of weight, displacement, mpg and price

Regression Analysis: horspwr versus weight, displace, milpgal, price

```
The regression equation is
horspwr = 98.1 - 0.00032 weight + 0.175 displace - 1.32 milpgal +0.000138
price
150 cases used 5 cases contain missing values
```

Predictor	Coef	SE Coef	T	P	VIF
Constant	98.14	16.05	6.11	0.000	
weight	-0.000324	0.005462	-0.06	0.953	10.3
displace	0.17533	0.03647	4.81	0.000	6.8
milpgal	-1.3194	0.2613	-5.05	0.000	3.5
price	0.0001379	0.0001438	0.96	0.339	1.3

```
S = 12.55      R-Sq = 74.3%     R-Sq(adj) = 73.6%
Analysis of Variance
```

Source	DF	SS	MS	F	P
Regression	4	66187	16547	105.00	0.000
Residual Error	145	22849	158		
Total	149	89036			

Engine displacement has a significant positive impact on horsepower, fuel mileage is negatively related to horsepower and price is not significant.

e. Explanatory power has marginally increased from the first model to the last. The estimated coefficient on price is not significantly different from zero. Displacement and fuel mileage have the expected signs. The coefficient on weight has the wrong sign; however, it is not significantly different from zero (p-value of .953).

13.16   A regression analysis has produced the following Analysis of Variance table

Given that SST = SSR + SSE, $s^2_e = \dfrac{SSE}{n-k-1}$, $R^2 = \dfrac{SSR}{SST} = 1 - \dfrac{SSE}{SST}$,

$\overline{R}^2 = 1 - \dfrac{SSE/(n-k-1)}{SST/(n-1)}$

a. $SSE = 2500$, $s^2_e = \dfrac{2500}{32-2-1} = 86.207$, $s_e = 9.2848$

b. SST = SSR + SSE = 7,000 + 2,500 = 9,500

c. $R^2 = \dfrac{7000}{9500} = 1 - \dfrac{2500}{9500} = .7368$, $\overline{R}^2 = 1 - \dfrac{2500/(29)}{9500/(31)} = .7187$

13.18   A regression analysis has produced the following Analysis of Variance table

Given that SST = SSR + SSE, $s^2_e = \dfrac{SSE}{n-k-1}$, $R^2 = \dfrac{SSR}{SST} = 1 - \dfrac{SSE}{SST}$,

$\overline{R}^2 = 1 - \dfrac{SSE/(n-k-1)}{SST/(n-1)}$

a. $SSE = 15,000$, $s^2_e = \dfrac{15,000}{206-5-1} = 75.0$, $s_e = 8.660$

b. SST = SSR + SSE = 80,000 + 15,000 = 95,000

c. $R^2 = \dfrac{80,000}{95,000} = 1 - \dfrac{15,000}{95,000} = .8421$, $\overline{R}^2 = 1 - \dfrac{10,000/(45)}{50,000/(49)} = .7822$

13.20   a. $R^2 = \dfrac{88.2}{162.1} = .5441$, therefore, 54.41% of the variability in milk consumption can be explained by the variations in weekly income and family size.

b. $\overline{R}^2 = 1 - \dfrac{73.9/(30-3)}{162.1/29} = .5103$

c. $R = \sqrt{.5441} = .7376$. This is the sample correlation between observed and predicted values of milk consumption.

13.22 a.

Regression Analysis: Y profit versus X2 offices
```
The regression equation is
Y profit = 1.55 -0.000120 X2  offices
Predictor          Coef      SE Coef          T        P
Constant         1.5460       0.1048      14.75    0.000
X2  offi   -0.00012033   0.00001434       -8.39    0.000


S = 0.07049     R-Sq = 75.4%     R-Sq(adj) = 74.3%
Analysis of Variance
Source             DF          SS          MS        F        P
Regression          1     0.34973     0.34973    70.38    0.000
Residual Error     23     0.11429     0.00497
Total              24     0.46402
```

b.

Regression Analysis: X1 revenue versus X2 offices
```
The regression equation is
X1 revenue = - 0.078 +0.000543 X2  offices

Predictor          Coef      SE Coef          T        P
Constant        -0.0781       0.2975       -0.26    0.795
X2  offi    0.00054280   0.00004070       13.34    0.000


S = 0.2000      R-Sq = 88.5%     R-Sq(adj) = 88.1%
Analysis of Variance
Source             DF          SS          MS        F        P
Regression          1      7.1166      7.1166   177.84    0.000
Residual Error     23      0.9204      0.0400
Total              24      8.0370
```

c.

Regression Analysis: Y profit versus X1 revenue
```
The regression equation is
Y profit = 1.33 - 0.169 X1 revenue
Predictor          Coef      SE Coef          T        P
Constant         1.3262       0.1386        9.57    0.000
X1 reven      -0.16913       0.03559       -4.75    0.000


S = 0.1009      R-Sq = 49.5%     R-Sq(adj) = 47.4%
Analysis of Variance
Source             DF          SS          MS        F        P
Regression          1     0.22990     0.22990    22.59    0.000
Residual Error     23     0.23412     0.01018
Total              24     0.46402
```

d.

Regression Analysis: X2 offices versus X1 revenue

```
The regression equation is
X2 offices = 957 + 1631 X1 revenue
Predictor        Coef      SE Coef          T        P
Constant        956.9        476.5       2.01    0.057
X1 reven       1631.3        122.3      13.34    0.000

S = 346.8        R-Sq = 88.5%    R-Sq(adj) = 88.1%
Analysis of Variance
Source            DF          SS           MS        F        P
Regression         1    21388013     21388013   177.84    0.000
Residual Error    23     2766147       120267
Total             24    24154159
```

13.24   Given the following results where the numbers in parentheses are the sample standard error of the coefficient estimates
  a. Compute two-sided 95% confidence intervals for the three regression slope coefficients

$b_j \pm t_{n-k-1,\alpha/2} s_{b_j}$

95% CI for $x_1 = 6.8 \pm 2.042\ (3.1)$; .4698 up to 13.1302

95% CI for $x_2 = 6.9 \pm 2.042\ (3.7)$; -6.4554 up to 14.4554

95% CI for $x_3 = -7.2 \pm 2.042\ (3.2)$; -13.7344 up to -.6656

  b. Test the hypothesis $H_0 : \beta_j = 0, H_1 : \beta_j > 0$

For x_1: $t = \dfrac{6.8}{3.1} = 2.194$ $t_{30,.05/.01} = 1.697, 2.457$

Therefore, reject H_0 at the 5% level but not at the 1% level

For x_2: $t = \dfrac{6.9}{3.7} = 1.865$ $t_{30,.05/.01} = 1.697, 2.457$

Therefore, reject H_0 at the 5% level but not at the 1% level

For x_3: $t = \dfrac{-7.2}{3.2} = -2.25$ $t_{30,.05/.01} = 1.697, 2.457$

Therefore, do not reject H_0 at the 5% level nor the 1% level

13.26   Given the following results where the numbers in parentheses are the sample standard error of the coefficient estimates
  a. Compute two-sided 95% confidence intervals for the three regression slope coefficients

$b_j \pm t_{n-k-1,\alpha/2} s_{b_j}$

95% CI for $x_1 = 17.8 \pm 2.021\ (7.1)$; 3.451 up to 32.149

95% CI for $x_2 = 26.9 \pm 2.021\ (13.7)$; -.7887 up to 54.588

95% CI for $x_3 = -9.2 \pm 2.021\ (3.8)$; -16.88 up to -1.52

b. Test the hypothesis $H_0 : \beta_j = 0, H_1 : \beta_j > 0$

For x_1: $t = \dfrac{17.8}{7.1} = 2.507$ $t_{35,.05/.01} \approx 1.697, 2.457$

Therefore, reject H_0 at the 5% level but not at the 1% level

For x_2: $t = \dfrac{26.9}{13.7} = 1.964$ $t_{35,.05/.01} \approx 1.697, 2.457$

Therefore, reject H_0 at the 5% level but not at the 1% level

For x_3: $t = \dfrac{-9.2}{3.8} = -2.421$ $t_{35,.05/.01} \approx 1.697, 2.457$

Therefore, do not reject H_0 at either level.

13.28 a. $H_0 : \beta_1 = 0; H_1 : \beta_1 > 0$

$t = \dfrac{.052}{.023} = 2.26$

$t_{27,.025/.01} = 2.052, 2.473$

Therefore, reject H_0 at the 2.5% level but not at the 1% level.

b. $t_{27,.05/.025/.005} = 1.703, 2.052, 2.771$

90% CI: $1.14 \pm 1.703(.35)$; .5439 up to 1.7361

95% CI: $1.14 \pm 2.052(.35)$; .4218 up to 1.8582

99% CI: $1.14 \pm 2.771(.35)$; .1701 up to 2.1099

13.30 a. $H_0 : \beta_3 = 0, H_1 : \beta_3 \neq 0$

$t = \dfrac{-.000191}{.000446} = -.428$, $t_{16,.10} = -1.337$. Therefore, do not reject H_0 at the 20% level

b. $H_0 : \beta_1 = \beta_2 = \beta_3 = 0, H_1 :$ At least one $\beta_i \neq 0, (i = 1, 2, 3)$

$F = \dfrac{16}{3} \dfrac{.71}{1 - .71} = 13.057$, $F_{3,16,.01} = 5.29$. Therefore, reject H_0 at the 1% level

13.32 a. All else being equal, an extra \$1 in mean per capita personal income leads to an expected extra \$.04 of net revenue per capita from the lottery

b. $b_2 = .8772, s_{b_2} = .3107, n = 29, t_{24,.025} = 2.064$

95% CI: $.8772 \pm 2.064(.3107)$, .2359 up to 1.5185

c. $H_0 : \beta_3 = 0, H_1 : \beta_3 < 0$

$t = \dfrac{-365.01}{263.88} = -1.383$, $t_{24,.10/.05} = -1.318, -1.711$. Therefore, reject H_0 at the 10% level but not at the 5% level

13.34 a. $n = 19, b_1 = .2, s_{b_1} = .0092, t_{16,.025} = 2.12$.

95% CI: $.2 \pm 2.12(.0092)$, .1805 up to .2195

b. $H_0 : \beta_2 = 0, H_1 : \beta_2 < 0$, $t = \dfrac{-.1}{.084} = -1.19$

$t_{16,.10} = -1.337$, Therefore, do not reject H_0 at the 10% level

13.36 a. $n = 39, b_5 = .0495, s_{b_1} = .01172, t_{30,.005} = 2.750$

99% CI: $.0495 \pm 2.750(.01172)$, .0173 up to .0817

b. $H_0 : \beta_4 = 0, H_1 : \beta_4 \neq 0$

$t = \dfrac{.48122}{.77954} = .617$, $t_{30,.10} = 1.31$. Therefore, do not reject H_0 at the 20% level

c. $H_0 : \beta_7 = 0, H_1 : \beta_7 \neq 0$, $t = \dfrac{.00645}{.00306} = 2.108$, $t_{30,.025/.01} = 2.042, 2.457$.

Therefore, reject H_0 at the 5% level but not at the 2% level

13.38 a. SST = 3.881, SSR = 3.549, SSE = .332

$H_0 : \beta_1 = \beta_2 = \beta_3 = 0, H_1$: At least one $\beta_i \neq 0, (i = 1, 2, 3)$

$F = \dfrac{3.549/3}{.332/23} = 81.955$

$F_{3,23,.01} = 4.76$

Therefore, reject H_0 at the 1% level

b. Analysis of Variance table:

Sources of variation	Sum of Squares	Degress of Freedom	Mean Squares	F-Ratio
Regressor	3.549	3	1.183	81.955
Error	.332	23	.014435	
Total	3.881	26		

13.40 a. SST = 162.1, SSR = 88.2, SSE = 73.9

$H_0 : \beta_1 = \beta_2 = 0, H_1$: At least one $\beta_i \neq 0, (i = 1, 2)$

$F = \dfrac{88.2/2}{73.9/27} = 16.113$, $F_{2,27,.01} = 5.49$

Therefore, reject H_0 at the 1% level

b. Analysis of Variance table:

Sources of variation	Sum of Squares	Degress of Freedom	Mean Squares	F-Ratio
Regressor	88.2	2	44.10	16.113
Error	73.9	27	2.737	
Total	162.1	29		

13.42 $H_0 : \beta_1 = \beta_2 = \beta_3 = \beta_4 = 0, H_1 :$ At least one $\beta_i \neq 0, (i = 1, 2, 3, 4)$

The test can be based directly on the coefficient of determination since

$$R^2 = \frac{SSR}{SST} = 1 - \frac{SSE}{SST}, \text{ and hence } \frac{R^2}{1 - R^2} = \frac{SSR/SST}{SSE/SST} = \frac{SSR}{SSE} = F, \text{ and }$$

$$F = \frac{n - K - 1}{K}\left(\frac{R^2}{1 - R^2}\right), \quad F = \frac{24}{4}\frac{.51}{1 - .51} = 6.2449, F_{4,24,.01} = 4.22. \text{ Therefore,}$$

reject H_0 at the 1% level

13.44 $H_0 : \beta_1 = \beta_2 = 0, H_1 :$ At least one $\beta_i \neq 0, (i = 1, 2)$

$$R^2 = \frac{SSR}{SST} = 1 - \frac{SSE}{SST}, \text{ and hence } \frac{R^2}{1 - R^2} = \frac{SSR/SST}{SSE/SST} = \frac{SSR}{SSE} = F, \text{ and }$$

$$F = \frac{n - K - 1}{K}\left(\frac{R^2}{1 - R^2}\right), \quad F = \frac{16}{2}\frac{.96 + (2/16)}{1 - .96} = 217, \ F_{2,16,.01} = 6.23$$

Therefore, reject H_0 at the 1% level

13.46 $$\frac{(SSE* - SSE)k_1}{SSE/(n - k - 1)} = \frac{n - k - 1}{k_1}\frac{(SSE* - SSE)/SST}{SSE/SST}$$

$$= \frac{n - k - 1}{k_1}\frac{1 - R^2* - (1 - R^2)}{1 - R^2} = \frac{n - k - 1}{k_1}\frac{R^2 - R^2*}{1 - R^2}$$

13.48   a. $$\bar{R}^2 = 1 - \frac{SSE/(n - k - 1)}{SST/(n - 1)} = 1 - \frac{n - 1}{n - k - 1}(1 - R^2)$$

$$= \frac{n - 1}{n - k - 1}R^2 - \frac{k}{n - k - 1} = \frac{(n - 1)R^2 - k}{n - k - 1}$$

b.   Since $\bar{R}^2 = \dfrac{(n - 1)R^2 - k}{n - k - 1}$, then $R^2 = \dfrac{(n - k - 1)\bar{R}^2 + k}{n - 1}$

c. $$\frac{SSR/k}{SSE/(n-k-1)} = \frac{n-k-1}{k}\frac{SSR/SST}{SSE/SST} = \frac{n-k-1}{k}\frac{R^2}{1-R^2} =$$

$$\frac{n-k-1}{k}\frac{[(n-k-1)\bar{R}^2+k]/(n-1)}{[n-1-(n-k-1)\bar{R}^2-k]/(n-1)} = \frac{n-k-1}{k}\frac{(n-k-1)\bar{R}^2+k}{(n-k-1)(1-\bar{R}^2)}$$

$$= \frac{n-k-1}{k}\frac{\bar{R}^2+k}{(1-\bar{R}^2)}$$

13.50 $\hat{Y} = 7.35 + .653(20) - 1.345(10) + .613(6) = 10.638$ pounds

13.52 $\hat{Y} = 2.0 + .661(1) + .065(7) - .018(50) = 2.216$ million worker hours

13.54   Compute values of y_i when $x_i = 1, 2, 4, 6, 8, 10$

Xi	1	2	4	6	8	10
$y_i = 4x^{1.5}$	4	11.3137	32	58.7878	90.5097	126.4611
$y_i = 1 + 2x_i + 2x_i^2$	5	13	41	85	145	221

13.56   Compute values of y_i when $x_i = 1, 2, 4, 6, 8, 10$

Xi	1	2	4	6	8	10
$y_i = 4x^{1.5}$	4	11.3137	32	58.7878	90.5097	126.4611
$y_i = 1 + 2x_i + 1.7x_i^2$	4.7	11.8	36.2	74.2	125.8	191

13.58   There are many possible answers. Relationships that can be approximated by a non-linear quadratic model include many supply functions, production functions and cost functions including average cost versus the number of units produced.

13.60   a. All else equal, 1% increase in annual consumption expenditures will be associated with a 1.1556% increase in expenditures on vacation travel.
        All else equal, a 1% increase in the size of the household will be associated with a .4408% decrease in expenditures on vacation travel.

   b. 16.8% of the variation in vacation travel expenditures can be explained by the variations in the log of total consumption expenditures and log of the number of members in the household

   c. $1.1556 \pm 1.96(.0546) = 1.049$ up to 1.2626

   d. $H_0 : \beta_2 = 0, H_1 : \beta_2 < 0$, $t = \dfrac{-.4408}{.0490} = -8.996$, Therefore, reject H_0 at the 1% level

13.62   a. All else equal, a 1% increase in the price of beef will be associated with a decrease of .529% in the tons of beef consumed annually in the U.S.

   b. All else equal, a 1% increase in the price of pork will be associated with an increase of .217% in the tons of beef consumed annually in the U.S.

c. $H_0 : \beta_4 = 0, H_1 : \beta_4 > 0$, $t = \dfrac{.416}{.163} = 2.552$, $t_{25,.01} = 2.485$, Therefore, reject

H_0 at the 1% level

d. $H_0 : \beta_1 = \beta_2 = \beta_3 = \beta_4 = 0, H_1 :$ At least one $\beta_i \neq 0, (i = 1,2,3,4)$

$F = \dfrac{n-k-1}{k} \dfrac{R^2}{1-R^2} = \dfrac{25}{4} \dfrac{.683}{1-.683} = 13.466$, $F_{4,25,.01} = 4.18$.   Therefore,

reject H_0 at the 1% level

e. If an important independent variable has been omitted, there may be specification bias. The regression coefficients produced for the misspecified model would be misleading.

13.64 a. Coefficients for exponential models can be estimated by taking the logarithm of both sides of the multiple regression model to obtain an equation that is linear in the logarithms of the variables.

$\log(Y) = \log(\beta_0) + \beta_1 \log(X_1) + \beta_2 \log(X_2) + \beta_3 \log(X_3) + \beta_4 (\log(X_4) + \log(\varepsilon)$

Substituting in the restrictions on the coefficients: $\beta_1 + \beta_2 = 1, \beta_2 = 1 - \beta_1$,

$\beta_3 + \beta_4 = 1, \beta_4 = 1 - \beta_3$

$\log(Y) = \log(\beta_0) + \beta_1 \log(X_1) + [1 - \beta_1]\log(X_2) + \beta_3 \log(X_3) + [1 - \beta_3](\log(X_4) + \log(\varepsilon)$

Simplify algebraically and estimate the coefficients. The coefficient β_2 can be found by subtracting β_1 from 1.0. Likewise the coefficient β_4 can be found by subtracting β_3 from 1.0.

b. Constant elasticity for Y versus X_4 is the regression slope coefficient on the X_4 term of the logarithm model.

13.66

Results for: GermanImports.xls
Regression Analysis: LogYt versus LogX1t, LogX2t

```
The regression equation is
LogYt = - 4.07 + 1.36 LogX1t + 0.101 LogX2t
Predictor          Coef      SE Coef          T          P       VIF
Constant        -4.0709       0.3100      -13.13      0.000
LogX1t          1.35935      0.03005       45.23      0.000       4.9
LogX2t          0.10094      0.05715        1.77      0.088       4.9

S = 0.04758     R-Sq = 99.7%      R-Sq(adj) = 99.7%


Analysis of Variance
Source            DF            SS           MS          F          P
Regression         2        21.345       10.673    4715.32      0.000
Residual Error    28         0.063        0.002
Total             30        21.409


Source         DF      Seq SS
LogX1t          1      21.338
LogX2t          1       0.007
```

13.68 What is the model constant when the dummy variable equals 1
    a. $\hat{y} = 5.78 + 4.87 x_1$
    b. $\hat{y} = 1.15 + 9.51 x_1$
    c. $\hat{y} = 13.67 + 8.98 x_1$

13.70 a. All else being equal, expected selling price is higher by \$3,219 if condo has a fireplace.
    b. All else being equal, expected selling price is higher by \$2,005 if condo has brick siding.
    c. 95% CI: $3219 \pm 1.96(947) = \$1,362.88$ up to \$5,075.12
    f. $H_0 : \beta_5 = 0, H_1 : \beta_5 > 0$, $t = \dfrac{2005}{768} = 2.611$, $t_{809,.005} = 2.576$
        Therefore, reject H_0 at the .5% level.

13.72 35.6% of the variation in overall performance in law school can be explained by the variation in undergraduate gpa, scores on the LSATs and whether the student's letter of recommendation are unusually strong. The overall model is significant since we can reject the null hypothesis that the model has no explanatory power in favor of the alternative hypothesis that the model has significant explanatory power. The individual regression coefficients that are significantly different than zero include the scores on the LSAT and whether the student's letters of recommendation were unusually strong. The coefficient on undergraduate gpa was not found to be significant at the 5% level.

13.74 a. All else equal, the average rating of a course is 6.21 units higher if a visiting lecturer is brought in than if otherwise.
    b. $H_0 : \beta_4 = 0, H_1 : \beta_4 > 0$, $t = \dfrac{6.21}{3.59} = 1.73$, $t_{20,.05} = 1.725$
        Therefore, reject H_0 at the 5% level
    c. 56.9% of the variation in the average course rating can be explained by the variation in the percentage of time spent in group discussions, the dollars spent on preparing the course materials, the dollars spent on food and drinks, and whether a guest lecturer is brought in.
        $H_0 : \beta_1 = \beta_2 = \beta_3 = \beta_4 = 0, H_1 :$ At least one $\beta_i \neq 0, (i = 1, 2, 3, 4)$

$$F = \frac{n-k-1}{k} \frac{R^2}{1-R^2} = \frac{20}{4} \frac{.569}{1-.569} = 6.6$$

        $F_{4,20,.01} = 4.43$
        Therefore, reject H_0 at the 1% level
    d. $t_{20,.025} = 2.086$
        95% CI: $.52 \pm 2.086(.21)$, .0819 up to .9581

13.76

Results for: Student Performance.xls
Regression Analysis: Y versus X1, X2, X3, X4, X5

```
The regression equation is
Y = 2.00 + 0.0099 X1 + 0.0763 X2 - 0.137 X3 + 0.064 X4 + 0.138 X5

Predictor        Coef     SE Coef         T         P       VIF
Constant        1.997       1.273      1.57     0.132
X1            0.00990     0.01654      0.60     0.556       1.3
X2            0.07629     0.05654      1.35     0.192       1.2
X3           -0.13652     0.06922     -1.97     0.062       1.1
X4             0.0636      0.2606      0.24     0.810       1.4
X5            0.13794     0.07521      1.83     0.081       1.1

S = 0.5416      R-Sq = 26.5%     R-Sq(adj) = 9.0%

Analysis of Variance
Source          DF          SS          MS         F         P
Regression       5      2.2165      0.4433      1.51     0.229
Residual Error  21      6.1598      0.2933
Total           26      8.3763
```

The model is not significant (p-value of the F-test = .229). The model only explains 26.5% of the variation in gpa with the hours spent studying, hours spent preparing for tests, hours spent in bars, whether or not students take notes or mark highlights when reading tests and the average number of credit hours taken per semester. The only independent variables that are marginally significant (10% level but not the 5% level) include number of hours spent in bars and average number of credit hours. The other independent variables are not significant at common levels of alpha.

13.78   Two variables are included as predictor variables. What is the effect on the estimated slope coefficients when these two variables have a correlation equal to

   a. $r = .78$. A large correlation among the independent variables will lead to a high variance for the estimated slope coefficients and will tend to have a small student's t statistic. Use the rule of thumb $|r| > \dfrac{2}{\sqrt{n}}$ to determine if the correlation is 'large'.

   b. $r = .08$. No correlation exists among the independent variables. No effect on the estimated slope coefficients.

   c. $r = .94$. A large correlation among the independent variables will lead to a high variance for the estimated slope coefficients and will tend to have a small student's t statistic.

   d. $r = .33$. Use the rule of thumb $|r| > \dfrac{2}{\sqrt{n}}$ to determine if the correlation is 'large'.

13.80   n = 47 with three independent variables. One of the independent variables has a correlation of .95 with the dependent variable.

Correlation between the independent variable and the dependent variable is not necessarily evidence of a small student's t statistic. A high correlation among the *independent* variables could result in a very small student's t statistic as the correlation creates a high variance.

13.82   Reports can be written by following the extended Case Study on the data file Cotton – see Section 13.9

13.84   Reports can be written by following the extended Case Study on the data file Cotton – see Section 13.9

13.86

Regression Analysis: y_FemaleLFPR versus x1_income, x2_yrsedu, ...

The regression equation is
y_FemaleLFPR = 0.2 +0.000406 x1_income + 4.84 x2_yrsedu - 1.55 x3_femaleun

Predictor	Coef	SE Coef	T	P	VIF
Constant	0.16	34.91	0.00	0.996	
x1_incom	0.0004060	0.0001736	2.34	0.024	1.2
x2_yrsed	4.842	2.813	1.72	0.092	1.5
x3_femal	-1.5543	0.3399	-4.57	0.000	1.3

S = 3.048   R-Sq = 54.3%   R-Sq(adj) = 51.4%

Analysis of Variance

Source	DF	SS	MS	F	P
Regression	3	508.35	169.45	18.24	0.000
Residual Error	46	427.22	9.29		
Total	49	935.57			

13.88

Regression Analysis: y_manufgrowt versus x1_aggrowth, x2_exportgro, ...

The regression equation is
y_manufgrowth = 2.15 + 0.493 x1_aggrowth + 0.270 x2_exportgrowth
         - 0.117 x3_inflation

Predictor	Coef	SE Coef	T	P	VIF
Constant	2.1505	0.9695	2.22	0.032	
x1_aggro	0.4934	0.2020	2.44	0.019	1.0
x2_expor	0.26991	0.06494	4.16	0.000	1.0
x3_infla	-0.11709	0.05204	-2.25	0.030	1.0

S = 3.624   R-Sq = 39.3%   R-Sq(adj) = 35.1%

Analysis of Variance

Source	DF	SS	MS	F	P
Regression	3	373.98	124.66	9.49	0.000
Residual Error	44	577.97	13.14		
Total	47	951.95			

13.90   The analysis of variance table identifies how the total variability of the dependent variable (SST) is split up between the portion of variability that is explained by the regression model (SSR) and the part that is unexplained (SSE). The Coefficient of Determination (R^2) is derived as the ratio of SSR to SST. The analysis of variance table also computes the F statistic for the test of the significance of the overall regression – whether all of the slope coefficients are jointly equal to zero. The associated p-value is also generally reported in this table.

13.92   If one model contains more explanatory variables, then SST remains the same for both models but SSR will be higher for the model with more explanatory variables. Since $SST = SSR_1 + SSE_1$ which is equivalent to $SSR_2 + SSE_2$ and given that $SSR_2 > SSR_1$, then $SSE_1 > SSE_2$. Hence, the coefficient of determination will be higher with a greater number of explanatory variables and the coefficient of determination must be interpreted in conjunction with whether or not the regression slope coefficients on the explanatory variables are significantly different from zero.

13.94

$$\sum e_i = \sum (y_i - a - b_1 x_{1i} - b_2 x_{2i})$$

$$\sum e_i = \sum (y_i - \overline{y} + b_1 \overline{x}_{1i} + b_2 \overline{x}_{2i} - b_1 x_{1i} - b_2 x_{2i})$$

$$\sum e_i = n\overline{y} - n\overline{y} + nb_1 \overline{x}_1 + nb_2 \overline{x}_2 - nb_1 \overline{x}_1 - nb_2 \overline{x}_2$$

$$\sum e_i = 0$$

13.96 a. All else equal, an increase of one question results in a decrease of 1.834 in expected percentage of responses received. All else equal, an increase in one word in length of the questionnaire results in a decrease of .016 in expected percentage of responses received.

   b. 63.7% of the variability in the percentage of responses received can be explained by the variability in the number of questions asked and the number of words

   c. $H_0 : \beta_1 = \beta_2 = 0, H_1 :$ At least one $\beta_i \neq 0, (i = 1, 2)$

$$F = \frac{n-k-1}{k} \frac{R^2}{1-R^2} = \frac{27}{2} \frac{.637}{1-.637} = 23.69$$

   $F_{2,27,.01} = 5.49$,   Therefore, reject H_0 at the 1% level

   d. $t_{27,.005} = 2.771$, 99% CI: $-1.8345 \pm 2.771(.6349)$. -3.5938 up to $-.0752$

   e. $t = -1.78$, $t_{27,.05/.025} = -1.703, -2.052$.

   Therefore, reject H_0 at the 5% level but not at the 2.5% level

13.98

Regression Analysis: y_rating versus x1_expgrade, x2_Numstudents

```
The regression equation is
y_rating = - 0.200 + 1.41 x1_expgrade - 0.0158 x2_Numstudents
Predictor        Coef     SE Coef          T        P       VIF
Constant      -0.2001      0.6968      -0.29    0.777
x1_expgr       1.4117      0.1780       7.93    0.000       1.5
x2_Numst    -0.015791     0.003783      -4.17    0.001       1.5


S = 0.1866      R-Sq = 91.5%      R-Sq(adj) = 90.5%
Analysis of Variance
Source           DF          SS          MS        F        P
Regression        2      6.3375      3.1687    90.99    0.000
Residual Error    17      0.5920      0.0348
Total             19      6.9295
```

13.100 a. All else equal, each extra point in the student's expected score leads to an expected increase of .469 in the actual score

b. $t_{103,.025} \approx 1.96$, therefore, the 95% CI: $3.369 \pm 1.96(.456) = 2.4752$ up to 4.26276

c. $H_0 : \beta_3 = 0, H_1 : \beta_3 \neq 0$, $t = \dfrac{3.054}{1.457} = 2.096$, $t_{103,.025} = 1.96$

Therefore, reject H_0 at the 5% level

d. 68.6% of the variation in the exam scores is explained by their linear dependence on the student's expected score, hours per week spent working on the course and the student's grade point average

e. $H_0 : \beta_1 = \beta_2 = \beta_3 = 0, H_1 :$ At least one $\beta_i \neq 0, (i = 1,2,3)$

$$F = \frac{n-k-1}{k} \frac{R^2}{1-R^2} = \frac{103}{3} \frac{.686}{1-.686} = 75.008, F_{3,103,.01} = 3.95$$

Reject H_0 at any common levels of alpha

f. $R = \sqrt{.686} = .82825$

g. $\hat{Y} = 2.178 + .469(80) + 3.369(8) + 3.054(3) = 75.812$

13.102 a. $t_{2669,.05} = 1.645$, therefore, the 90% CI: $480.04 \pm 1.645(224.9) = 110.0795$ up to 850.0005

b. $t_{2669,.005} = 2.576$, therefore, the 99% CI: $1350.3 \pm 2.576(212.3) = 803.4152$ up to 1897.1848

c. $H_0 : \beta_8 = 0, H_1 : \beta_8 < 0$, $t = \dfrac{-891.67}{180.87} = -4.9299$

$t_{2669,.005} = 2.576$, therefore, reject H_0 at the .5% level

d. $H_0 : \beta_9 = 0, H_1 : \beta_9 > 0$, $t = \dfrac{722.95}{110.98} = 6.5142$

$t_{2669,.005} = 2.576$, therefore, reject H_0 at the .5% level

e. 52.39% of the variability in minutes played in the season can be explained by the variability in all 9 variables.

f. $R = \sqrt{.5239} = .7238$

13.104 A report can be written by following the Case Study and testing the significance of the model. See section 13.9

13.106

Correlations: Salary, age, Experien, yrs_asoc, yrs_full, Sex_1Fem, Market, C8

	Salary	age	Experien	yrs_asoc	yrs_full	Sex_1Fem	Market
age	0.749						
	0.000						
Experien	0.883	0.877					
	0.000	0.000					
yrs_asoc	0.698	0.712	0.803				
	0.000	0.000	0.000				
yrs_full	0.777	0.583	0.674	0.312			
	0.000	0.000	0.000	0.000			
Sex_1Fem	-0.429	-0.234	-0.378	-0.367	-0.292		
	0.000	0.004	0.000	0.000	0.000		
Market	0.026	-0.134	-0.150	-0.113	-0.017	0.062	
	0.750	0.103	0.067	0.169	0.833	0.453	
C8	-0.029	-0.189	-0.117	-0.073	-0.043	-0.094	-0.107
	0.721	0.020	0.155	0.373	0.598	0.254	0.192

The correlation matrix indicates that several of the independent variables are likely to be significant, however, multicollinearity is also a likely result. The regression model with all independent variables is:

Regression Analysis: Salary versus age, Experien, ...
```
The regression equation is
Salary = 23725 - 40.3 age + 357 Experien + 263 yrs_asoc + 493 yrs_full
         - 954 Sex_1Fem + 3427 Market + 1188 C8
Predictor        Coef      SE Coef         T          P        VIF
Constant        23725         1524     15.57      0.000
age            -40.29        44.98     -0.90      0.372        4.7
Experien       356.83        63.48      5.62      0.000       10.0
yrs_asoc       262.50        75.11      3.49      0.001        4.0
yrs_full       492.91        59.27      8.32      0.000        2.6
Sex_1Fem       -954.1        487.3     -1.96      0.052        1.3
Market         3427.2        754.1      4.54      0.000        1.1
C8             1188.4        597.5      1.99      0.049        1.1

S = 2332        R-Sq = 88.2%      R-Sq(adj) = 87.6%
Analysis of Variance
Source            DF          SS           MS           F          P
Regression         7  5776063882    825151983      151.74      0.000
Residual Error   142   772162801      5437766
Total            149  6548226683

Source        DF       Seq SS
age            1   3669210599
Experien       1   1459475287
yrs_asoc       1      1979334
yrs_full       1    500316356
Sex_1Fem       1     22707368
Market         1    100860164
```

Since age is insignificant and has the smallest t-statistics, it is removed from the model: The conditional F test for age is:

$$F_{X_2} = \frac{SSR_F - SSR_R}{s^2_{Y|X}} = \frac{5,766,064,000 - 5,771,700,736}{(2332)^2} = .80$$

Which is well below any common critical value of F. Thus, age is removed from the model. The remaining independent variables are all significant at the .05 level of significance and hence, become the final regression model. Residual analysis to determine if the assumption of linearity holds true follows:

Regression Analysis: Salary versus Experien, yrs_asoc, ...
```
The regression equation is
Salary = 22455 + 324 Experien + 258 yrs_asoc + 491 yrs_full - 1043 Sex_1Fem
         + 3449 Market + 1274 C8
Predictor        Coef      SE Coef         T          P        VIF
Constant       22455.2        557.7     40.26      0.000
Experien       324.24        51.99      6.24      0.000        6.7
yrs_asoc       257.88        74.88      3.44      0.001        4.0
yrs_full       490.97        59.19      8.29      0.000        2.6
Sex_1Fem      -1043.4        476.7     -2.19      0.030        1.2
Market         3449.4        753.2      4.58      0.000        1.1
C8             1274.5        589.3      2.16      0.032        1.1

S = 2330        R-Sq = 88.1%      R-Sq(adj) = 87.6%
Analysis of Variance
Source            DF          SS           MS           F          P
Regression         6  5771700580    961950097      177.15      0.000
Residual Error   143   776526103      5430252
Total            149  6548226683
```

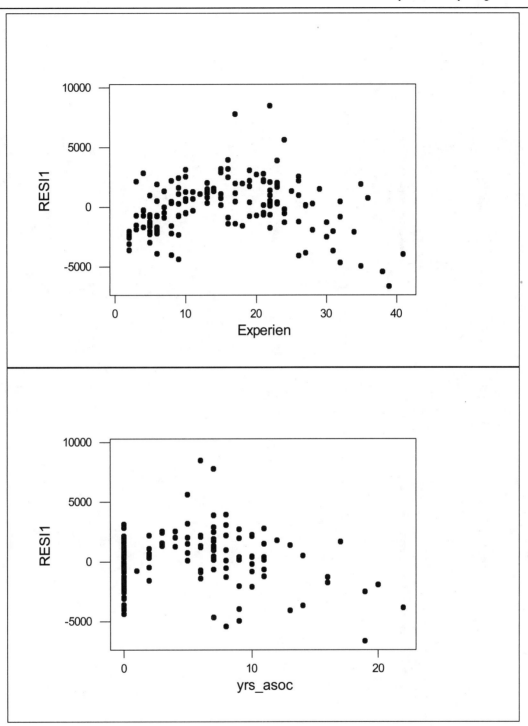

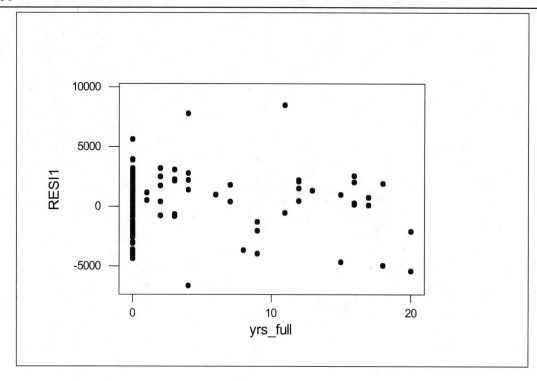

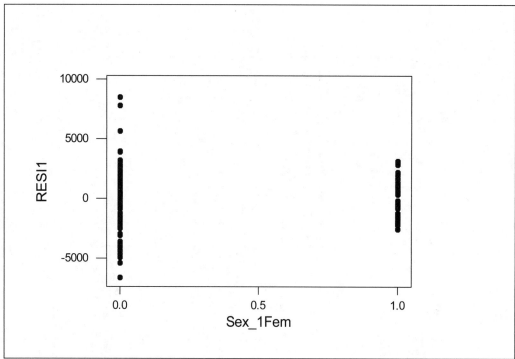

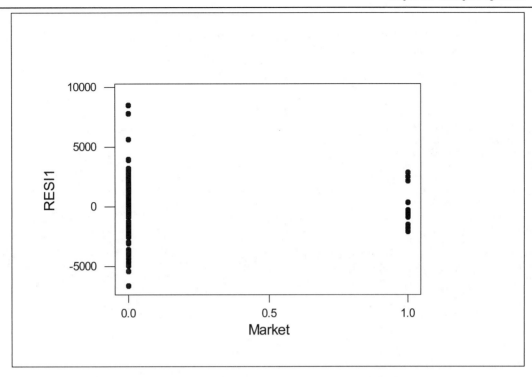

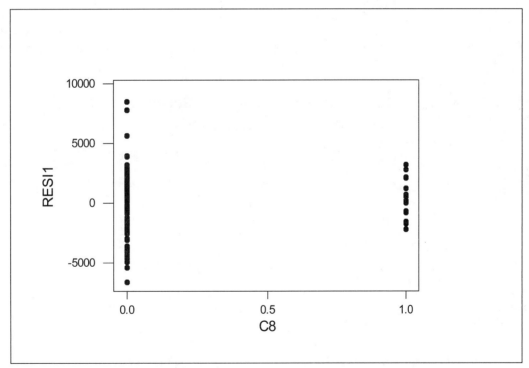

The residual plot for Experience shows a relatively strong quadratic relationship between Experience and Salary. Therefore, a new variable, taking into account the quadratic relationship is generated and added to the model. None of the other residual plots shows strong evidence of non-linearity.

Regression Analysis: Salary versus Experien, ExperSquared, ...

```
The regression equation is
Salary = 18915 + 875 Experien - 15.9 ExperSquared + 222 yrs_asoc + 612 yrs_full
         - 650 Sex_1Fem + 3978 Market + 1042 C8
```

Predictor	Coef	SE Coef	T	P	VIF
Constant	18915.2	583.2	32.43	0.000	
Experien	875.35	72.20	12.12	0.000	20.6
ExperSqu	-15.947	1.717	-9.29	0.000	16.2
yrs_asoc	221.58	59.40	3.73	0.000	4.0
yrs_full	612.10	48.63	12.59	0.000	2.8
Sex_1Fem	-650.1	379.6	-1.71	0.089	1.2
Market	3978.3	598.8	6.64	0.000	1.1
C8	1042.3	467.1	2.23	0.027	1.1

```
S = 1844        R-Sq = 92.6%      R-Sq(adj) = 92.3%
Analysis of Variance
```

Source	DF	SS	MS	F	P
Regression	7	6065189270	866455610	254.71	0.000
Residual Error	142	483037413	3401672		
Total	149	6548226683			

Source	DF	Seq SS
Experien	1	5109486518
ExperSqu	1	91663414
yrs_asoc	1	15948822
yrs_full	1	678958872
Sex_1Fem	1	12652358
Market	1	139540652
C8	1	16938635

The squared term for experience is statistically significant; however, the Sex_1Fem is no longer significant at the .05 level and hence is removed from the model:

Regression Analysis: Salary versus Experien, ExperSquared, ...

```
The regression equation is
Salary = 18538 + 888 Experien - 16.3 ExperSquared + 237 yrs_asoc + 624 yrs_full
         + 3982 Market + 1145 C8
```

Predictor	Coef	SE Coef	T	P	VIF
Constant	18537.8	543.6	34.10	0.000	
Experien	887.85	72.32	12.28	0.000	20.4
ExperSqu	-16.275	1.718	-9.48	0.000	16.0
yrs_asoc	236.89	59.11	4.01	0.000	3.9
yrs_full	624.49	48.41	12.90	0.000	2.8
Market	3981.8	602.9	6.60	0.000	1.1
C8	1145.4	466.3	2.46	0.015	1.0

```
S = 1857        R-Sq = 92.5%      R-Sq(adj) = 92.2%
Analysis of Variance
```

Source	DF	SS	MS	F	P
Regression	6	6055213011	1009202168	292.72	0.000
Residual Error	143	493013673	3447648		
Total	149	6548226683			

This is the final model with all of the independent variables being conditionally significant, including the quadratic transformation of Experience. This would indicate that a non-linear relationship exists between experience and salary.

13.108   a. Correlation matrix:

Correlations: deaths, vehwt, impcars, lghttrks, carage

	deaths	vehwt	impcars	lghttrks
vehwt	0.244			
	0.091			
impcars	-0.284	-0.943		
	0.048	0.000		
lghttrks	0.726	0.157	-0.175	
	0.000	0.282	0.228	
carage	-0.422	0.123	0.011	-0.329
	0.003	0.400	0.943	0.021

Crash deaths are positively related to vehicle weight and percentage of light trucks and negatively related to percent imported cars and car age. Light trucks will have the strongest linear association of any independent variable followed by car age. Multicollinearity is likely to exist due to the strong correlation between impcars and vehicle weight.

b.

Regression Analysis: deaths versus vehwt, impcars, lghttrks, carage

The regression equation is
deaths = 2.60 +0.000064 vehwt - 0.00121 impcars + 0.00833 lghttrks
            - 0.0395 carage

Predictor	Coef	SE Coef	T	P	VIF
Constant	2.597	1.247	2.08	0.043	
vehwt	0.0000643	0.0001908	0.34	0.738	10.9
impcars	-0.001213	0.005249	-0.23	0.818	10.6
lghttrks	0.008332	0.001397	5.96	0.000	1.2
carage	-0.03946	0.01916	-2.06	0.045	1.4

S = 0.05334   R-Sq = 59.5%   R-Sq(adj) = 55.8%
Analysis of Variance

Source	DF	SS	MS	F	P
Regression	4	0.183634	0.045909	16.14	0.000
Residual Error	44	0.125174	0.002845		
Total	48	0.308809			

Light trucks is a significant positive variable. Since impcars has the smallest t-statistic, it is removed from the model:

Regression Analysis: deaths versus vehwt, lghttrks, carage

The regression equation is
deaths = 2.55 +0.000106 vehwt + 0.00831 lghttrks - 0.0411 carage

Predictor	Coef	SE Coef	T	P	VIF
Constant	2.555	1.220	2.09	0.042	
vehwt	0.00010622	0.00005901	1.80	0.079	1.1
lghttrks	0.008312	0.001380	6.02	0.000	1.2
carage	-0.04114	0.01754	-2.34	0.024	1.2

S = 0.05277   R-Sq = 59.4%   R-Sq(adj) = 56.7%
Analysis of Variance

Source	DF	SS	MS	F	P
Regression	3	0.183482	0.061161	21.96	0.000
Residual Error	45	0.125326	0.002785		
Total	48	0.308809			

Also, remove vehicle weight using the same argument:

Regression Analysis: deaths versus lghttrks, carage

```
The regression equation is
deaths = 2.51 + 0.00883 lghttrks - 0.0352 carage
Predictor        Coef     SE Coef         T        P        VIF
Constant        2.506       1.249      2.01    0.051
lghttrks     0.008835    0.001382      6.39    0.000        1.1
carage       -0.03522     0.01765     -2.00    0.052        1.1


S = 0.05404     R-Sq = 56.5%     R-Sq(adj) = 54.6%
Analysis of Variance
Source           DF          SS          MS        F        P
Regression        2    0.174458    0.087229    29.87    0.000
Residual Error   46    0.134351    0.002921
Total            48    0.308809
```

The model has light trucks and car age as the significant variables. Note that car age is marginally significant (p-value of .052) and hence could also be dropped from the model.

c. The regression modeling indicates that the percentage of light trucks is conditionally significant in all of the models and hence is an important predictor in the model. Car age and imported cars are marginally significant predictors when only light trucks is included in the model.

13.110 a. Correlation matrix and descriptive statistics

Correlations: hseval, sizehse, Taxhse, Comper, incom72, totexp

```
           hseval    sizehse    Taxhse    Comper    incom72
sizehse     0.542
            0.000
Taxhse      0.248      0.289
            0.019      0.006
Comper     -0.335     -0.278    -0.114
            0.001      0.008     0.285
incom72     0.426      0.393     0.261    -0.198
            0.000      0.000     0.013     0.062
totexp      0.261     -0.022     0.228     0.269     0.376
            0.013      0.834     0.030     0.010     0.000
```

The correlation matrix shows that multicollinearity is not likely to be a problem in this model since all of the correlations among the independent variables are relatively low.

Descriptive Statistics: hseval, sizehse, Taxhse, Comper, incom72, totexp

```
Variable          N       Mean     Median     TrMean     StDev    SE Mean
hseval           90     21.031     20.301     20.687     4.957      0.522
sizehse          90     5.4778     5.4000     5.4638     0.2407     0.0254
Taxhse           90     130.13     131.67     128.31     48.89      5.15
Comper           90     0.16211    0.15930    0.16206    0.06333    0.00668
incom72          90     3360.9     3283.0     3353.2     317.0      33.4
totexp           90    1488848    1089110    1295444    1265564    133402

Variable     Minimum    Maximum         Q1         Q3
hseval        13.300     35.976     17.665     24.046
sizehse       5.0000     6.2000     5.3000     5.6000
Taxhse         35.04     399.60      98.85     155.19
Comper       0.02805    0.28427    0.11388    0.20826
incom72       2739.0     4193.0     3114.3     3585.3
totexp        361290    7062330     808771    1570275
```

The range for applying the regression model (variable means + / - 2 standard errors):

Hseval	21.03 +/- 2(4.957) = 11.11 to 30.94
Sizehse	5.48 +/- 2(.24) = 5.0 to 5.96
Taxhse	130.13 +/- 2(48.89) = 32.35 to 227.91
Comper	.16 +/- 2(.063) = .034 to .286
Incom72	3361 +/- 2(317) = 2727 to 3995
Totexp	1488848 +/- 2(1265564) = not a good approximation

b. Regression models:

Regression Analysis: hseval versus sizehse, Taxhse, ...

```
The regression equation is
hseval = - 31.1 + 9.10 sizehse - 0.00058 Taxhse - 22.2 Comper + 0.00120 incom72
         +0.000001 totexp
Predictor        Coef      SE Coef        T        P       VIF
Constant       -31.07        10.09     -3.08    0.003
sizehse          9.105        1.927      4.72    0.000      1.3
Taxhse        -0.000584     0.008910    -0.07    0.948      1.2
Comper        -22.197         7.108     -3.12    0.002      1.3
incom72        0.001200      0.001566     0.77    0.445      1.5
totexp       0.00000125    0.00000038     3.28    0.002      1.5

S = 3.785      R-Sq = 45.0%     R-Sq(adj) = 41.7%


Analysis of Variance
Source          DF          SS         MS        F        P
Regression       5       982.98     196.60    13.72    0.000
Residual Error  84      1203.65      14.33
Total           89      2186.63
```

Taxhse is not conditionally significant, nor is income; however, dropping one variable at a time, eliminate Taxhse first, then eliminate income:

Regression Analysis: hseval versus sizehse, Comper, totexp

```
The regression equation is
hseval = - 29.9 + 9.61 sizehse - 23.5 Comper +0.000001 totexp
Predictor        Coef      SE Coef        T        P       VIF
Constant       -29.875        9.791     -3.05    0.003
sizehse          9.613        1.724      5.58    0.000      1.1
Comper        -23.482         6.801     -3.45    0.001      1.2
totexp       0.00000138    0.00000033     4.22    0.000      1.1

S = 3.754      R-Sq = 44.6%     R-Sq(adj) = 42.6%

Analysis of Variance
Source          DF          SS         MS        F        P
Regression       3       974.55     324.85    23.05    0.000
Residual Error  86      1212.08      14.09
Total           89      2186.63
```

This is the final regression model. All of the independent variables are conditionally significant.

Both the size of house and total government expenditures enhances market value of homes while the percent of commercial property tends to reduce market values of homes.

c. In the final regression model, the tax variable was not found to be conditionally significant and hence it is difficult to support the developer's claim.

13.112 a.

Correlations: FRH, FBPR, FFED, FM2, GDPH, GH

	FRH	FBPR	FFED	FM2	GDPH
FBPR	0.510				
	0.000				
FFED	0.244	0.957			
	0.001	0.000			
FM2	0.854	0.291	0.077		
	0.000	0.000	0.326		
GDPH	0.934	0.580	0.287	0.987	
	0.000	0.000	0.000	0.000	
GH	0.907	0.592	0.285	0.977	0.973
	0.000	0.000	0.000	0.000	0.000

The correlation matrix shows that both interest rates have a significant positive impact on residential investment. The money supply, GDP and government expenditures also have a significant linear association with residential investment. Note the high correlation between the two interest rate variables, which, as expected, would create significant problems if both variables are included in the regression model. Hence, the interest rates will be developed in two separate models.

Regression Analysis: FRH versus FBPR, FM2, GDPH, GH

The regression equation is
FRH = 70.0 - 3.79 FBPR - 0.0542 FM2 + 0.0932 GDPH - 0.165 GH
166 cases used 52 cases contain missing values

Predictor	Coef	SE Coef	T	P	VIF
Constant	70.00	24.87	2.82	0.005	
FBPR	-3.7871	0.6276	-6.03	0.000	1.2
FM2	-0.054210	0.009210	-5.89	0.000	46.8
GDPH	0.093223	0.007389	12.62	0.000	58.1
GH	-0.16514	0.03747	-4.41	0.000	28.7

S = 23.42   R-Sq = 86.7%   R-Sq(adj) = 86.3%

Analysis of Variance

Source	DF	SS	MS	F	P
Regression	4	573700	143425	261.42	0.000
Residual Error	161	88331	549		
Total	165	662030			

This will be the final model with prime rate as the interest rate variable since all of the independent variables are conditionally significant. Note the significant multicollinearity that exists between the independent variables.

Regression Analysis: FRH versus FFED, FM2, GDPH, GH
```
The regression equation is
FRH = 55.0 - 2.76 FFED - 0.0558 FM2 + 0.0904 GDPH - 0.148 GH
166 cases used 52 cases contain missing values
Predictor        Coef      SE Coef          T       P      VIF
Constant        55.00        26.26       2.09   0.038
FFED          -2.7640       0.6548      -4.22   0.000      1.2
FM2           -0.05578      0.01007     -5.54   0.000     50.7
GDPH          0.090402     0.007862     11.50   0.000     59.6
GH            -0.14752      0.03922     -3.76   0.000     28.5

S = 24.61       R-Sq = 85.3%      R-Sq(adj) = 84.9%
Analysis of Variance
Source            DF           SS           MS       F       P
Regression         4       564511       141128  233.00   0.000
Residual Error   161        97519          606
Total            165       662030
```

The model with the federal funds rate as the interest rate variable is also the final model with all of the independent variables conditionally significant. Again, high correlation among the independent variables will be a problem with this regression model.

b. 95% confidence intervals for the slope coefficients on the interest rate term: Bank prime rate as the interest rate variable:

$$\hat{\beta}_1 \pm t(S_{\hat{\beta}_1}): \; -3.7871 +/- 1.96(.6276) = -3.7871 +/- 1.23$$

Federal funds rate as the interest rate variable:

$$\hat{\beta}_1 \pm t(S_{\hat{\beta}_1}): \; -2.764 +/- 1.96(.6548) = -2.764 +/- 1.2834$$

13.114 a.

Correlations: Salary, age, yrs_asoc, yrs_full, Sex_1Fem, Market, C8
```
             Salary        age  yrs_asoc  yrs_full  Sex_1Fem    Market
age           0.749
              0.000
yrs_asoc      0.698      0.712
              0.000      0.000
yrs_full      0.777      0.583     0.312
              0.000      0.000     0.000
Sex_1Fem     -0.429     -0.234    -0.367    -0.292
              0.000      0.004     0.000     0.000
Market        0.026     -0.134    -0.113    -0.017     0.062
              0.750      0.103     0.169     0.833     0.453
C8           -0.029     -0.189    -0.073    -0.043    -0.094    -0.107
              0.721      0.020     0.373     0.598     0.254     0.192
```

The correlation matrix indicates several independent variables that should provide good explanatory power in the regression model. We would expect that age, years at Associate professor and years at full professor are likely to be conditionally significant:

Regression Analysis: Salary versus age, yrs_asoc, ...

```
The regression equation is
Salary = 21107 + 105 age + 532 yrs_asoc + 690 yrs_full - 1312 Sex_1Fem
         + 2854 Market + 1101 C8
```

Predictor	Coef	SE Coef	T	P	VIF
Constant	21107	1599	13.20	0.000	
age	104.59	40.62	2.58	0.011	3.1
yrs_asoc	532.27	63.66	8.36	0.000	2.4
yrs_full	689.93	52.66	13.10	0.000	1.7
Sex_1Fem	-1311.8	532.3	-2.46	0.015	1.3
Market	2853.9	823.3	3.47	0.001	1.0
C8	1101.0	658.1	1.67	0.097	1.1

```
S = 2569        R-Sq = 85.6%     R-Sq(adj) = 85.0%
```

Analysis of Variance

Source	DF	SS	MS	F	P
Regression	6	5604244075	934040679	141.49	0.000
Residual Error	143	943982608	6601277		
Total	149	6548226683			

Dropping the C8 variable yields:

Regression Analysis: Salary versus age, yrs_asoc, ...

```
The regression equation is
Salary = 21887 + 90.0 age + 539 yrs_asoc + 697 yrs_full - 1397
Sex_1Fem
         + 2662 Market
```

Predictor	Coef	SE Coef	T	P	VIF
Constant	21887	1539	14.22	0.000	
age	90.02	39.92	2.26	0.026	3.0
yrs_asoc	539.48	63.91	8.44	0.000	2.4
yrs_full	697.35	52.80	13.21	0.000	1.7
Sex_1Fem	-1397.2	533.2	-2.62	0.010	1.2
Market	2662.3	820.3	3.25	0.001	1.0

```
S = 2585        R-Sq = 85.3%     R-Sq(adj) = 84.8%
```

Analysis of Variance

Source	DF	SS	MS	F	P
Regression	5	5585766862	1117153372	167.14	0.000
Residual Error	144	962459821	6683749		
Total	149	6548226683			

This is the final model. All of the independent variables are conditionally significant and the model explains a sizeable portion of the variability in salary.

b. To test the hypothesis that the rate of change in female salaries as a function of age is less than the rate of change in male salaries as a function of age, the dummy variable Sex_1Fem is used to see if the slope coefficient for age (X1) is different for males and females. The following model is used:

$$Y = \beta_0 + (\beta_1 + \beta_6 X_4)X_1 + \beta_2 X_2 + \beta_3 X_3 + \beta_4 X_4 + \beta_5 X_5$$
$$= \beta_0 + \beta_1 X_1 + \beta_6 X_4 X_1 + \beta_2 X_2 + \beta_3 X_3 + \beta_4 X_4 + \beta_5 X_5$$

Create the variable $X_4 X_1$ and then test for conditional significance in the regression model. If it proves to be a significant predictor of salaries then there is strong evidence to conclude that the rate of change in female salaries as a function of age is different than for males:

Regression Analysis: Salary versus age, femage, ...
```
The regression equation is
Salary = 22082 + 85.1 age + 11.7 femage + 543 yrs_asoc + 701 yrs_full
         - 1878 Sex_1Fem + 2673 Market
Predictor         Coef      SE Coef         T         P       VIF
Constant         22082         1877     11.77     0.000
age              85.07        48.36      1.76     0.081       4.4
femage           11.66        63.89      0.18     0.855      32.2
yrs_asoc        542.85        66.73      8.13     0.000       2.6
yrs_full        701.35        57.35     12.23     0.000       2.0
Sex_1Fem         -1878         2687     -0.70     0.486      31.5
Market          2672.8        825.1      3.24     0.001       1.0

S = 2594       R-Sq = 85.3%    R-Sq(adj) = 84.7%
Analysis of Variance
Source            DF           SS           MS          F         P
Regression         6   5585990999    930998500     138.36     0.000
Residual Error   143    962235684      6728921
Total            149   6548226683
```

The regression shows that the newly created variable of femage is not conditionally significant. Thus, we cannot conclude that the rate of change in female salaries as a function of age differs from that of male salaries.

13.116   a. Correlation matrix:

Correlations: EconGPA, sex, Acteng, ACTmath, ACTss, ACTcomp, HSPct

	EconGPA	sex	Acteng	ACTmath	ACTss	ACTcomp
sex	0.187					
	0.049					
Acteng	0.387	0.270				
	0.001	0.021				
ACTmath	0.338	-0.170	0.368			
	0.003	0.151	0.001			
ACTss	0.442	-0.105	0.448	0.439		
	0.000	0.375	0.000	0.000		
ACTcomp	0.474	-0.084	0.650	0.765	0.812	
	0.000	0.478	0.000	0.000	0.000	
HSPct	0.362	0.216	0.173	0.290	0.224	0.230
	0.000	0.026	0.150	0.014	0.060	0.053

There exists a positive relationship between EconGPA and all of the independent variables, which is expected. Note that there is a high correlation between the composite ACT score and the individual components, which is again, as expected. Thus, high correlation among the independent variables is likely to be a serious concern in this regression model.

Regression Analysis: EconGPA versus sex, Acteng, ...

```
The regression equation is
EconGPA = - 0.050 + 0.261 sex + 0.0099 Acteng + 0.0064 ACTmath + 0.0270
ACTss
          + 0.0419 ACTcomp + 0.00898 HSPct
71 cases used 41 cases contain missing values
```

Predictor	Coef	SE Coef	T	P	VIF
Constant	-0.0504	0.6554	-0.08	0.939	
sex	0.2611	0.1607	1.62	0.109	1.5
Acteng	0.00991	0.02986	0.33	0.741	2.5
ACTmath	0.00643	0.03041	0.21	0.833	4.3
ACTss	0.02696	0.02794	0.96	0.338	4.7
ACTcomp	0.04188	0.07200	0.58	0.563	12.8
HSPct	0.008978	0.005716	1.57	0.121	1.4

```
S = 0.4971    R-Sq = 34.1%    R-Sq(adj) = 27.9%
Analysis of Variance
```

Source	DF	SS	MS	F	P
Regression	6	8.1778	1.3630	5.52	0.000
Residual Error	64	15.8166	0.2471		
Total	70	23.9945			

As expected, high correlation among the independent variables is affecting the results. A strategy of dropping the variable with the lowest t-statistic with each successive model causes the dropping of the following variables (in order): 1) ACTmath, 2) ACTeng, 3) ACTss, 4) HSPct. The two variables that remain are the final model of gender and ACTcomp:

Regression Analysis: EconGPA versus sex, ACTcomp

```
The regression equation is
EconGPA = 0.322 + 0.335 sex + 0.0978 ACTcomp
73 cases used 39 cases contain missing values
```

Predictor	Coef	SE Coef	T	P	VIF
Constant	0.3216	0.5201	0.62	0.538	
sex	0.3350	0.1279	2.62	0.011	1.0
ACTcomp	0.09782	0.01989	4.92	0.000	1.0

```
S = 0.4931    R-Sq = 29.4%    R-Sq(adj) = 27.3%
Analysis of Variance
```

Source	DF	SS	MS	F	P
Regression	2	7.0705	3.5352	14.54	0.000
Residual Error	70	17.0192	0.2431		
Total	72	24.0897			

Both independent variables are conditionally significant.

b. The model could be used in college admission decisions by creating a predicted GPA in economics based on sex and ACT comp scores. This predicted GPA could then be used with other factors in deciding admission. Note that this model predicts that females will outperform males with equal test scores. Using this model as the only source of information may lead to charges of unequal treatment.

Chapter 14:

Additional Topics in Regression Analysis

14.2 $Y_i = \beta_0 + \beta_1 X_{1i} + \beta_2 X_{2i} + \beta_3 X_{3i} + \beta_4 X_{4i} + \beta_5 X_{5i} + \varepsilon_i$

where Y_i = wages

   X_1 = Years of experience

   X_2 = 1 for Germany, 0 otherwise

   X_3 = 1 for Great Britain, 0 otherwise

   X_4 = 1 for Japan, 0 otherwise

   X_5 = 1 for Turkey, 0 otherwise

The excluded category consists of wages in the United States

14.4 a. For any observation, the values of the dummy variables sum to one. Since the equation has an intercept term, there is perfect multicollinearity and the existence of the "dummy variable trap".

   b. β_3 measures the expected difference between demand in the first and fourth quarters, all else equal. β_4 measures the expected difference between demand in the second and fourth quarters, all else equal. β_5 measures the expected difference between demand in the third and fourth quarters, all else equal.

14.6 $Y_i = \beta_0 + \beta_1 X_{1i} + \beta_2 X_{2i} + \beta_3 X_{3i} + \beta_4 X_{4i} + \beta_5 X_{5i} + \varepsilon_i$

where Y_i = per capita cereal sales

X_1 = cereal price

X_2 = price of competing cereals

X_3 = mean per capita income

X_4 = % college graduates

X_5 = mean annual temperature

X_6 = mean annual rainfall

X_7 = 1 for cities east of the Mississippi, 0

otherwise

X_8 = 1 for high per capita income, 0 otherwise

X_9 = 1 for intermediate per capita income, 0

otherwise

$X_{10} = 1$ for northwest, 0 otherwise

$X_{11} = 1$ for southwest, 0 otherwise

$X_{12} = 1$ for northeast, 0 otherwise

$X_{13} = X_1 X_7$ – interaction term between price and cities east of the Mississippi

The model specification includes continuous independent variables, dichotomous indicator variables and slope dummy variables. Based on economic demand theory, we would expect the coefficient on cereal price to be negative due to the law of demand. Prices of substitutes are expected to have a positive impact on per capita cereal sales. If the cereal is deemed a normal good, mean per capita income will have a positive impact on sales. The signs and sizes of other variables may be empirically determined. While the functional form can be linear, non-linearity could be introduced based on an initial analysis of the scatterplots of the relationships. High correlation among the independent variables could also be detected, for example, per capita income and % college graduates may very well be collinear. Several iterations of the model could be conducted to find the optimal combinations of variables.

14.8   Define the following variables for the experiment

   Y = worker compensation

   X_1 = years of experience

   X_2 = job classification level

      1.   Apprentice

      2.   Professional

      3.   Master

   X_3 = individual ability

   X_4 = gender

      1.   male

      2.   female

   X_5 = race

      1.   White

      2.   Black

      3.   Latino

Two different dependent variables can be developed from the salary data. Base compensation will be one analysis that can be conducted. The incremental salaries can also be analyzed. Dummy variables are required to analyze the impact of job classifications on salary. Discrimination can be measured by the size of the dummy variable on gender and on race. For each dummy variable, (k-1) categories are required to avoid the 'dummy variable trap.' The F-test for the significance of the overall regression will be utilized to determine whether the model has significant explanatory power. And the t-test for the significance of the individual regression slope coefficients will be utilized to determine the impact of each independent variable. Model diagnostics will be based on R-square and the behavior of the residuals.

14.10   What is the long term effect of a one unit increase in x in period t?

a. $\dfrac{\beta_j}{(1-\gamma)} = \dfrac{2}{(1-.34)} = 3.03$

b. $\dfrac{\beta_j}{(1-\gamma)} = \dfrac{2.5}{(1-.24)} = 3.289$

c. $\dfrac{\beta_j}{(1-\gamma)} = \dfrac{2}{(1-.64)} = 5.556$

d. $\dfrac{\beta_j}{(1-\gamma)} = \dfrac{4.3}{(1-.34)} = 6.515$

14.12

Regression Analysis: Y Retail Sales versus X Income, Ylag1
```
The regression equation is
Y  Retail Sales = 1752 + 0.367 X  Income + 0.053 Ylag1
21 cases used 1 cases contain missing values

Predictor         Coef      SE Coef          T        P
Constant        1751.6        500.0       3.50    0.003
X  Incom       0.36734      0.08054       4.56    0.000
Ylag1           0.0533       0.2035       0.26    0.796

S = 153.4        R-Sq = 91.7%      R-Sq(adj) = 90.7%
```

$t = \dfrac{.0533}{.2035} = .2619;$ $t_{18,.10} = 1.33$, therefore, do not reject H_0 at the 20% level.

14.14

Regression Analysis: Y_%stocks versus X_Return, Y_lag%stocks
```
The regression equation is
Y_%stocks = 1.65 + 0.228 X_Return + 0.950 Y_lag%stocks
24 cases used 1 cases contain missing values

Predictor         Coef      SE Coef          T        P
Constant         1.646        2.414       0.68    0.503
X_Return       0.22776      0.03015       7.55    0.000
Y_lag%st       0.94999      0.04306      22.06    0.000

S = 2.351        R-Sq = 95.9%      R-Sq(adj) = 95.5%
Analysis of Variance
Source           DF           SS          MS        F        P
Regression        2       2689.6      1344.8   243.38    0.000
Residual Error   21        116.0         5.5
Total            23       2805.6

Source          DF      Seq SS
X_Return         1         0.7
Y_lag%st         1      2688.9

Unusual Observations
Obs   X_Return   Y_%stock        Fit    SE Fit   Residual   St Resid
 20      -26.5     56.000     60.210     1.160     -4.210     -2.06R
```

14.16

Regression Analysis: Y_Birth versus X_1stmarriage, Y_lagBirth

```
The regression equation is
Y_Birth = 21262 + 0.485 X_1stmarriage + 0.192 Y_lagBirth

19 cases used 1 cases contain missing values
```

Predictor	Coef	SE Coef	T	P
Constant	21262	5720	3.72	0.002
X_1stmar	0.4854	0.1230	3.94	0.001
Y_lagBir	0.1923	0.1898	1.01	0.326

```
S = 2513        R-Sq = 93.7%     R-Sq(adj) = 93.0%
Analysis of Variance
```

Source	DF	SS	MS	F	P
Regression	2	1515082551	757541276	119.93	0.000
Residual Error	16	101062160	6316385		
Total	18	1616144711			

Source	DF	Seq SS
X_1stmar	1	1508597348
Y_lagBir	1	6485203

```
Unusual Observations
```

Obs	X_1stmar	Y_Birth	Fit	SE Fit	Residual	St Resid
15	105235	95418	89340	982	6078	2.63R

14.18

Regression Analysis: Y_logCons versus X_LogDI, Y_laglogCons

```
The regression equation is
Y_logCons = 0.405 + 0.373 X_LogDI + 0.558 Y_laglogCons

28 cases used 1 cases contain missing values
```

Predictor	Coef	SE Coef	T	P
Constant	0.4049	0.1051	3.85	0.001
X_LogDI	0.3734	0.1075	3.47	0.002
Y_laglog	0.5577	0.1243	4.49	0.000

```
S = 0.03023     R-Sq = 99.6%     R-Sq(adj) = 99.6%
Analysis of Variance
```

Source	DF	SS	MS	F	P
Regression	2	6.1960	3.0980	3389.90	0.000
Residual Error	25	0.0228	0.0009		
Total	27	6.2189			

Source	DF	Seq SS
X_LogDI	1	6.1776
Y_laglog	1	0.0184

```
Unusual Observations
```

Obs	X_LogDI	Y_logCon	Fit	SE Fit	Residual	St Resid
9	5.84	5.80814	5.72298	0.01074	0.08517	3.01R

```
Durbin-Watson statistic = 1.63
```

14.20   a. In the special case where the sample correlations between x_1 and x_2 is zero, the estimate for β_1 will be the same whether or not x_2 is included in the regression equation. In the simple linear regression of y on x_1, the intercept term will embody the influence of x_2 on y, under these special circumstances.

b.

$$b_1 = \frac{\sum (x_{2i} - \bar{x}_2)^2 \sum (x_{1i} - \bar{x}_1)(y_{1i} - \bar{y}) - \sum (x_{1i} - \bar{x}_1)(x_{2i} - \bar{x}_2) \sum (x_{2i} - \bar{x}_2)(y_i - \bar{y})}{\sum (x_{1i} - \bar{x}_1)^2 \sum (x_{2i} - \bar{x}_2)^2 - [\sum (x_{1i} - \bar{x}_1) \sum (x_{2i} - \bar{x}_2)]^2}$$

If the sample correlation between x_1 and x_2 is zero, then

$\sum (x_{1i} - \bar{x}_1)(x_{2i} - \bar{x}_2) = 0$ and the slope coefficient equation can be simplified.

The result is $b_1 = \dfrac{\sum (x_{1i} - \bar{x}_1)(y_{1i} - \bar{y})}{\sum (x_{1i} - \bar{x}_1)^2}$ which is the estimated slope coefficient

for the bivariate linear regression of y on x_1.

14.22

Results for: CITYDAT.XLS
Regression Analysis: hseval versus Comper, Homper, ...
```
The regression equation is
hseval = - 19.0 - 26.4 Comper - 12.1 Homper - 15.5 Indper + 7.22 sizehse
         + 0.00408 incom72
Predictor         Coef      SE Coef          T         P
Constant        -19.02        13.20      -1.44     0.153
Comper         -26.393         9.890      -2.67     0.009
Homper         -12.123         7.508      -1.61     0.110
Indper         -15.531         8.630      -1.80     0.075
sizehse          7.219         2.138       3.38     0.001
incom72       0.004081      0.001555       2.62     0.010


S = 3.949      R-Sq = 40.1%     R-Sq(adj) = 36.5%
Analysis of Variance
Source            DF            SS          MS          F         P
Regression         5        876.80      175.36      11.25     0.000
Residual Error    84       1309.83       15.59
Total             89       2186.63


Source      DF      Seq SS
Comper       1      245.47
Homper       1        1.38
Indper       1      112.83
sizehse      1      409.77
incom72      1      107.36


Unusual Observations
Obs     Comper      hseval         Fit      SE Fit     Residual     St Resid
 23      0.100      20.003      28.296       1.913       -8.294       -2.40RX
 24      0.103      20.932      29.292       2.487       -8.360       -2.73RX
 29      0.139      16.498      19.321       1.872       -2.823       -0.81 X
 30      0.141      16.705      19.276       1.859       -2.570       -0.74 X
 75      0.112      35.976      24.513       0.747       11.463        2.96R
 76      0.116      35.736      24.418       0.749       11.317        2.92R
R denotes an observation with a large standardized residual
X denotes an observation whose X value gives it large influence.
Durbin-Watson statistic = 1.03
```

Dropping the insignificant independent variables: Homper and Indper yields:

Regression Analysis: hseval versus Comper, sizehse, incom72

```
The regression equation is
hseval = - 34.2 - 13.9 Comper + 8.27 sizehse + 0.00364 incom72

Predictor         Coef      SE Coef          T         P
Constant        -34.24        10.44      -3.28     0.002
Comper         -13.881         6.974      -1.99     0.050
sizehse          8.270         1.957       4.23     0.000
incom72       0.003636      0.001456       2.50     0.014

S = 3.983        R-Sq = 37.6%      R-Sq(adj) = 35.4%
Analysis of Variance
Source           DF           SS          MS         F         P
Regression        3       822.53      274.18     17.29     0.000
Residual Error   86      1364.10       15.86
Total            89      2186.63

Source       DF     Seq SS
Comper        1     245.47
sizehse       1     478.09
incom72       1      98.98

Unusual Observations
Obs    Comper    hseval        Fit     SE Fit    Residual    St Resid
 49     0.282    29.810     23.403      1.576       6.407     1.75 X
 50     0.284    30.061     23.380      1.583       6.681     1.83 X
 75     0.112    35.976     24.708      0.674      11.268     2.87R
 76     0.116    35.736     24.659      0.667      11.077     2.82R

R denotes an observation with a large standardized residual
X denotes an observation whose X value gives it large influence.
Durbin-Watson statistic = 1.02
```

Excluding median rooms per residence (Sizehse):

Regression Analysis: hseval versus Comper, incom72

```
The regression equation is
hseval = 4.69 - 20.4 Comper + 0.00585 incom72
Predictor         Coef      SE Coef          T         P
Constant         4.693        5.379       0.87     0.385
Comper         -20.432        7.430      -2.75     0.007
incom72       0.005847      0.001484       3.94     0.000

S = 4.352        R-Sq = 24.7%      R-Sq(adj) = 22.9%
Analysis of Variance
Source           DF           SS          MS         F         P
Regression        2       539.20      269.60     14.24     0.000
Residual Error   87      1647.44       18.94
Total            89      2186.63

Source       DF     Seq SS
Comper        1     245.47
incom72       1     293.73
Durbin-Watson statistic = 0.98
```

Note that the coefficient on percent of commercial property for both of the models is negative; however, it is larger in the second model where the median rooms variable is excluded.

14.24   If y is, in fact, strongly influenced by x_2, dropping it from the regression equation could lead to serious specification bias. Instead of dropping the variable, it is preferable to acknowledge that, while the group as a whole is clearly influential, the data does not contain information to allow the disentangling of the separate effects of each of the explanatory variables with some degree of precision.

14.26   a. Graphical check for heteroscedasticity shows no evidence of strong heteroscedasticity.

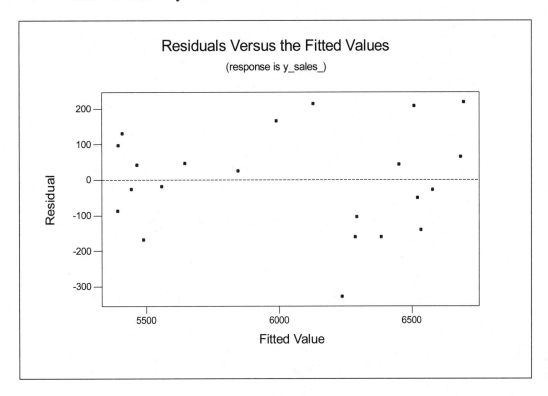

b.   The auxiliary regression is $e^2 = -63310.41 + 13.75\hat{y}$

$n = 22, \quad R^2 = .06954, \quad nR^2 = 1.5299 < 2.71 = \chi^2_{1,.1}$

therefore, do not reject H_0 the error terms have constant variance at the 10% level.

14.28 a. Compute the multiple regression of Y on x_1, x_2 and x_3.

Results for: Household Income.MTW
Regression Analysis: y versus X1, X2, X3

```
The regression equation is
y = 0.2 + 0.000406 X1 + 4.84 X2 - 1.55 X3
Predictor        Coef     SE Coef       T       P    VIF
Constant         0.16       34.91    0.00   0.996
X1          0.0004060   0.0001736    2.34   0.024    1.2
X2              4.842       2.813    1.72   0.092    1.5
X3            -1.5543      0.3399   -4.57   0.000    1.3

S = 3.04752   R-Sq = 54.3%   R-Sq(adj) = 51.4%
Analysis of Variance
Source          DF        SS       MS       F       P
Regression       3    508.35   169.45   18.24   0.000
Residual Error  46    427.22     9.29
Total           49    935.57


Unusual Observations
Obs      X1        y     Fit   SE Fit   Residual   St Resid
  4   22456   52.600  59.851    0.850     -7.251     -2.48R
 13   14174   44.200  50.840    1.166     -6.640     -2.36R
R denotes an observation with a large standardized residual.
Durbin-Watson statistic = 1.75105
```

b. Graphical check for heteroscedasticity shows no evidence of strong heteroscedasticity

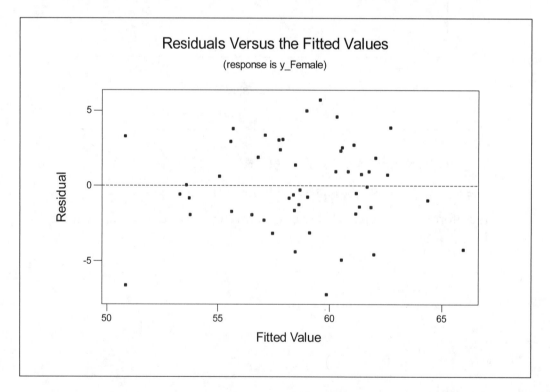

c. The auxiliary regression is $e^2 = 20.34 - .201\hat{y}$

$n = 50$, $R^2 = .00322$, $nR^2 = .161 < 2.71 = \chi^2_{1,.1}$, therefore, do not reject the H_0 that the error terms have constant variance at the 10% level.

14.30   Test for the presence of autocorrelation.

$H_0 : \rho = 0, H_1 : \rho > 0$, d = .50, n = 28, K = 2, $\alpha = .05$: $d_L = 1.26$ and $d_U = 1.56$

$\alpha = .01$: $d_L = 1.04$ and $d_U = 1.32$

Reject the null hypothesis based on the Durbin-Watson test at both the 5% and 1% levels. Estimate of the autocorrelation coefficient: $r = 1 - \dfrac{d}{2} = r = 1 - \dfrac{.5}{2} = .75$

a. $H_0 : \rho = 0, H_1 : \rho > 0$, d = .80, n = 28, K = 2,

$\alpha = .05$: $d_L = 1.26$ and $d_U = 1.56$

$\alpha = .01$: $d_L = 1.04$ and $d_U = 1.32$

Reject the null hypothesis based on the Durbin-Watson test at both the 5% and 1% levels. Estimate of the autocorrelation coefficient: $r = 1 - \dfrac{d}{2} =$

$r = 1 - \dfrac{.8}{2} = .60$

b. $H_0 : \rho = 0, H_1 : \rho > 0$, d = 1.10, n = 28, K = 2,

$\alpha = .05$: $d_L = 1.26$ and $d_U = 1.56$

$\alpha = .01$: $d_L = 1.04$ and $d_U = 1.32$

Reject the null hypothesis based on the Durbin-Watson test at the 5% level. The test is inconclusive at the 1% level.

Estimate of the autocorrelation coefficient: $r = 1 - \dfrac{d}{2} = r = 1 - \dfrac{1.10}{2} = .45$

c. $H_0 : \rho = 0, H_1 : \rho > 0$, d = 1.25, n = 28, K = 2,

$\alpha = .05$: $d_L = 1.26$ and $d_U = 1.56$

$\alpha = .01$: $d_L = 1.04$ and $d_U = 1.32$

The test is inconclusive at the 1% level. There is evidence of first-order positive autocorrelation of the residuals at the .05 level.

d. $H_0 : \rho = 0, H_1 : \rho > 0$, d = 1.70, n = 28, K = 2,

$\alpha = .05$: $d_L = 1.26$ and $d_U = 1.56$

$\alpha = .01$: $d_L = 1.04$ and $d_U = 1.32$

Do not reject the null hypothesis at either the 5% level or the 1% level. There is insufficient evidence to suggest autocorrelation exists in the residuals.

14.32   Given that $Var(\varepsilon_i) = Kx^2_i$ $(K > 0)$

$$Var(\varepsilon_i / x_i) = \frac{1}{x^2_i} Var(\varepsilon_i) = \frac{1}{x^2_i} Kx^2_i = K$$

If the squared relationship can be found between the variance of the error terms and x_i such as $Var(\varepsilon_i) = Kx^2_i$, the problem of heteroscedasticity can be removed by dividing both sides of the regression equation by x_i

14.34   The regression model associated with Exercise 14.13 includes the lagged value of the dependent variable as an independent variable. In the presence of a lagged dependent variable used as an independent variable, the Durbin-Watson statistic is no longer valid. Instead, use of Durbin's h statistic is appropriate:

$H_0 : \rho = 0, H_1 : \rho > 0$

$$r = 1 - \frac{d}{2} = 1 - \frac{1.65}{2} = .175, \quad s_c^2 = (.1266)^2 = .0160,$$

$$h = r\sqrt{\frac{n}{1 - n(s_c^2)}} = .175\sqrt{\frac{27}{1 - 27(.0160)}} = 1.21$$

$z_{.1} = 1.28$, therefore, do not reject H_0 at the 10% level

14.36   With a low Durbin-Watson statistic of .85, test for the presence of positive autocorrelation

$H_0 : \rho = 0, H_1 : \rho > 0$, d=.85, n=24, K = 4, $\alpha = .05$: $d_L = 1.01$ and $d_U = 1.78$

$\alpha = .01$: $d_L = .80$ and $d_U = 1.53$. Reject H_0 at the 5% level, test is inconclusive at 1% level.

14.38   d = .8529. $H_0 : \rho = 0, H_1 : \rho > 0$, n = 25, K = 1, $\alpha = .01$: $d_L = 1.05$ and $d_U = 1.21$

Reject H_0 at the 1% level, therefore, a misspecified regression model with an omitted variable can result in the presence of autocorrelation of the residuals

14.40   a. Dummy Variables: Dummy variables are used whenever a factor is not readily quantifiable. For example, if we wished to determine the effect of trade barriers on output growth rates, we could include a dummy variable which takes the value of one when trade barriers are imposed and zero otherwise. This could then be used to distinguish between different trade barrier levels.

   b. Lagged dependent variables: Lagged dependent variables are useful when time series data are analyzed. For example, one might wish to include lagged growth rates in a model used to explain fluctuations in output

   c. Logarithmic transformation: Logarithmic transformations allows inherently linear statistical techniques such as least squares linear regression to estimate non-linear functions. For example, cost functions where cost is some function of output produced is typically non-linear. The log transformation allows us to express non-linear relationships in linear form and hence use linear estimation techniques to estimate the model.

14.42   The statement is not valid. The summation of several bivariate (simple) linear regressions does not equal the results obtained from a multiple regression. Therefore, while separating the independent variables may give some indication of the statistical significance of the individual effects, they will not provide any information about the influence on the dependent variable when the independent variables are taken together. It is preferable to acknowledge that the group as a whole is clearly influential but the data are not sufficiently informative to allow the disentangling, with any precision, of each independent variable's separate effects.

14.44 a. $H_0 : \beta_1 = 0, \quad H_1 : \beta_1 > 0, \ t = \dfrac{2.11}{1.79} = 1.179$

Do not reject H_0 at the 10% level since $t < 1.282 \approx t_{84,.1}$

b. $H_0 : \beta_2 = 0, \quad H_1 : \beta_2 > 0, \ t = \dfrac{.96}{1.94} = .495$

Do not reject H_0 at the 10% level since $t < 1.282 \approx t_{84,.1}$

c. The difference in results are likely due to the existence of multicollinearity between earnings per share (x_1) and funds flow per share (x_2)

14.46   Based on the t-ratios, none of the gender dummy variables has been found to be statistically different from zero. We have not found strong evidence to suggest that the gender of the student or the gender of the instructor, or gender taken together has a significant impact on total student score in the intermediate economics course.

14.48 a. All else being equal, a 1% increase in value of new orders leads to expected decrease of .82% in number of failures.

b. $H_0 : \rho = 0, H_1 : \rho > 0$, d = .49, n=30, K = 3, $\alpha = .01$: $d_L = 1.01$ and $d_U = 1.42$

Reject H_0 at the 1% level

c. Given that the residuals are autocorrelated, the hypothesis test results of part b are not valid. The model must be reestimated taking into account the autocorrelated errors

d. $r = 1 - \dfrac{.49}{2} = .755$

14.50 a. 95% CI: $.253 \pm 2.052(.106)$: $.035 < \beta < .471$

b. $.253 increase in current period, further $.138 increase next period, $.075 increase two periods ahead, and so on. Total expected increase of $.557.

c. $H_0 : \rho = 0, H_1 : \rho > 0$

Note that due to the presence of a lagged dependent variable used as an independent variable, Durbin's h statistic is relevant

$$r = 1 - \frac{d}{2} = 1 - \frac{1.86}{2} = .07, \quad s^2_c = (.134)^2 = .01796$$

$$h = r \sqrt{\frac{n}{1 - ns_c^2}} = .07 \sqrt{\frac{30}{1 - 30(.01796)}} = .56449$$

$z_{.1} = 1.28$, therefore, do not reject H_0 at the 10% level

14.52

Regression Analysis: y_log versus x1_log, x2_log

The regression equation is

y_log = - 2.14 + 0.909 x1_log + 0.195 x2_log

Predictor	Coef	SE Coef	T	P
Constant	-2.1415	0.2000	-10.71	0.000
x1_log	0.90947	0.03518	25.85	0.000
x2_log	0.19451	0.07126	2.73	0.018

S = 0.07721   R-Sq = 99.6%   R-Sq(adj) = 99.5%

Analysis of Variance

Source	DF	SS	MS	F	P
Regression	2	16.7802	8.3901	1407.52	0.000
Residual Error	12	0.0715	0.0060		
Total	14	16.8517			

Source	DF	Seq SS
x1_log	1	16.7358
x2_log	1	0.0444

Durbin-Watson statistic = 1.67

$H_0 : \rho = 0, H_1 : \rho > 0$, d = 1.67, n=15, K = 2, $\alpha = .05$: d_L = .95 and d_U = 1.54

Do not reject H_0 at the 5% level.

14.54

Regression Analysis: y_log versus x1_log, x2_log, y_laglog_1

The regression equation is

y_log = 0.435 - 0.101 x1_log + 0.237 x2_log + 0.666 y_laglog_1

34 cases used 1 cases contain missing values

Predictor	Coef	SE Coef	T	P
Constant	0.4352	0.4360	1.00	0.326
x1_log	-0.10116	0.03822	-2.65	0.013
x2_log	0.2365	0.1017	2.32	0.027
y_laglog	0.6658	0.1174	5.67	0.000

S = 0.04039   R-Sq = 75.1%   R-Sq(adj) = 72.6%

Analysis of Variance

Source	DF	SS	MS	F	P
Regression	3	0.147751	0.049250	30.18	0.000
Residual Error	30	0.048952	0.001632		
Total	33	0.196704			

Unusual Observations

Obs	x1_log	y_log	Fit	SE Fit	Residual	St Resid
20	0.410	4.58497	4.59677	0.02689	-0.01181	-0.39 X
35	-0.119	4.68398	4.59012	0.01650	0.09386	2.55R

R denotes an observation with a large standardized residual
X denotes an observation whose X value gives it large influence.
Durbin-Watson statistic = 2.22

Test for autocorrelation. Note that the lagged variable removes one observation from the original 35 observations.

$$r = 1 - \frac{d}{2} = 1 - \frac{2.22}{2} = -.11, \quad s^2_c = (.1174)^2 = .01378$$

$$h = r\sqrt{\frac{n}{1 - ns_c^2}} = -.11\sqrt{\frac{34}{1 - 34(.01378)}} = -.880$$

p-value = 2[1-Fz(.880))] = .3788, do not reject H_0 at any common level of alpha

14.56

Regression Analysis: y_log versus x1_log, x2_log, x3_log

```
The regression equation is
y_log = 2.72 - 0.0252 x1_log + 0.315 x2_log + 0.379 x3_log

Predictor         Coef      SE Coef           T          P
Constant       2.71584      0.08821       30.79      0.000
x1_log        -0.02519      0.04049       -0.62      0.543
x2_log         0.31472      0.05689        5.53      0.000
x3_log          0.3788       0.2009        1.89      0.078

S = 0.03611      R-Sq = 91.7%      R-Sq(adj) = 90.2%
Analysis of Variance
Source            DF           SS           MS          F          P
Regression         3     0.231282     0.077094      59.14      0.000
Residual Error    16     0.020859     0.001304
Total             19     0.252140
Durbin-Watson statistic = 1.75
```

Test for autocorrelation:

$H_0 : \rho = 0, H_1 : \rho > 0$, d = 1.75, n = 20, K = 3, $\alpha = .05$: $d_L = 1.00$

and $d_U = 1.68$

$\alpha = .01$: $d_L = .77$ and $d_U = 1.41$, do not reject H_0 at the 1% level or 5% level.

14.58   a. predict consumption of service goods (CSH) as a function of GDP (GDPH)

Regression Analysis: CSH versus GDPH

```
The regression equation is
CSH = - 207 + 0.417 GDPH
214 cases used 4 cases contain missing values

Predictor         Coef      SE Coef           T          P
Constant      -207.440        6.920      -29.98      0.000
GDPH          0.416931     0.001430      291.66      0.000

S = 44.42        R-Sq = 99.8%      R-Sq(adj) = 99.8%
Analysis of Variance
Source            DF           SS           MS          F          P
Regression         1    167815352    167815352   85064.28      0.000
Residual Error   212       418235         1973
Total            213    168233587
Durbin-Watson statistic = 0.11
```

Test for autocorrelation:

$H_0 : \rho = 0, H_1 : \rho > 0$, d =.11, n = 214, K = 1,

$\alpha = .01$: $d_L = 1.52$ and $d_U = 1.56$

Reject H_0 at the 1% level and accept the alternative that significant first order positive autocorrelation exists in the residuals.

The model shows extremely large explanatory power ($R^2 = 99.8\%$); however, there is significant autocorrelation in the residuals (d = .11).

b.

Regression Analysis: CSH versus GDPH, FBPR, CSH_lag

```
The regression equation is
CSH = - 4.30 + 0.0178 GDPH - 0.504 FBPR + 0.965 CSH_lag
210 cases used 8 cases contain missing values

Predictor          Coef        SE Coef           T          P
Constant         -4.302          2.661       -1.62      0.108
GDPH           0.017760       0.004441        4.00      0.000
FBPR            -0.5040         0.1676       -3.01      0.003
CSH_lag         0.96547        0.01077       89.64      0.000

S = 6.976       R-Sq = 100.0%    R-Sq(adj) = 100.0%
Analysis of Variance
Source            DF             SS          MS          F          P
Regression         3      162823334    54274445  1.115E+06      0.000
Residual Error   206          10024          49
Total            209      162833358
Durbin-Watson statistic = 1.66
```

Test for autocorrelation:

$$r = 1 - \frac{d}{s} = 1 - \frac{1.66}{2} = .17, \quad s^2{}_c = (.01077)^2 = .000116$$

$$h = r \sqrt{\frac{n}{1 - ns_c^2}} = .17 \sqrt{\frac{210}{1 - 210(.000116)}} = 2.494$$

p-value = $2[1-Fz(2.49))]$ = .0128, therefore, do not reject H_0 at the 1% level, reject at 5% level.

Including the lagged value of the dependent variable as an independent variable has reduced the problem of autocorrelation of the residuals, however, multicollinearity has likely resulted between the independent variables.

14.60 a. Estimate with the statistically significant independent variables

Regression Analysis: hseval versus sizehse, taxrate, totexp, Comper
The regression equation is
hseval = - 23.4 + 9.21 sizehse - 178 taxrate +0.000001 totexp - 20.4 Comper

Predictor	Coef	SE Coef	T	P
Constant	-23.433	8.986	-2.61	0.011
sizehse	9.210	1.564	5.89	0.000
taxrate	-177.53	39.87	-4.45	0.000
totexp	0.00000142	0.00000030	4.80	0.000
Comper	-20.370	6.199	-3.29	0.001

S = 3.400   R-Sq = 55.1%   R-Sq(adj) = 52.9%
Analysis of Variance

Source	DF	SS	MS	F	P
Regression	4	1203.84	300.96	26.03	0.000
Residual Error	85	982.79	11.56		
Total	89	2186.63			

Source	DF	Seq SS
sizehse	1	643.12
taxrate	1	244.06
totexp	1	191.82
Comper	1	124.84

Unusual Observations

Obs	sizehse	hseval	Fit	SE Fit	Residual	St Resid
23	5.70	20.003	27.850	0.806	-7.847	-2.38R
49	5.60	29.810	28.522	1.708	1.288	0.44 X
50	5.60	30.061	28.178	1.687	1.883	0.64 X
75	5.70	35.976	24.490	0.535	11.486	3.42R
76	5.70	35.736	25.093	0.553	10.643	3.17R

R denotes an observation with a large standardized residual
X denotes an observation whose X value gives it large influence.
Durbin-Watson statistic = 1.20

Since all of the independent variables are statistically, significant, leave all of the independent variables in the regression model.

b.

The auxiliary regression is

Regression Analysis: ResiSq versus FITS1
The regression equation is
ResiSq = - 15.1 + 1.24 FITS1

Predictor	Coef	SE Coef	T	P
Constant	-15.09	11.96	-1.26	0.210
FITS1	1.2370	0.5604	2.21	0.030

S = 19.44   R-Sq = 5.2%   R-Sq(adj) = 4.2%

$$e^2 = -15.1 + 1.24\hat{y}, \ n = 90, \quad R^2 = .052, \ nR^2 = 4.68 > 3.84 = \chi^2_{1,.05}$$, therefore, reject the null hypothesis that the error terms have constant variance at the 5% level and the economist is correct that heteroscedasticity is likely to be a problem.

c. Use population as the weighting variable. The constant term has been suppressed.

Regression Analysis: hseval/pop versus sizehse/pop, taxrate/pop, ...

```
The regression equation is
hseval/pop = 5.02 sizehse/pop - 191 taxrate/pop + 0.000002 totexp/pop
             - 25.6 comper/pop
Predictor         Coef      SE Coef      T      P
Noconstant
sizehse/pop      5.0208      0.2433    20.63   0.000
taxrate/pop     -191.06       33.12    -5.77   0.000
totexp/pop    0.00000166  0.00000068    2.45   0.016
comper/pop      -25.575       5.119    -5.00   0.000
S = 0.000354555

Analysis of Variance
Source           DF         SS          MS       F      P
Regression        4   0.00044572  0.00011143  886.42  0.000
Residual Error   86   0.00001081  0.00000013
Total            90   0.00045653
```

The partial regression slope coefficients in the weighted least squares model have smaller rates of response than the unweighted model. The coefficients all have the same sign are significantly different from zero at the .02 level of significance. F-calc has increased from 26.03 up to 886.42.

Chapter 15:

Nonparametric Statistics

15.2 $H_0 : P = 0.50$ (there is no overall improvement in comprehension levels following completion of the program)

$H_1 : P > 0.50$ (the level of comprehension is increased by the program)

$n = 9$. For 8 scores higher "After" and a one-sided test,

$P(X \geq 8) = .0176 + .002 = .0196$. Reject H_0 at levels of alpha in excess of 1.96%

15.4 $H_0 : P = 0.50$ (positive and negative returns are equally likely)

$H_1 : P > 0.50$ (positive returns are more likely)

$n = 57$. $\hat{p} = 39/57 = .6842$

$\mu = nP = 57(0.5) = 28.5$ $\sigma = .5\sqrt{n} = .5\sqrt{57} = 3.7749$

$$Z = \frac{S * -\mu}{\sigma} = \frac{38.5 - 28.5}{3.7749} = 2.65, \text{ p-value} = 1 - F_z(2.65)$$

$= 1 - .9960 = .0040$

Therefore, reject H_0 at levels of alpha in excess of .40%

15.6 $H_0 : P = 0.50$ (economists' profession is equally divided on whether the inflation rate will increase)

$H_1 : P \neq 0.50$ (otherwise)

$n = 49$, $\hat{p} = 29/49 = .5918$

$\mu = nP = 49(0.5) = 24.5$ $\sigma = .5\sqrt{n} = .5\sqrt{49} = 3.50$

$$Z = \frac{S * -\mu}{\sigma} = \frac{28.5 - 24.5}{3.50} = 1.14, \text{ p-value} = 2[1 - F_z(1.14)]$$

$= 2[1 - .8729] = .2542$

Therefore, reject H_0 at levels of alpha in excess of 25.42%

15.8 H_0: no preference for domestic vs. imported beer

H_1: imported beer is preferred

Wilcoxon Signed Rank Test: Diff
Test of median = 0.000000 versus median < 0.000000

	N	N for Wilcoxon Test	Statistic	P	Estimated Median
Diff	10	9	7.0	0.038	-1.500

$n = 9$, $T = 7.0$, $T_{.05} = 9$. Reject H_0 at levels of alpha in excess of 3.8%

15.10 H_0: both courses rated equally interesting

H_1: statistics course is rated more interesting

$T = 281$, $\mu_T = n(n+1)/4 = 40(41)/4 = 410$

$\sigma^2_T = n(n+1)(2n+1)/24 = 40(41)(81)/24 = 5535$

$z = \dfrac{281 - 410}{\sqrt{5535}} = -1.73$, p-value = 1-$F_Z(1.73)$ = 1- .9582 = .0418

Therefore, reject H_0 at levels in excess of 4.18%

15.12 H_0: time allocated equally

H_1: time not allocated equally

$T = 1502$, $\mu_T = 80(81)/4 = 1620$, $\sigma^2_T = 80(81)(161)/24 = 43,470$

$z = \dfrac{1502 - 1620}{\sqrt{43470}} = -.57$, p-value = 2[1-$F_Z(.57)$] = 2[1- .7157] = .5686

Therefore, do not reject H_0 at any common level

15.14 H_0: there is no difference in returns

H_1: the 'buy list' has a higher percentage return (one-tailed test)
Sum of ranks for 'buy list' = 137

$R_1 = 137, n_1 = 10, n_2 = 10$

$U = n_1 n_2 + n_1(n_1 + 1)/2 - R_1 = 100 + 110/2 - 137 = 18$

$\mu_U = n_1 n_2 / 2 = 100/2 = 50, \sigma^2_U = n_1 n_2(n_1 + n_2 + 1)/12 = 100(21)/12 = 175$

$z = \dfrac{18 - 50}{\sqrt{175}} = -2.42$, p-value = 1-$F_Z(2.42)$ = 1- .9922 = .0078

Therefore, reject H_0 at levels in excess of .78%

15.16 H_0: no preference between marketing and finance majors

H_1: finance majors are preferred (one-tailed test)
Sum of ranks for the finance students = 171, $T = 171$, $n_1 = 14, n_2 = 10$

$E(T) = \mu_T = n_1(n_1 + n_2 + 1)/2 = 175$

$Var(T) = \sigma^2_T = n_1 n_2(n_1 + n_2 + 1)/12 = 291.667$

$$z = \frac{171-174}{\sqrt{291.667}} = -0.234, \text{p-value} = [1-F_Z(.23)] = [1-.5910] = 0.4090$$

Therefore, reject H_0 at levels in excess of 40.9%

15.18 H_0: population rates of return are equal

H_1: 'Highest rated' funds achieve higher rates of return

Sum of ranks for 'Highest rated' = 113.5

$T = 113.5, n_1 = 10, n_2 = 10$, $E(T) = \mu_T = n_1(n_1 + n_2 + 1)/2 = 105$

$$Var(T) = \sigma_T^2 = n_1 n_2 (n_1 + n_2 + 1)/12 = 175, \quad z = \frac{113.5 - 105}{\sqrt{175}} = 0.64$$

p-value = $[1-F_Z(.64)] = [1-.7389] = .2611$

Therefore, reject H_0 at levels in excess of 26.11%

15.20 H_0: time taken in days from year-end to release a

preliminary profit report is no different for firms

with clean audit reports vs. 'subject to' conditions

H_1: 'subject to' firms take longer

$T = 9,686, n_1 = 86, n_2 = 120$, $E(T) = \mu_T = n_1(n_1 + n_2 + 1)/2 = 8,901$

$Var(T) = \sigma_T^2 = n_1 n_2 (n_1 + n_2 + 1)/12 = 178,020$

$$z = \frac{9,686 - 8,901}{\sqrt{178,020}} = 1.86, \text{ p-value} = 0.0314$$

Reject H_0 at levels in excess of 3.14%

15.22   a. Obtain rankings of the two variables

RankExam	RankProject
6	5.5
1	3.0
4	2.0
5	5.5
10	9.0
2	1.0
3	8.0
7	4.0
9	10.0
8	7.0

Therefore, pearson correlation between rankings of variables is the spearman rank correlation coefficient:

Correlations: RankExam, RankProject
Pearson correlation of RankExam and RankProject = 0.717

b. H_0: no association between scores on the exam vs on the project

H_1: an association exists (two-tailed test)

$n = 10, r_{s.025} = .648, r_{s.010} = .745$. Therefore, reject H_0 of no association between the two variables at the .05 level but not at .02 level (two-tailed test).

15.24 Nonparametric tests make no assumption about the behavior of the population distribution. The advantages of the tests are less restrictive assumptions, easily calculated tests that can be used on nominal or ordinal data. And less weight is placed on outliers by nonparametric tests.

15.26 $H_0 : P = 0.50$ (sales next year are the same as this year)

$H_1 : P \neq 0.50$ (otherwise)

n = 9. For 2 "in favor" and a two-sided test,
P(2 ≥ X ≥ 7) = 2P(X ≤ 2) = 2[.002 + .0176 + .0703] = .1798
Therefore, reject H_0 at levels of alpha in excess of 17.98%

15.28 $H_0 : P = 0.50$ (more students expect a higher standard of living)

$H_1 : P < 0.50$ (more students expect a lower standard of living, compared with their parents)

$n = 78, \hat{p} = 35 / 78 = .4487$

$\mu = nP = 78(.5) = 39 \quad \sigma = .5\sqrt{n} = .5\sqrt{78} = 4.4159$

$Z = \dfrac{S*-\mu}{\sigma} = \dfrac{35.5-39}{4.4159} = -.79$

p-value= $1 - F_z(.79) = 1 - .7852 = .2148$

Therefore, reject H_0 at levels of alpha in excess of 21.48%.

15.30 H_0: corporate analysts are more optimistic about the prospects for their own companies
than for the economy at large

H_1: otherwise (one-tailed test)

$n = 8, \quad T = \min(T_+, T_-) = \min(25, 11) = 11$

From Appendix Table 10, $T_{0.10} = 9$. Do not reject H_0 at the 10% level.

Chapter 16:

Goodness-of-Fit and Contingency Tables

16.2 H_0: Mutual fund performance is equally likely to be in the 5 quintiles.

   H_1: otherwise

Mutual funds	Top 20%	2nd 20%	3rd 20%	4th 20%	5th 20%	Total
Observed Number	13	20	18	11	13	75
Probability (Ho)	0.2	0.2	0.2	0.2	0.2	1
Expected Number	15	15	15	15	15	75
Chi-square calculation	0.266667	1.666667	0.6	1.066667	0.266667	3.8667

Chi-square calculation: $\chi^2 = \sum \dfrac{(O_i - E_i)^2}{Ei} = 3.8667$

$\chi^2_{(4,.1)} = 7.78$ Therefore, do not reject H_0 at the 10% level.

16.4 H_0: Quality of the output conforms to the usual pattern.

   H_1: otherwise

Electronic component	No faults	1 fault	>1 fault	Total
Observed Number	458	30	12	500
Probability (Ho)	0.93	0.05	0.02	1
Expected Number	465	25	10	500
Chi-square calculation	0.105376344	1	0.4	1.505376

Chi-square calculation: $\chi^2 = \sum \dfrac{(O_i - E_i)^2}{Ei} = 1.505$

$\chi^2_{(2,.05)} = 5.99$ $\chi^2_{(2,.10)} = 4.61$ Therefore, do not reject H_0 at the 5% or the 10% level.

16.6 H_0: Student opinion of business courses is the same as that for all courses

H_1: otherwise

Opinion	Very useful	Somewhat	Worthless	Total
Observed Number	68	18	14	100
Probability (Ho)	0.6	0.2	0.2	1
Expected Number	60	20	20	100
Chi-square calculation	1.066666667	0.2	1.8	3.066667

Chi-square calculation: $\chi^2 = \sum \dfrac{(O_i - E_i)^2}{Ei} = 3.067$

$\chi^2_{(2,.10)} = 4.61$ Therefore, do not reject H_0 at the 10% level.

16.8 H_0: Consumer preferences for soft drinks are equally spread across 5 soft drinks

H_1: otherwise

Drink	A	B	C	D	E	Total
Observed Number	20	25	28	15	27	115
Probability (Ho)	0.2	0.2	0.2	0.2	0.2	1
Expected Number	23	23	23	23	23	115
Chi-square calculation	0.391304	0.173913	1.086957	2.782609	0.695652	5.130435

$\chi^2 = \sum \dfrac{(O_i - E_i)^2}{Ei} = 5.130, \quad \chi^2_{(4,.10)} = 7.78$

Do not reject H_0 at the 10% level.

16.10 H_0: Statistics professors preferences for software packages are equally divided across 4 packages

H_1: otherwise

Software	M	E	S	P	Total
Observed Number	100	80	35	35	250
Probability (Ho)	0.25	0.25	0.25	0.25	1
Expected Number	62.5	62.5	62.5	62.5	250
Chi-square calculation	22.5	4.9	12.1	12.1	51.6

Chi-square calculation: $\chi^2 = \sum \dfrac{(O_i - E_i)^2}{Ei} = 51.6$

$\chi^2_{(3,.005)} = 12.84$ Therefore, reject H_0 at the .5% level.

16.12 H_0: population distribution of arrivals per minute is Poisson

   H_1: otherwise

Arrivals	0	1	2	3	4+	Total
Observed Number	10	26	35	24	5	100
Probability (Ho)	0.1496	0.2842	0.27	0.171	0.1252	1
Expected Number	14.96	28.42	27	17.1	12.52	100
Chi-square calculation	1.644492	0.206066	2.37037	2.784211	4.516805	**11.52194**

Chi-square calculation: $\chi^2 = \sum \frac{(O_i - E_i)^2}{Ei} = 11.52$

$\chi^2_{(3,.01)} = 11.34$ $\chi^2_{(3,.005)} = 12.84$.   Reject H_0 at the 1% level but not at the .5% level.

16.14 H_0: resistance of electronic components is normally distributed

   H_1: otherwise

$$B = 100 \left[\frac{(.63)^2}{6} + \frac{(3.85-3)^2}{24} \right] = 9.625$$

From Table 16.7 – Significance points of the Bowman-Shelton statistic; 5% point (n=100) is 4.29.   Therefore, reject H_0 at the 5% level.

16.16 H_0: monthly balances for credit card holders of a particular card are normally distributed

   H_1: otherwise

$$B = 125 \left[\frac{(.55)^2}{6} + \frac{(2.77-3)^2}{24} \right] = 6.578$$

From Table 16.7 – Significance points of the Bowman-Shelton statistic; 5% point (n = 125) is 4.34.   Therefore, reject H_0 at the 5% level.

16.18 a. H_0: No association exists between gpa and major

H_1: otherwise

Chi-Square Test: GPA<3, GPA3+
Expected counts are printed below observed counts

	GPA<3	GPA3+	Total
1	50	35	85
	46.75	38.25	
2	45	30	75
	41.25	33.75	
3	15	25	40
	22.00	18.00	
Total	110	90	200

Chi-Sq = 0.226 + 0.276 + 0.341 + 0.417 + 2.227 + 2.722 = 6.209
DF = 2, P-Value = 0.045

$\chi^2_{(2,.05)} = 5.99$ Therefore, reject H_0 of no association at the 5% level

16.20 a. Complete the contingency table:

		Method of learning about product		
Age		Friend	Ad	col. total
<21		30	20	50
21-35		60	30	90
35+		18	42	60
row total		108	92	200

b. H_0: No association exists between the method of learning about the product and the age of the respondent

H_1: otherwise

Chi-Square Test: Friend, Ad
Expected counts are printed below observed counts

	Friend	Ad	Total
1	30	20	50
	27.00	23.00	
2	60	30	90
	48.60	41.40	
3	18	42	60
	32.40	27.60	
Total	108	92	200

Chi-Sq = 0.333 + 0.391 + 2.674 + 3.139 + 6.400 + 7.513 = 20.451
DF = 2, P-Value = 0.000

$\chi^2_{(2,.005)} = 10.6$ Therefore, reject H_0 of no association at the .5% level

16.22 H_0: No association exists between write-downs of assets and merger activity

H_1: otherwise

Chi-Square Test: Yes, No

Expected counts are printed below observed counts

	Yes	No	Total
1	32	48	80
	28.15	51.85	
2	25	57	82
	28.85	53.15	
Total	57	105	162

Chi-Sq = 0.527 + 0.286 + 0.514 + 0.279 = 1.607

DF = 1, P-Value = 0.205

$\chi^2_{(1,.10)} = 2.71$ Therefore, do not reject H_0 at the 10% level

16.24 H_0: No association exists between personnel rating and college major

H_1: otherwise

Chi-Square Test: Excellent, Strong, Average

Expected counts are printed below observed counts

	Excellent	Strong	Average	Total
1	21	18	10	49
	19.11	18.42	11.47	
2	19	15	5	39
	15.21	14.66	9.13	
3	10	5	5	20
	7.80	7.52	4.68	
4	5	15	13	33
	12.87	12.40	7.72	
Total	55	53	33	141

Chi-Sq = 0.186 + 0.010 + 0.188 + 0.943 + 0.008 + 1.867 + 0.620 + 0.843 + 0.022 + 4.814 + 0.543 + 3.605 = 13.648

DF = 6, P-Value = 0.034

1 cells with expected counts less than 5.0

$\chi^2_{(6,.05)} = 12.59$ Therefore, reject H_0 at the 5% level

16.26 H_0: No association exists between graduate studies and college major

   H_1: otherwise

Chi-Square Test: Business, Law, Theology

Expected counts are printed below observed counts

	Business	Law	Theology	Total
1	30	20	10	60
	18.00	27.00	15.00	
2	6	34	20	60
	18.00	27.00	15.00	
Total	36	54	30	120

Chi-Sq = 8.000 + 1.815 + 1.667 + 8.000 + 1.815 + 1.667 = 22.963

DF = 2, P-Value = 0.000

$\chi^2_{(2,.005)} = 10.60$ Therefore, reject H_0 at the .5% level

16.28 H_0: No association exists between primary election candidate preferences and voting district

   H_1: otherwise

Chi-Square Test: A, B, C, D

Expected counts are printed below observed counts

	A	B	C	D	Total
1	52	34	80	34	200
	46.46	31.69	92.00	29.85	
2	33	15	78	24	150
	34.85	23.77	69.00	22.38	
3	66	54	141	39	300
	69.69	47.54	138.00	44.77	
Total	151	103	299	97	650

Chi-Sq = 0.660 + 0.168 + 1.565 + 0.578 + 0.098 + 3.235 + 1.174 + 0.117 + 0.196 + 0.878 + 0.065 + 0.743 = 9.478

DF = 6, P-Value = 0.148

$\chi^2_{(6,.10)} = 10.64$ Therefore, do not reject H_0 at the 10% level

16.30 H_0: No association exists between years of experience and parts produced per hour

   H_1: otherwise

Chi-Square Test: Subgroup1, Subgroup2, Subgroup3

Expected counts are printed below observed counts

	Subgroup1	Subgroup2	Subgroup3	Total
1	10	30	10	50
	10.00	20.00	20.00	
2	10	20	20	50
	10.00	20.00	20.00	
3	10	10	30	50
	10.00	20.00	20.00	
Total	30	60	60	150

Chi-Sq = 0.000 + 5.000 + 5.000 + 0.000 + 0.000 + 0.000 + 0.000 + 5.000 + 5.000 = 20.000

DF = 4, P-Value = 0.000

$\chi^2_{(4,.005)} = 14.86$ Therefore, reject H_0 at the .5% level

16.32 a. H_0: No association exists between package weight and package source

H_1: otherwise

Chi-Square Test: <3lb, 4-10lb, 11-75lb

Expected counts are printed below observed counts

	<3 lb	4-10lb	11-75lb	Total
1	40	40	20	100
	37.85	36.62	25.54	
2	119	63	18	200
	75.69	73.23	51.08	
3	18	71	111	200
	75.69	73.23	51.08	
4	69	64	17	150
	56.77	54.92	38.31	
Total	246	238	166	650

Chi-Sq = 0.123 + 0.313 + 1.201 + 24.779 + 1.429 + 21.420 + 43.973 + 0.068 + 70.301 + 2.635 + 1.500 + 11.852 = 179.594

DF = 6, P-Value = 0.000

$\chi^2_{(6,.005)} = 18.55$ Therefore, reject H_0 at the .5% level

b. The combinations with the largest percentage gap between observed and expected frequencies are 1) between factories and 11-75 pound packages, and 2) between factories and under 3 pound packages.

16.34 a. H_0 : No association exists between the age of the company and the owner's opinion regarding the effectiveness of digital signatures

H_1 : otherwise

Chi-Square Test: Yes, No, Uncertain

Expected counts are printed below observed counts

	Yes	No	Uncertain	Total
1	80	68	10	158
	71.27	74.29	12.44	
2	60	90	15	165
	74.43	77.59	12.99	
3	72	63	12	147
	66.31	69.12	11.57	
Total	212	221	37	470

Chi-Sq = 1.070 + 0.533 + 0.478 + 2.796 + 1.987 + 0.311 + 0.489 + 0.542 + 0.016 = 8.222

DF = 4, P-Value = 0.084

$\chi^2_{(4,.05)} = 9.49$ $\chi^2_{(4,.10)} = 7.78$. Therefore, do not reject H_0 at the 5% level; but reject at 10%

16.36 a. H_0 : No association exists between reason for moving to Florida and industry type

H_1 : otherwise

Chi-Square Test: Manufacturing, Retail, Tourism

Expected counts are printed below observed counts

	Manufacturing	Retail	Tourism	Total
1	53	25	10	88
	42.04	28.31	17.66	
2	67	36	20	123
	58.76	39.56	24.68	
3	30	40	33	103
	49.20	33.13	20.67	
Total	150	101	63	314

Chi-Sq = 2.858 + 0.386 + 3.320 + 1.156 + 0.321 + 0.887 + 7.495 + 1.424 + 7.362 = 25.210

DF = 4, P-Value = 0.000

$\chi^2_{(4,.005)} = 14.86$ Therefore, reject H_0 at the .5% level

16.38 H_0 : No association exists between opinions on stricter advertising controls of weight loss products and useage of quick weight reduction product

H_1 : otherwise

Chi-Square Test: Yes, No

Expected counts are printed below observed counts

	Yes	No	Total
1	85	40	125
	64.25	60.75	
2	25	64	89
	45.75	43.25	
Total	110	104	214

Chi-Sq = 6.700 + 7.086 + 9.410 + 9.952 = 33.148

DF = 1, P-Value = 0.000

$\chi^2_{(1,.005)} = 7.88$ Therefore, reject H_0 at the .5% level

16.40 H_0: No difference in current and past customer preferences

H_1: otherwise

	A	B	C	D
observed frequency	56	70	28	126
expected frequency	56	92.4	56	75.6
$(O_i - E_i)^2 / E_i$	0	5.43	14	33.6

Chi-square Test Statistic = 53.03

$\chi^2_{(3,.005)} = 12.84$ Therefore, reject H_0 at the .5% level

16.42 a. H_0: No association exists between class standing and opinions on whether library hours should be extended

H_1: otherwise

Here we used Mintab and included only the responses from 340 students who had an opinion about the extension of the library hours.

Tabulated statistics: Class, Hours Extension

Rows: Class   Columns: Hours Extension

	1	2	All
1	86	53	139
	98.12	40.88	139.00
2	79	21	100
	70.59	29.41	100.00
3	46	15	61
	43.06	17.94	61.00
4	29	11	40
	28.24	11.76	40.00
Missing	0	1	*
	*	*	*
All	240	100	340
	240.00	100.00	340.00

Cell Contents: Count
                     Expected count

Pearson Chi-Square = 9.250, DF = 3, P-Value = 0.026

Likelihood Ratio Chi-Square = 9.262, DF = 3, P-Value = 0.026

$\chi^2_{(3,0.025)} = 9.35$ Do not reject H_0 at the 2.5% level

b. Recommendations should include better orientation with the freshmen class in order to better acquaint the students with the library and the hours that the library is open. Also, extending library hours, particularly during heavy usage, would be appropriate.

16.44   Answers will vary.

16.46 H_0: No association exists between method of filing tax returns and the person's age

H_1: otherwise

Chi-Square Test: Age and 1040, Other, Extension
```
Expected counts are printed below observed counts
Chi-Square contributions are printed below expected counts

Age     1040   Other  Extension  Total
< 25      35      8          7      50
        35.00   8.00       7.00

25-45     60     20         10      90
        63.00  14.40      12.60

> 45      45      4         11      60
        42.00   9.60       8.40

Total    140     32         28     200
Chi-Sq = 7.143, DF = 4, P-Value = 0.129
```

$\chi^2_{(4,.10)} = 7.78$ Therefore, do not reject H_0 at the 10% level

There is not a statistically significant relationship between the method of filing income tax returns and the person's age.

Chapter 17:

Analysis of Variance

17.2 Given the Analysis of Variance table, compute mean squares for between and for within groups. Compute the F ratio and test the hypothesis that the group means are equal.

$H_0 : \mu_1 = \mu_2 = \mu_3 = \mu_4, H_1 : otherwise$

$$MSG = \frac{SSG}{k-1}, MSW = \frac{SSW}{n-k}, F = \frac{MSG}{MSW}$$

$$MSG = \frac{879}{3}, MSW = \frac{798}{16}, F = \frac{293}{49.875} = 5.875$$

$F_{3,16,.05} = 3.24, F_{3,16,.01} = 5.29$, Therefore, reject H_0 at the 1% level.

17.4 a. $\bar{x}_1 = 62, \bar{x}_2 = 53, \bar{x}_3 = 52$

n=16, SSW = 1028 + 1044 + 1536 = 3608

SSG = $7(62 - 56.0625)^2 + 6(53 - 56.0625)^2 + 6(52 - 56.0625)^2 =$ 340.9375

SST = 3948.9375

b. Complete the anova table

One-way ANOVA: SodaSales versus CanColor
```
Analysis of Variance for SodaSale
Source      DF        SS         MS        F         P
CanColor     2       341        170      0.61     0.556
Error       13      3608        278
Total       15      3949
                                  Individual 95% CIs For Mean
                                  Based on Pooled StDev
Level        N      Mean      StDev   -+---------+---------+---------+-----
1            6     62.00      14.34                 (------------*-----------)
2            5     53.00      16.16      (------------*-------------)
3            5     52.00      19.60      (------------*-------------)
                                        -+---------+---------+---------+-----
Pooled StDev =     16.66               36        48        60        72
```

$H_0 : \mu_1 = \mu_2 = \mu_3, H_1 : otherwise$

$F_{2,13,.05} = 3.81$, do not reject H_0 at the 5% level.

17.6 a. $\bar{x}_1 = 32, \bar{x}_2 = 24.3333, \bar{x}_3 = 34.8333$, complete the anova table

One-way ANOVA: Nonconforming versus Supplier

```
Analysis of Variance for Nonconfo
Source      DF       SS       MS       F       P
Supplier     2     354.1    177.1    10.45   0.001
Error       15     254.2     16.9
Total       17     608.3
                                Individual 95% CIs For Mean
                                Based on Pooled StDev
Level     N      Mean    StDev  ---------+---------+---------+-------
1         6    32.000    3.347                 (------*------)
2         6    24.333    5.007    (------*------)
3         6    34.833    3.817                          (------*------)
                                ---------+---------+---------+-------
Pooled StDev =    4.116            25.0      30.0      35.0
```

b. $H_0 : \mu_1 = \mu_2 = \mu_3, H_1 : otherwise$

$F_{2,15,.01} = 6.36$, reject H_0 at the 1% level.

17.8 a. $\bar{x}_1 = 71.7143, \bar{x}_2 = 75.2857, \bar{x}_3 = 76.5714$, complete the anova table

One-way ANOVA: Scores versus Class

```
Analysis of Variance for Scores
Source      DF       SS       MS       F       P
Class        2       89       44     0.28    0.756
Error       18     2813      156
Total       20     2901
                                Individual 95% CIs For Mean
                                Based on Pooled StDev
Level     N     Mean    StDev  --+---------+---------+---------+----
1         7    71.71    13.16  (-------------*--------------)
2         7    75.29    11.19       (--------------*-------------)
3         7    76.57    13.05          (-------------*--------------)
                                --+---------+---------+---------+----
Pooled StDev =   12.50         63.0      70.0      77.0      84.0
```

b. $H_0 : \mu_1 = \mu_2 = \mu_3, H_1 : otherwise$

$F_{2,18,.05} = 3.55$, do not reject H_0 at the 5% level.

17.10   a. $\bar{x}_1 = 11.3333$, $\bar{x}_2 = 12.5$, $\bar{x}_3 = 8$, set out the anova table

One-way ANOVA: Time versus Rank

```
Analysis of Variance for Time
Source    DF        SS        MS        F        P
Rank       2     51.40     25.70     3.27    0.074
Error     12     94.33      7.86
Total     14    145.73
                                     Individual 95% CIs For Mean
                                     Based on Pooled StDev
Level      N      Mean     StDev   ---+---------+---------+---------+---
1          6    11.333     3.011                 (--------*-------)
2          4    12.500     3.317                    (----------*---------)
3          5     8.000     2.000     (--------*-------)
                                     ---+---------+---------+---------+---
Pooled StDev =    2.804             6.0       9.0      12.0      15.0
```

b. $H_0 : \mu_1 = \mu_2 = \mu_3$, $H_1 : otherwise$

$F_{2,12,.05} = 3.89$, do not reject H$_0$ at the 5% level.

17.12

One-way ANOVA: TrueCon, People, Newsweek

```
Source   DF       SS        MS       F       P
Factor    2    48.96     24.48    4.07   0.039
Error    15    90.13      6.01
Total    17   139.09
S = 2.451   R-Sq = 35.20%   R-Sq(adj) = 26.56%
                                   Individual 95% CIs For Mean Based on
                                   Pooled StDev
Level      N     Mean   StDev    -------+---------+---------+---------+--
TrueCon    6   10.402   2.268                    (----------*----------)
People     6    7.045   2.182      (---------*----------)
Newsweek   6    6.777   2.850    (---------*----------)
                                  -------+---------+---------+---------+--
                                     6.0       8.0      10.0      12.0
Pooled StDev = 2.451
```

$H_0 : \mu_1 = \mu_2 = \mu_3$, $H_1 : otherwise$

$F_{2,15,.05} = 3.68$, reject H$_0$ at the 5% level.

17.14   a. $\hat{\mu} = 8.0744$

b. $\hat{G}_1 = 10.4017 - 8.0744 = 2.3273$, $\hat{G}_2 = 7.045 - 8.0744 = -1.0294$

   $\hat{G}_3 = 6.7767 - 8.0744 = -1.2977$

c. $\hat{\varepsilon}_{32} = 11.15 - 10.4017 = .7483$

17.16

$$H_0 : \mu_1 = \mu_2 = \mu_3 = \mu_4, H_1 : otherwise$$

$$R_1 = 49, \quad R_2 = 84, \quad R_3 = 76, \quad R_4 = 81$$

$$W = \frac{12}{23(24)} \left[(49^2 / 4) + (84^2 / 6) + (76^2 / 7) + (81^2 / 6) \right] - 3(24) = 8.32$$

$\chi^2_{(2,.05)} = 5.99$, therefore, reject H_0 at the 5% level

17.18 $H_0 : \mu_1 = \mu_2 = \mu_3, H_1 : otherwise$

$$R_1 = 61, \quad R_2 = 37, \quad R_3 = 38$$

$$W = \frac{12}{16(17)} \left[(3721/6) + (1396/5) + (1444/5) \right] - 3(17) = 1.18$$

$\chi^2_{(2,.10)} = 4.61$, therefore, do not reject H_0 at the 10% level

Using Minitab:

Kruskal-Wallis Test: SodaSales versus CanColor

```
Kruskal-Wallis Test on SodaSale
CanColor    N    Median    Ave Rank        Z
1           6     60.00        10.2     1.08
2           5     52.00         7.4    -0.62
3           5     53.00         7.6    -0.51
Overall    16                   8.5
H = 1.18  DF = 2  P = 0.554
H = 1.19  DF = 2  P = 0.553 (adjusted for ties)
```

17.20 $H_0 : \mu_1 = \mu_2 = \mu_3, H_1 : otherwise$

$$R_1 = 63.5, \quad R_2 = 26, \quad R_3 = 81.5$$

$$W = \frac{12}{18(19)} \left[(4032.25 + 676 + 6642.25) / 6 \right] - 3(19) = 9.3772$$

$\chi^2_{(2,.01)} = 9.21$, therefore, reject H_0 at the 1% level

Using Minitab:

Kruskal-Wallis Test: Nonconforming versus Supplier

```
Kruskal-Wallis Test on Nonconfo
Supplier    N    Median    Ave Rank        Z
1           6     32.00        10.6     0.61
2           6     24.50         4.3    -2.90
3           6     35.00        13.6     2.29
Overall    18                   9.5
H = 9.38  DF = 2  P = 0.009
H = 9.47  DF = 2  P = 0.009 (adjusted for ties)
```

17.22 $H_0 : \mu_1 = \mu_2 = \mu_3, H_1 : otherwise$

$R_1 = 66, \quad R_2 = 79.5, \quad R_3 = 85.5$

$$W = \frac{12}{21(22)}[(4356 + 6320.25 + 7310.25)/7] - 3(22) = .7403$$

$\chi^2_{(2,.10)} = 4.61$, therefore, do not reject H$_0$ at the 10% level.

17.24 $H_0 : \mu_1 = \mu_2 = \mu_3, H_1 : otherwise$

$R_1 = 54.5, \quad R_2 = 43.5, \quad R_3 = 22$

$$W = \frac{12}{15(16)}[(2970.25/6) + (1892.25/4) + (484/5)] - 3(16) = 5.2452$$

$\chi^2_{(2,.10)} = 4.61$, therefore, reject H$_0$ at the 10% level

17.26   a.   The null hypothesis tests the equality of the population mean ratings across the   classes

   b. $H_0 : \mu_1 = \mu_2 = \mu_3, H_1 : otherwise$

   $W = .17$, $\chi^2_{(2,.10)} = 4.61$, therefore, do not reject H$_0$ at the 10% level

17.28

$$MSG = \frac{SSG}{K-1}, MSB = \frac{SSB}{H-1}, MSE = \frac{SSE}{(K-1)(H-1)}$$

Test of K population group means all the same:

Reject Ho if $\dfrac{MSG}{MSE} > F_{K-1,(K-1)(H-1),\alpha}$

Test of H population block means all the same:

Reject Ho if $\dfrac{MSB}{MSE} > F_{H-1,(K-1)(H-1),\alpha}$

$$MSG = \frac{380}{6} = 63.333, MSB = \frac{232}{5} = 46.4, MSE = \frac{387}{(6)(5)} = 12.90$$

$$\frac{MSB}{MSE} = \frac{46.4}{12.90} = 3.597, F_{5,30,.05} = 2.53, F_{5,30,.01} = 3.70$$

Reject at the 5% level, do not reject H$_0$ at the 1% level that the block means differ.

$$\frac{MSG}{MSE} = \frac{63.333}{12.90} = 4.91, F_{6,30,.05} = 2.42, F_{6,30,.01} = 3.47$$

Reject H$_0$ at the 1% level. Evidence suggests the group means differ

17.30   a. two-way ANOVA table:

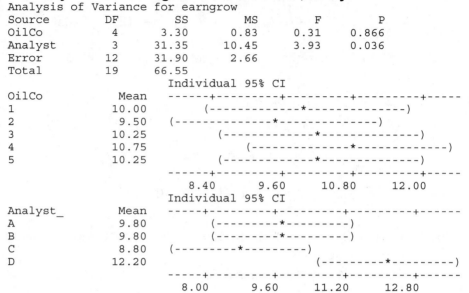

Two-way ANOVA: earngrowth versus OilCo, Analyst
```
Analysis of Variance for earngrow
Source       DF        SS        MS         F        P
OilCo         4       3.30      0.83      0.31     0.866
Analyst       3      31.35     10.45      3.93     0.036
Error        12      31.90      2.66
Total        19      66.55
                             Individual 95% CI
OilCo       Mean    ------+---------+---------+---------+-----
1           10.00              (-------------*--------------)
2            9.50        (---------------*--------------)
3           10.25             (-------------*---------------)
4           10.75                (-------------*-------------)
5           10.25             (-------------*---------------)
                    ------+---------+---------+---------+-----
                        8.40      9.60     10.80     12.00
                             Individual 95% CI
Analyst_    Mean    -----+---------+---------+---------+------
A            9.80            (---------*---------)
B            9.80            (---------*---------)
C            8.80        (---------*---------)
D           12.20                        (---------*---------)
                    -----+---------+---------+---------+------
                        8.00      9.60     11.20     12.80
```

b. $H_0 : \mu_1 = \mu_2 = \mu_3 = \mu_4 = \mu_5, H_1 : Otherwise$

$F_{4,12,.05} = 3.26 > .31$, therefore, do not reject H_0 at the 5% level

17.32   a. two-way ANOVA table:

Two-way ANOVA: sales versus Quarter, soup
```
Analysis of Variance for sales
Source       DF        SS         MS        F        P
Quarter_      3      615.0      205.0      2.10     0.202
Soup          2        6.2        3.1      0.03     0.969
Error         6      586.5       97.7
Total        11     1207.7
                             Individual 95% CI
Quarter_    Mean    ----------+---------+---------+---------+-
1           56.3         (-----------*-----------)
2           67.3                   (-----------*-----------)
3           66.7                  (-----------*---------)
4           50.3     (-----------*-----------)
                    ----------+---------+---------+---------+-
                            48.0      60.0      72.0      84.0
                             Individual 95% CI
Soup        Mean    ---+---------+---------+---------+--------
A           60.3        (---------------*----------------)
B           59.3     (----------------*----------------)
C           61.0        (----------------*----------------)
                    ---+---------+---------+---------+--------
                       49.0      56.0      63.0      70.0
```

b. $H_0 : \mu_1 = \mu_2 = \mu_3, H_1 : otherwise$

$F_{2,6,.05} = 5.14 > .03$, therefore, do not reject H_0 at the 5% level

17.34   a. two-way ANOVA table:

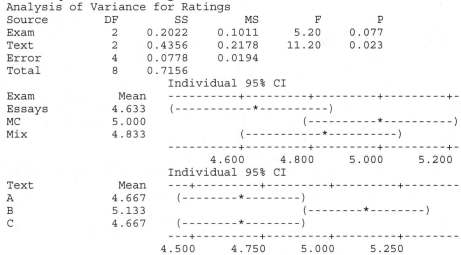

Two-way ANOVA: Ratings versus Exam, Text
```
Analysis of Variance for Ratings
Source     DF        SS        MS        F         P
Exam        2     0.2022    0.1011     5.20     0.077
Text        2     0.4356    0.2178    11.20     0.023
Error       4     0.0778    0.0194
Total       8     0.7156
                            Individual 95% CI
Exam            Mean    ----------+---------+---------+---------+-
Essays          4.633   (-----------*----------)
MC              5.000                       (----------*----------)
Mix             4.833             (-----------*----------)
                        ----------+---------+---------+---------+-
                            4.600     4.800     5.000     5.200
                            Individual 95% CI
Text            Mean    ---+---------+---------+---------+--------
A               4.667   (--------*-------)
B               5.133                     (--------*--------)
C               4.667   (--------*-------)
                        ---+---------+---------+---------+--------
                          4.500     4.750     5.000     5.250
```

b. $H_0 : \mu_1 = \mu_2 = \mu_3$, $H_1 : otherwise$ [texts]

$F_{2,4,.05} = 6.94 < 11.20$, therefore, reject H_0 at the 5% level

c. $H_0 : \mu_1 = \mu_2 = \mu_3$, $H_1 : otherwise$ [exam type]

$F_{2,4,.05} = 6.94 > 5.20$, therefore, do not reject H_0 at the 5% level

17.36

$\hat{G}_3 = -.1556 \quad \hat{B}_1 = .1778 \quad \hat{\varepsilon}_{31} = .0556$

17.38   a. complete the ANOVA table:

Source of Variation	Sum of Squares	df	Mean square	F Ratio
Fertilizers	135.6	3	45.20	6.0916
Soil Types	81.7	5	16.34	2.2022
Error	111.3	15	7.42	
Total	328.6	23		

b. $H_0 : \mu_1 = \mu_2 = \mu_3 = \mu_4$, $H_1 : otherwise$ [fertilizers]

$F_{3,15,.01} = 5.42 < 6.0916$, therefore, reject H_0 at the 1% level

c. $H_0 : \mu_1 = \mu_2 = \mu_3 = \mu_4 = \mu_5 = \mu_6$, $H_1 : Otherwise$ [soil types]

$F_{5,15,.05} = 2.90 > 2.2021$, therefore, do not reject H_0 at the 5% level

17.40   Given, say, ten pairs observations, the F statistic would have 1, 9 degrees of freedom. The test is in the form of a two-tailed test. With alpha = .05, the critical value of F would be 5.12. For a matched –pairs test, the degrees of freedom would be 9, and the area in each tail would be .025. The critical value for t would be 2.262 (which is the square root of the F statistic of 5.12). Therefore, the two tests are equivalent.

17.42

$$MSG = \frac{SSG}{K-1}, \; MSB = \frac{SSB}{H-1}, \; MSI = \frac{SSI}{(K-1)(H-1)}, \; MSE = \frac{SSE}{KH(L-1)}, \; F = \frac{MSG}{MSE}, \frac{MSB}{MSE}, \frac{MSI}{MSE}$$

$$MSG_A = \frac{86}{4} = 21.5, \; MSG_B = \frac{75}{5} = 15, \; MSI = \frac{75}{20} = 3.75, \; MSE = \frac{300}{90} = 3.33$$

$$F \; Ratio : Interaction = \frac{MSI}{MSE} = \frac{3.75}{3.33} = 1.125, \; F_{30,80,.05} \approx 1.65, \; F_{30,80,.01} \approx 2.03$$

Do not reject H_0 at the 5% level. No significant interaction exists between treatment groups A and B. Therefore, go on to test the main effects of each treatment group.

$$F \; Ratio : Treatment \; A = \frac{MSG_A}{MSE} = \frac{21.5}{3.33} = 6.456,$$

$F_{4,80,.05} \approx 2.53, \; F_{4,80,.01} \approx 3.65$ Reject H_0 at the 1% level, there is a significant main effect for group A.

$$F \; Ratio : Treatment \; B = \frac{MSG_B}{MSE} = \frac{15}{3.33} = 4.505,$$

$F_{5,80,.05} \approx 2.37, \; F_{5,80,.01} \approx 3.34$ Reject H_0 at the 1% level, there is a significant main effect for group B.

17.44   a. ANOVA table:

Source of Variation	Sum of Squares	df	Mean square	F Ratio
Contestant	364.50	21	17.3571	19.2724
Judges	.81	8	.1013	.1124
Interaction	4.94	168	.0294	.0326
Error	1069.94	1188	.9006	
Total	1440.19	1385		

H_0: Mean value for all 22 contestants is the same

H_1: Otherwise, $F_{21,1188,.01} \approx 1.88 < 19.2724$, therefore, reject H_0 at the 1% level

H_0: Mean value for all 9 judges is the same

H_1: Otherwise, $F_{8,1188,.05} \approx 1.94 > .1124$, do not reject H_0 at the 5% level

H_0: No interaction exists between contestants and judges

H_1: Otherwise, $F_{168,1188,.05} \approx 1.22 > .0326$, do not reject H_0 at the 5% level

17.46   a. ANOVA table:

Source of Variation	Sum of Squares	df	Mean square	F Ratio
Test type	57.5556	2	28.7778	4.7091
Subject	389.0000	3	129.6667	21.2182
Interaction	586.0000	6	97.66667	15.9818
Error	146.6667	24	6.1111	
Total	1179.2223	35		

   b. H_0: No interaction exists between contestants and judges

   H_1: Otherwise

   $F_{6,24,.01} = 3.67 < 15.9818$, therefore, reject H_0 at the 1% level

17.48   a. The implied assumption is that there is no interaction effect between student year and dormitory ratings

   b. Using Minitab:

General Linear Model: Ratings_36 versus Dorm_36, Year_36
```
Factor      Type Levels Values
Dorm_36     fixed     4 A B C D
Year_36     fixed     4 1 2 3 4

Analysis of Variance for Ratings_, using Adjusted SS for Tests
Source      DF    Seq SS    Adj SS    Adj MS      F      P
Dorm_36      3    20.344    20.344     6.781   4.91  0.008
Year_36      3    10.594    10.594     3.531   2.56  0.078
Error       25    34.531    34.531     1.381
Total       31    65.469
```

Source of Variation	Sum of Squares	df	Mean square	F Ratio
Dorm	20.344	3	6.781	4.91
Year	10.594	3	3.531	2.56
Error	34.531	25	1.381	
Total	65.469	31		

c. H_0: Mean ratings for all 4 dormitories is the same
H_1: Otherwise
$F_{3,25,.01} = 4.68 < 4.91$, therefore, reject H_0 at the 1% level

d. H_0: Mean ratings for all 4 student years is the same
H_1: Otherwise
$F_{3,25,.05} = 2.99 > 2.56$, therefore, do not reject H_0 at the 5% level

17.50

Source of Variation	Sum of Squares	df	Mean square	F Ratio
Color	243.250	2	121.625	11.3140
Region	354.000	3	118.000	10.9767
Interaction	189.750	6	31.625	2.9419
Error	129.000	12	10.750	
Total	916.000	23		

H_0: No interaction exists between region and can color, H_1: Otherwise
$F_{6,12,.01} = 4.82 > 2.9419$, therefore, do not reject H_0 at the 1% level

Main effects are significant for both Color and Region

17.52   One-way ANOVA examines the effect of a single factor (having three or more conditions). Two-way ANOVA recognizes situations in which more than one factor may be significant.

17.54

Source of Variation	Sum of Squares	df	Mean square	F Ratio
Between	5156	2	2578.000	21.4458
Within	120802	1005	120.201	
Total	125967	1007		

$F_{2,1005,.01} = 4.61 < 21.4458$, therefore, reject H_0 at the 1% level

17.56   a. Use result from Exercise 50b to find SSG, then compute MSG and finally, find SSW using the fact that SSW = $(n-k)\dfrac{MSG}{F}$

Source of Variation	Sum of Squares	df	Mean square	F Ratio
Between	221.3400	3	73.7800	25.6
Within	374.6640	130	2.8820	
Total	596.0040	133		

b. H_0: Mean salaries are the same for managers in all 4 groups
H_1: Otherwise
$F_{3,130,.01} \approx 3.95 < 25.6$, therefore, reject H_0 at the 1% level

17.58

Source of Variation	Sum of Squares	df	Mean square	F Ratio
Between	11438.3028	2	5719.1514	.7856
Within	109200.000	15	7280.000	
Total	120638.3028	17		

H_0: Mean sales levels are the same for all three periods
H_1: Otherwise
$F_{2,15,.05} = 3.68 > .7856$, therefore, do not reject H_0 at the 5% level

17.60

$$H_0 : \mu_1 = \mu_2 = \mu_3 = \mu_4, H_1 : otherwise$$

$$R_1 = 48.5, \quad R_2 = 55, \quad R_3 = 74, \quad R_4 = 32.5$$

$$W = \frac{12}{20(21)}\left[(2352.25 + 3025 + 5476 + 1056.25)/5\right] - 3(21) = 5.0543$$

$$\chi^2_{(3,.10)} = 6.25 \text{ , therefore, do not reject } H_0 \text{ at the 10% level}$$

17.62 a. $SSW = \displaystyle\sum_{j=1}^{K}\sum_{i=1}^{n_i}(x_{ij} - \overline{x}_i)^2$

$$= \sum_{j=1}^{K}\left[\sum_{i=1}^{n_i}x^2_{ij} - 2n_i\overline{x}^2_i + n_i\overline{x}^2_i\right]$$

$$= \sum_{j=1}^{K}\sum_{i=1}^{n_i}x^2_{ij} - \sum_{i=1}^{K}n_i\overline{x}^2_i$$

b. $SSG = \displaystyle\sum_{j=1}^{K}n_i(\overline{x}_i - \overline{x})^2$

$$= \sum_{i=1}^{K}n_i\overline{x}^2_i - 2\overline{x}\sum_{i=1}^{k}n_i\overline{x}_i + n\overline{x}^2$$

$$= \sum_{i=1}^{K}n_i\overline{x}^2_i - 2n\overline{x}^2 + n\overline{x}^2$$

$$= \sum_{i=1}^{K}n_i\overline{x}^2_i - n\overline{x}^2$$

c. $SST = \sum_{i=1}^{K} \sum_{j=1}^{n_i} (x_{ij} - \overline{x}_i)^2$

$= \sum_{i=1}^{K} \left[\sum_{i=1}^{n_i} x^2_{ij} - 2\overline{x} \sum_{i=1}^{n_i} x_i + n_i \overline{x}^2_i \right]$

$= \sum_{i=1}^{K} \sum_{i=1}^{n_i} (x^2_{ij} - 2n_i \overline{x}\, \overline{x}_i + n_i x^2)$

$= \sum_{i=1}^{K} \sum_{j=1}^{n_i} x^2_{ij} - n\overline{x}^2$

17.64

Source of Variation	Sum of Squares	df	Mean square	F Ratio
Consumers	37571.5	124	302.996	1.3488
Brands	32987.3	2	16493.65	73.4226
Error	55710.7	248	224.6399	
Total	126269.5	374		

H_0: Mean perception levels are the same for all three brands
H_1: Otherwise
$F_{2,248,.01} \approx 4.79 < 73.4226$, therefore, reject H_0 at the 1% level

17.66 Using Minitab:

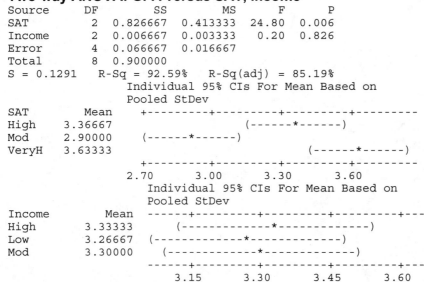

Two-way ANOVA: GPA versus SAT, Income
```
Source    DF       SS        MS      F       P
SAT        2  0.826667  0.413333  24.80   0.006
Income     2  0.006667  0.003333   0.20   0.826
Error      4  0.066667  0.016667
Total      8  0.900000
S = 0.1291   R-Sq = 92.59%   R-Sq(adj) = 85.19%
                 Individual 95% CIs For Mean Based on
                 Pooled StDev
SAT       Mean    +---------+---------+---------+---------
High    3.36667                  (------*------)
Mod     2.90000    (------*------)
VeryH   3.63333                           (------*------)
                  +---------+---------+---------+---------
                2.70      3.00      3.30      3.60
                 Individual 95% CIs For Mean Based on
                 Pooled StDev
Income    Mean   ------+---------+---------+---------+---
High    3.33333        (-------------*-------------)
Low     3.26667   (-------------*-------------)
Mod     3.30000     (-------------*-------------)
                 ------+---------+---------+---------+---
                    3.15      3.30      3.45      3.60
```

Source of Variation	Sum of Squares	df	Mean square	F Ratio
Income	.0067	2	.0033	.2000
SAT Score	.8267	2	.4133	24.8000
Error	.0667	4	.0167	
Total	.9000	8		

H_0: Mean gpa's are the same for all three income groups

H_1: Otherwise

$F_{2,4,.05} = 6.94 > .2000$, therefore, do not reject H_0 at the 5% level

H_0: Mean gpa's are the same for all three SAT score groups

H_1: Otherwise

$F_{2,4,.01} = 18.0 < 24.8$, therefore, reject H_0 at the 1% level

Descriptive Statistics: GPA
```
Variable    Mean   SE Mean  StDev   Variance  Minimum    Q1   Median     Q3
GPA        3.300    0.112   0.335     0.112    2.800   2.950   3.400   3.600

Variable  Maximum     IQR
GPA         3.700   0.650
```

17.68 a. $\hat{\mu} = 3.3$

b. $\hat{G}_2 = 0.0$

c. $\hat{B}_2 = .0667$

d. $\hat{\varepsilon}_{22} = .1333$

17.70 a. ANOVA table:

Source of Variation	Sum of Squares	df	Mean square	F Ratio
Prices	.178	2	.0890	.0944
Countries	4.365	2	2.1825	2.3151
Interaction	1.262	4	.3155	.3347
Error	93.330	99	.9427	
Total	99.135	107		

H_0: Mean quality ratings for all three prices levels is the same

H_1: Otherwise

$F_{2,99,.05} \approx 3.07 > .0944$, therefore, do not reject H_0 at the 5% level

H_0: Mean quality ratings for all three countries is the same

H_1: Otherwise

$F_{2,99,.05} \approx 3.07 > 2.3151$, therefore, do not reject H_0 at the 5% level

H_0: No interaction exists between price and country

H_1: Otherwise

$F_{4,99,.05} \approx 2.45 > .3347$, therefore, do not reject H_0 at the 5% level

17.72 a. ANOVA table:

Source of Variation	Sum of Squares	df	Mean square	F Ratio
Income	.0178	2	.0089	.5333
SAT score	2.2011	2	1.1006	66.0333
Interaction	.1022	4	.0256	1.5333
Error	.1500	9	.0167	
Total	2.4711	17		

b. H_0: Mean gpa's for all three income groups is the same

H_1: Otherwise

$F_{2,9,.05} = 4.26 > .5333$, therefore, do not reject H_0 at the 5% level

c. H_0: Mean gpa's for all three SAT score groups is the same

H_1: Otherwise

$F_{2,9,.01} = 8.02 < 66.0333$, therefore, reject H_0 at the 1% level

d. H_0: No interaction exists between income and SAT score group

H_1: Otherwise

$F_{4,9,.05} = 3.63 > 1.5333$, therefore, do not reject H_0 at the 5% level

Chapter 18:

Introduction to Quality

18.2 Various answers.

18.4 Various answers.

18.6 a. $\hat{\sigma} = \bar{s} / c_4 = 5.42 / .959 = 5.6517$

   b. CL $= \bar{\bar{X}} = 192.6$

   LCL $= \bar{\bar{X}} - A_3\bar{s}$, where $A_3 = \dfrac{3}{c_4\sqrt{n}} = 192.6 - 1.18(5.42) = 186.2044$

   UCL $= \bar{\bar{X}} + A_3\bar{s}$, where $A_3 = \dfrac{3}{c_4\sqrt{n}} = 192.6 + 1.18(5.42) = 198.9956$

   c. CL $= 5.42$
       LCL $= .12(5.42) = .6504$, UCL $= 1.88(5.42) = 10.1896$

18.8 a. $\hat{\sigma} = 1.23 / .965 = 1.2746$
   b. CL $= 19.86$
       LCL $= 19.86 - 1.1(1.23) = 18.507$, UCL $= 19.86 + 1.1(1.23) = 21.213$
   c. CL $= 1.23$
       LCL $= .18(1.23) = .2214$, UCL $= 1.82(1.23) = 2.2386$

18.10 a. $\bar{\bar{x}} = 4999.4 / 30 = 149.98$
   b. $\bar{s} = 179.67 / 30 = 5.989$
   c. $\hat{\sigma} = 5.989 / .965 = 6.2062$
   d. CL $= 149.98$
       LCL $= 149.98 - 1.1(5.989) = 143.3921$
       UCL $= 149.98 + 1.1(5.989) = 156.5679$
   e. The $\bar{X}$ chart shows that the 26th observation is below the LCL. This would be an unusual occurrence for a process that is in control.

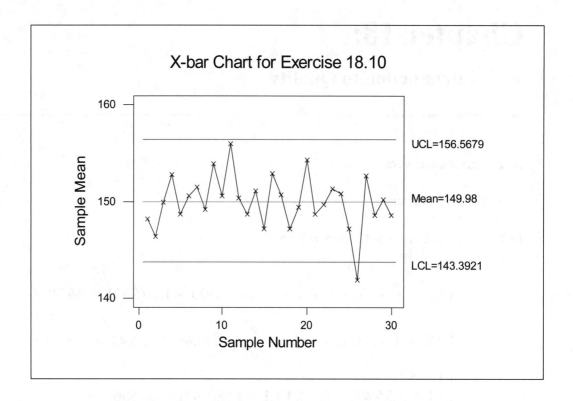

f.   CL = 5.989, LCL = .18(5.989) = 1.078, UCL = 1.82(5.989) = 10.9

g. S-chart

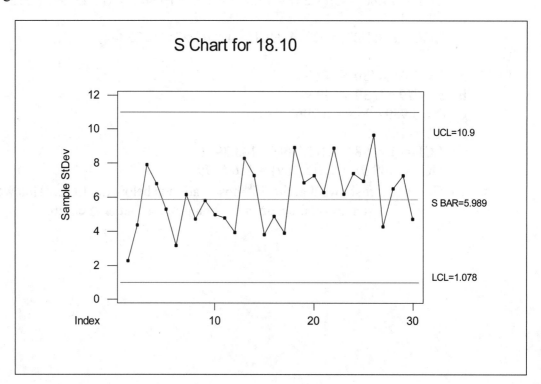

18.12   a. $192.6 \pm 3(5.6517)$: $(175.6449, 209.5551)$
These values lie within the tolerance limits

   b. $C_p = \dfrac{215-170}{6(5.6517)} = 1.327$ The process is not capable since $C_p < 1.33$

   c. $C_{pk} = \dfrac{215-192.6}{3(5.6517)} = 1.321$ The process is not capable since $C_{pk} < 1.33$

18.14   a. $19.86 \pm 3(1.2746)$: $(16.0362, 23.6838)$
These limits are beyond the tolerances set by management

   b. $C_p = \dfrac{22-18}{6(1.2746)} = .523$ The process is not capable since $C_p < 1.33$

   c. $C_{pk} = \dfrac{19.86-18}{3(1.2746)} = .486$ The process is not capable since $C_{pk} < 1.33$

18.16   a. $19.84 \pm 3(2.0903)$: $(13.5691, 26.1109)$
These limits are beyond the tolerances set by management

   b. $C_p = \dfrac{24-16}{6(2.0903)} = .638$ The process is not capable since $C_p < 1.33$

   c. $C_{pk} = \dfrac{19.84-16}{3(2.0903)} = .612$ The process is not capable since $C_{pk} < 1.33$

18.18 $CL = .018$, $LCL = 0$, $UCL = .018 + 3\sqrt{\dfrac{.018(.982)}{500}} = .0358$

18.20   a. $\bar{p} = 1.02/20 = .051$, $CL = .051$, $LCL = .051 - 3\sqrt{.051(.949)/500} = .0215$
$UCL = .051 + 3\sqrt{.051(.949)/500} = .0805$

b. p-chart

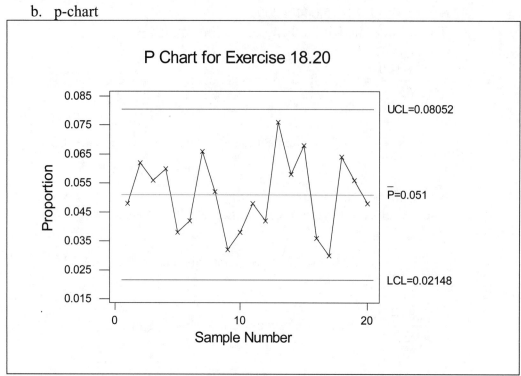

No evidence that the process is out of statistical control

18.22 a. $\bar{c} = 112 / 20 = 5.6$

b. CL = 5.6,   LCL = 0,   UCL = $5.6 + 3\sqrt{5.6} = 12.70$

c. C chart

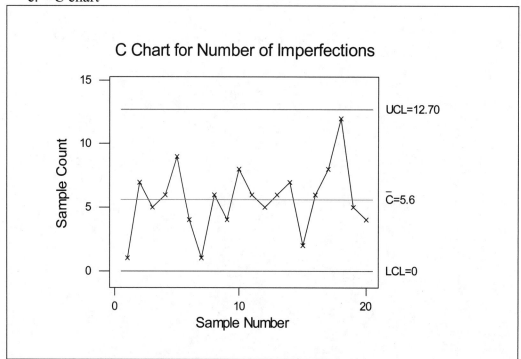

No evidence that the process is out of statistical control

18.24 a. $\bar{c} = 208/15 = 13.8667$

b. CL = 13.8667, LCL = $13.8667 - 3\sqrt{13.8667} = 2.6953$

UCL = $13.8667 + 3\sqrt{13.8667} = 25.0381$

c. c-chart

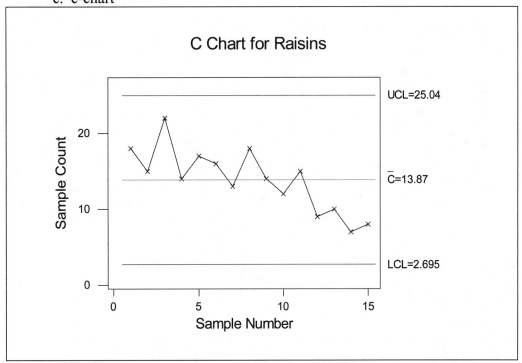

No evidence of a process out of control; however, keep monitoring the process because of the recent downward trend.

18.26   From the control charts in Exercise 18.25 and given below, we see that the process is not stable.

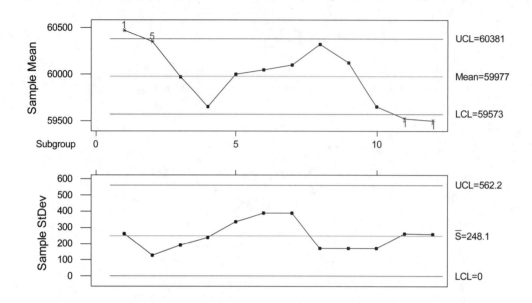

a. Capability process (normal) is meaningless since the process of manufacturing precision bolts is not stable (see Exercise 18.25).

b. Capability sixpack (normal) is meaningless since the process of manufacturing precision bolts is not stable (see Exercise 18.25).

a. c-chart for Exercise 18.22

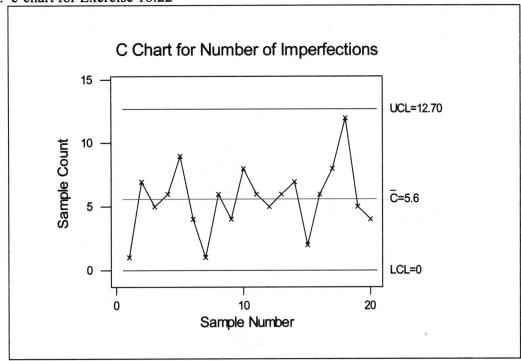

b. c-chart for Exercise 18.23

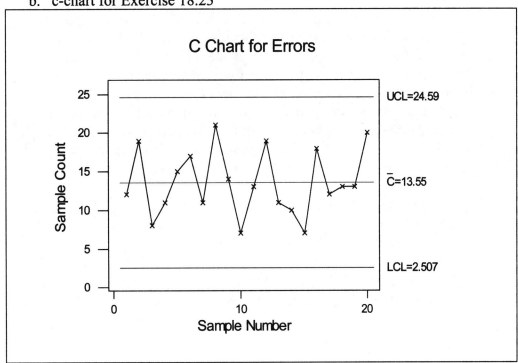

c.   c-chart for Exercise 18.24

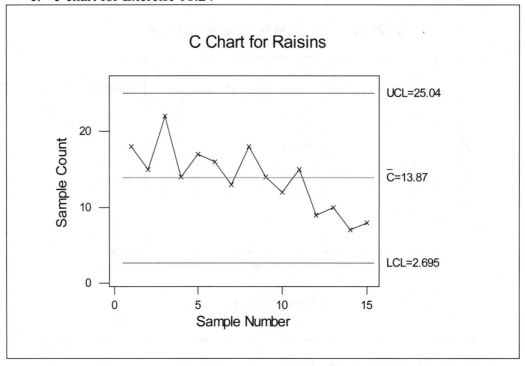

18.30   There are two types of errors that can be made – 1) identifying a special
or assignable cause of variation when there is none and 2) ignoring a
special cause by assuming that it is due to natural variability. Control
limits that are 'too narrow' will incorrectly flag natural causes of
variability as a special cause and the researcher is sent off to find a special
cause of variability that does not exist. Control limits that are 'too wide'
imply that the researcher is not going off to correct processes that are out
of control. The use of the three sigma limits as control limits was set by
Shewhart as an appropriate balance between the two types of errors.

18.32   a. $\bar{\bar{x}} = 8760.4 / 25 = 350.416$

b. $\bar{s} = 140.05 / 25 = 5.602$

c. $\hat{\sigma} = 5.602 / .965 = 5.8052$

d.   CL = 350.416
LCL = 350.416 – 1.1(5.602) = 344.2538
UCL = 350.416 + 1.1(5.602) = 356.5782

e. The X-bar chart provides no evidence that the process is out of control.

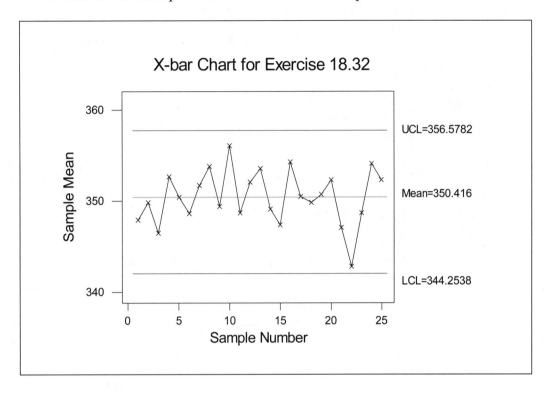

f. CL = 5.602
       LCL = .18(5.602) = 1.0084
       UCL = 1.82(5.602) = 10.1956

g. s-chart

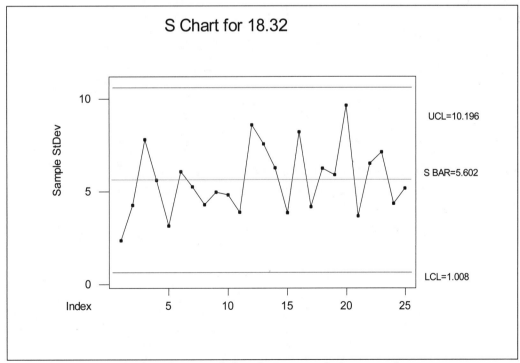

No pattern analysis rules are violated. Process is in control.

h.   i) $350.416 \pm 3(5.8052)$: $(333.0004, 367.8316)$

ii) $C_p = \dfrac{375 - 325}{6(5.8052)} = 1.435 > 1.33$. Therefore, the process is capable

iii) $C_{pk} = \dfrac{375 - 350.416}{3(5.8052)} = 1.412 > 1.33$. Therefore, the process is capable

18.34   a. $\bar{c} = 270/18 = 15$

b. CL = 15

LCL $= 15 - 3\sqrt{15} = 3.381$

UCL $= 15 + 3\sqrt{15} = 26.619$

c., d. C chart shows no evidence of a process that is out of statistical control.

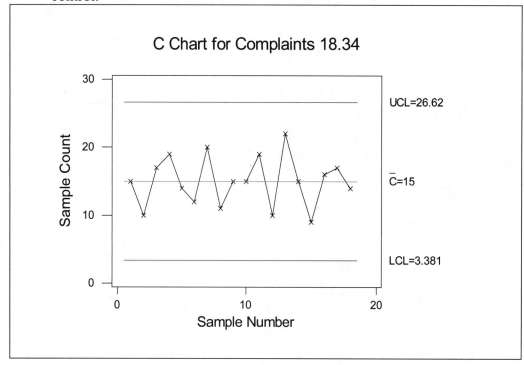

18.36 a. Common cause – affects all workers within the process

b. Common cause – affects all workers within the process

c. Assignable cause

d. Assignable cause

e. Assignable cause

18.38   a. Machine 1: X bar – s chart:

Xbar/S Chart for Machine 1

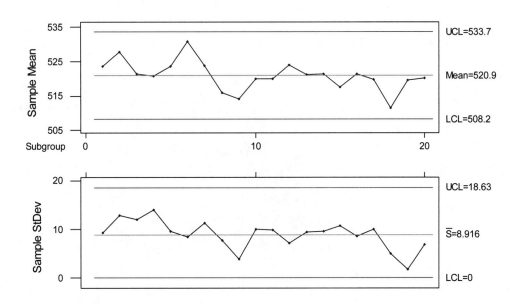

Machine 1 shows no evidence of being 'out of statistical control'

b. Machine 2: X bar – s chart:

Xbar/S Chart for Machine 2

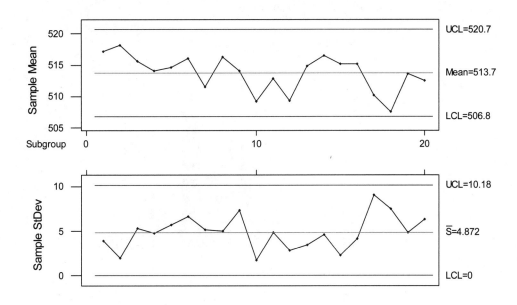

Likewise, Machine 2 shows no evidence of being 'out of statistical control'

c. Machine 1: capability analysis shows that Cp =0.44 and Cpk=0.14. Machine 1 is not capable of meeting specifications.

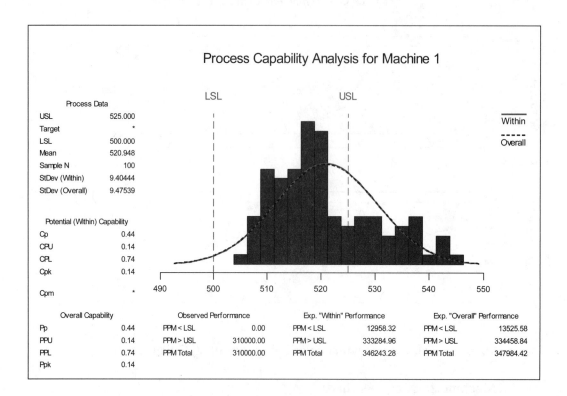

d. Machine 2: capability analysis shows that Cp = 0.80 and Cpk = 0.72. Machine 2 is not capable of meeting specifications.

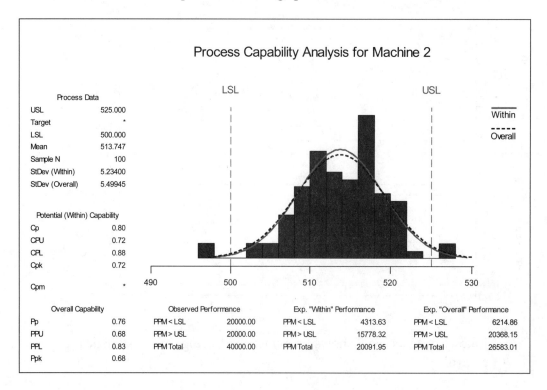

e. Neither machine is capable of meeting specifications. Both of the machines produce a product with greater variability than the specification limits call for. Note that Machine 1 has greater variability than Machine 2.

18.40   X bar chart for TOC data:

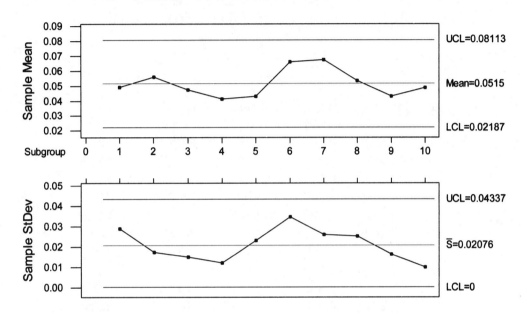

Xbar/S Chart for Leak Rates

All data points are within the control limits. No pattern analysis rule has been violated.

Chapter 19:

Time Series Analysis and Forecasting

19.2 Refer to Figure 19.4 Compute the revised Laspeyres Quantity Index for years 1 through 6 if the year one prices are 1.45 (wheat), 1.21 (corn), and 2.98 (soybeans).

Year	Wheat	Corn	Soybeans	Total Cost	Laspeyres Quantity Index
	1.45	1.21	2.98		
1	1,352	4,152	1,127	10,343	100.0
2	1,618	5,641	1,176	12,676	122.6
3	1,545	5,573	1,271	12,771	123.5
4	1,705	5,647	1,547	13,915	134.5
5	2,122	5,829	1,547	14,740	142.5
6	2,142	6,266	1,288	14,526	140.4
7	2,026	6,357	1,716	15,743	152.2
8	1,799	7,082	1,843	16,670	161.2
9	2,134	7,939	2,268	19,459	188.1
10	2,370	6,648	1,817	16,895	163.4

19.4

    a. e.g., $I_2 = 100(35.875 / 35) = 102.5$

    b. e.g., $I_1 = 100(35 / 34.375) = 101.82$

Week	Price	BaseWeek1	BaseWeek4
1	35	100.00	101.82
2	35.875	102.50	104.36
3	34.75	99.29	101.09
4	34.375	98.21	100.00
5	35	100.00	101.82
6	34.875	99.64	101.45
7	35	100.00	101.82
8	34.75	99.29	101.09
9	34.75	99.29	101.09
10	35.25	100.71	102.55
11	38.75	110.71	112.73
12	37.125	106.07	108.00

19.6   a. Unweighted average index

Year	Average	Index of Average
1	11.8	100.00
2	12.43	105.37
3	12.93	109.60
4	13.30	112.71
5	13.63	115.54
6	13.83	117.23

b. Laspeyres index

Year	$\sum q_{oi} p_{1i}$	Laspeyres Index
1	1120.4	100.00
2	1174.30	104.81
3	1237.90	110.49
4	1256.40	112.14
5	1296.40	115.71
6	1316.10	117.47

19.8   A price index for energy is helpful in that it allows us to say something about price movements over time for a group of commodities, namely, energy prices. A weighted index of prices allows one to compare the cost of a group of products across periods.

19.10 A time series contains 50 observations, find the probability that the number of runs
   a. is less than 14

$$Z = \frac{R - \frac{n}{2} - 1}{\sqrt{\frac{n^2 - 2n}{4(n-1)}}} = Z = \frac{14 - \frac{50}{2} - 1}{\sqrt{\frac{50^2 - 2(50)}{4(50-1)}}} = -3.43 \quad P(Z < -3.43) = .0003$$

   b.   is less than 17

$$Z = \frac{R - \frac{n}{2} - 1}{\sqrt{\frac{n^2 - 2n}{4(n-1)}}} = Z = \frac{17 - \frac{50}{2} - 1}{\sqrt{\frac{50^2 - 2(50)}{4(50-1)}}} = -2.57 \quad P(Z < -2.57) = .0051$$

c.   is greater than 38

$$Z = \frac{R - \frac{n}{2} - 1}{\sqrt{\frac{n^2 - 2n}{4(n-1)}}} = Z = \frac{38 - \frac{50}{2} - 1}{\sqrt{\frac{50^2 - 2(50)}{4(50-1)}}} = 3.43 \quad P(Z > 3.43) = .0003$$

19.12 Runs test on Value of the exchange rate

Runs Test: Value
```
Value    K =    99.8500
The observed number of runs =    6
    The expected number of runs =    7.0000
      6 Observations above K    6 below
 * N Small -- The following approximation may be invalid
              The test is significant at   0.5448
              Cannot reject at alpha = 0.05
```

Do not reject Ho that the data series is random. There is no evidence of nonrandom patterns in the data.

19.14   Runs test on Stock Market Return

Runs Test: Return
```
Return  K =    17.5000
   The observed number of runs =    9
   The expected number of runs =    8.0000
     7 Observations above K    7 below
  * N Small -- The following approximation may be invalid
              The test is significant at   0.5780
```

Do not reject Ho that the data series is random. There is no evidence of nonrandom patterns in the data.

19.16 a. Runs test on Housing Starts

Runs Test: Starts
```
Starts  K =    7.3500
   The observed number of runs =   10
   The expected number of runs =  13.0000
   12 Observations above K    12 below
              The test is significant at  0.2105
              Cannot reject at alpha = 0.05
```

Do not reject Ho that the data series is random. There is no evidence of nonrandom patterns in the data.

b. From the time series plot below, strong cyclical behavior is evident.

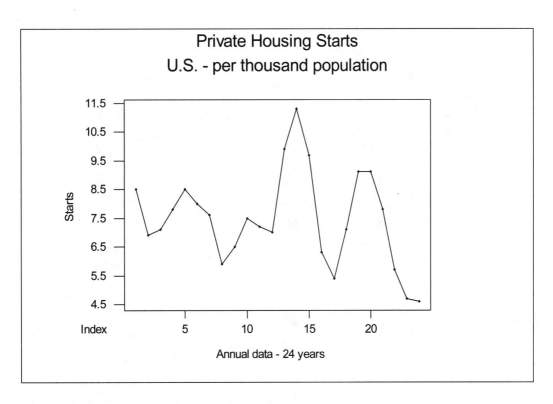

19.18 a. Time series plot of Quarterly sales
Data patterns evident in the time series plot include; strong seasonality and a strong upward trend

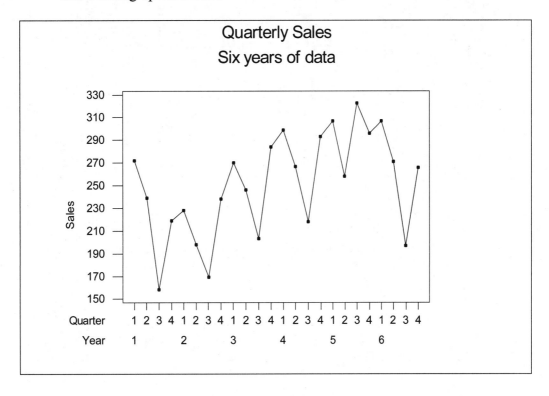

b.

Period	4 Period MA	$100\dfrac{X_t}{X_t^*}$	Seas. Factor	Adj. Series
1-1			112.848	241.032
2			99.609	239.938
3	216.500	72.979	79.826	197.930
4	205.875	106.375	107.716	203.312
2-1	202.125	112.802		202.041
2	205.875	96.175		198.777
3	213.500	79.157		211.709
4	224.750	105.895		220.951
3-1	235.000	114.894		239.259
2	245.000	100.408		246.966
3	254.375	79.803		254.302
4	260.625	108.969		263.656
4-1	265.125	112.777		264.958
2	268.125	99.580		268.048
3	270.250	80.666		273.093
4	270.125	108.468		272.011
5-1	270.750	113.389		272.047
2	272.875	94.549		259.013
3	273.250	84.904		290.631
4	274.875	107.685		274.796
6-1	272.125	112.816		272.047
2	264.000	102.652		272.064
3				246.786
4				246.945

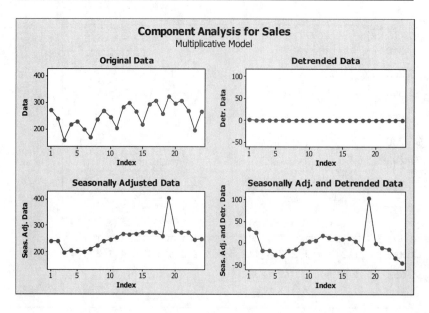

Component Analysis for Sales
Multiplicative Model

Original Data

Detrended Data

Seasonally Adjusted Data

Seasonally Adj. and Detrended Data

The seasonally adjusted series no longer shows the regular quarterly cycle. There is an unusual point in the third quarter of 2003. The value is much higher than expected.

19.20 3-period centered moving average – year-end gold price

Year	3-point Moving Avg
1	*
2	176.000
3	308.667
4	450.333
5	507.667
6	480.000
7	411.333
8	381.000
9	340.667
10	347.333
11	406.667
12	433.667
13	421.667
14	*

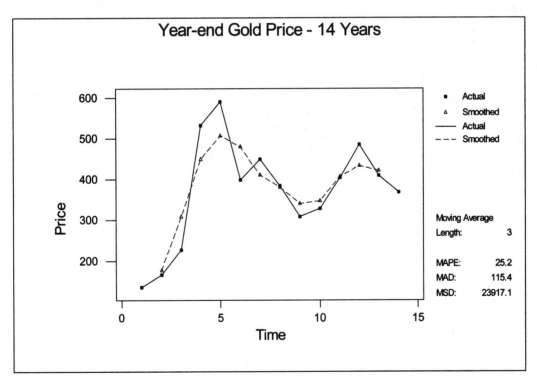

The resulting data shows strong cyclical behavior

19.22

Year	7ptMA
1	*
2	*
3	*
4	30.4429
5	25.3429
6	23.0000
7	23.4286
8	22.7429
9	21.1286
10	20.6000
11	23.1286
12	28.1000
13	32.0857
14	33.8000
15	35.1571
16	35.7143
17	34.9714
18	31.5143
19	27.4571
20	27.0857
21	34.3286
22	40.5429
23	43.7143
24	48.6000
25	54.4286
26	*
27	*
28	*

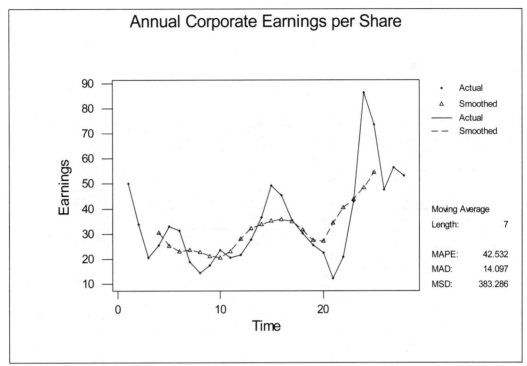

The smoothed data exhibits a cyclical data pattern

19.24 a.

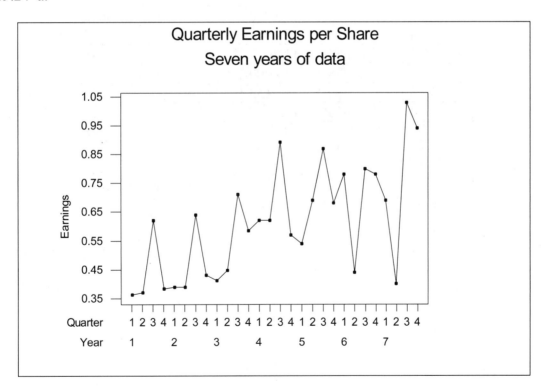

The data series exhibits a strong seasonal component.

b.

Period	4 Period MA	$100\dfrac{X_t}{X_t^*}$	Seas. Factor	Adj. Series
1-1			90.930	.3981
2			86.020	.4301
3	.438	141.902	130.400	.4762
4	.443	86.608	92.649	.4145
2-1	.448	86.830		.4278
2	.456	85.284		.4522
3	.465	137.493		.4900
4	.475	90.761		.4652
3-1	.491	83.643		.4520
2	.520	86.216		.5208
3	.565	126.046		.5460
4	.613	95.347		.6303
4-1	.656	94.458		.6818
2	.677	91.581		.7208
3	.665	133.935		.6833
4	.664	85.843		.6152
5-1	.670	80.582		.5939
2	.681	101.284		.8021
3	.725	120.000		.6672
4	.724	93.955		.7340
6-1	.684	114.077		.8578
2	.688	64.000		.5115
3	.689	116.153		.6135
4	.673	115.985		.8419
7-1	.696	99.102		.7588
2	.745	53.691		.4650
3				.7899
4				1.0146

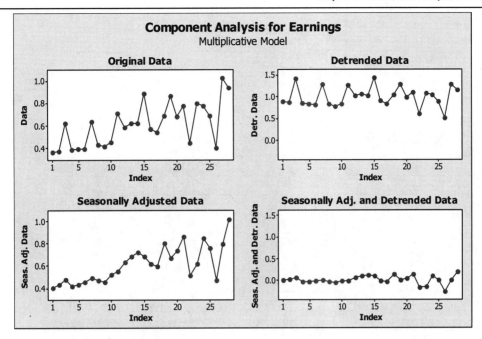

Seasonally adjusted series shows an upward trend in the data with increasing variability.

19.26

Period	4 Period MA	$100\dfrac{X_t}{X_t^*}$	Seas. Factor	Adj. Series
1-1			93.701	574.165
2			97.648	634.935
3			119.127	729.476
4			101.932	832.911
5			102.038	928.084
6			97.450	955.365
7	767.750	97.167	99.356	750.834
8	773.750	95.638	100.300	737.789
9	775.000	84.387	87.504	747.395
10	770.333	113.457	113.255	771.707
11	759.667	99.912	98.563	770.069
12	743.000	85.734	89.127	714.721
2-1	730.250	87.094		678.752
2	725.750	91.767		682.043
3	721.458	118.233		716.045
4	712.542	105.678		738.730
5	699.542	112.502		771.280
6	689.458	100.224		709.084
7	684.000	99.415		684.406
8	678.917	102.811		695.915
9	668.208	88.745		677.684
10	651.750	110.625		636.614
11	630.917	95.100		608.751
12	611.417	90.609		621.586
3-1	598.167	98.300		627.526
2	583.625	101.435		606.260
3	570.375	117.467		562.426
4	563.542	96.000		530.748
5	558.250	89.387		489.033
6	551.917	92.586		524.373
7				545.512
8				485.545
9				555.403
10				586.286
11				537.730
12				529.583

19.28   Use smoothing constant of .7 (alpha of .3) in Minitab. Set initial
smoothing value at the average of the first '1' observations

Single Exponential Smoothing

```
Data          Price
Length        14.0000
NMissing      0
Smoothing Constant
Alpha: 0.7
Accuracy Measures
MAPE:     20.7
MAD:      84.3
MSD:   13759.9
```

Row	Time	Price	SMOO2	FITS2	Error
1	1	135	135.000	135.000	0.000
2	2	166	156.700	135.000	31.000
3	3	227	205.910	156.700	70.300
4	4	533	434.873	205.910	327.090
5	5	591	544.162	434.873	156.127
6	6	399	442.549	544.162	-145.162
7	7	450	447.765	442.549	7.451
8	8	385	403.829	447.765	-62.765
9	9	308	336.749	403.829	-95.829
10	10	329	331.325	336.749	-7.749
11	11	405	382.897	331.325	73.675
12	12	486	455.069	382.897	103.103
13	13	410	423.521	455.069	-45.069
14	14	369	385.356	423.521	-54.521

Row	Period	Forecast	Lower	Upper
1	15	385.356	178.884	591.828
2	16	385.356	178.884	591.828
3	17	385.356	178.884	591.828
4	18	385.356	178.884	591.828
5	19	385.356	178.884	591.828

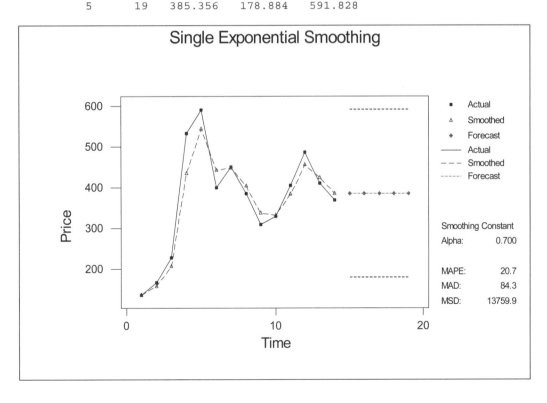

19.30   a. Forecasts for smoothing constants of .2, .4, .6, .8:

Period	Xt	Alpha = .2	Alpha = .4	Alpha = .6	Alpha = .8
1	3.63	3.6300	3.6300	3.6300	3.6300
2	3.62	3.6220	3.6240	6.6260	3.6280
3	3.66	3.6524	3.6456	3.6396	3.6344
4	5.31	4.9785	4.6442	4.3078	3.9695
5	6.14	5.9077	5.5417	5.0407	4.4036
6	6.42	6.3175	6.0687	5.5924	4.8069
7	7.01	6.8715	6.6335	6.1594	5.2475
8	6.37	6.4703	6.4754	6.2437	5.4720
9	5.82	5.9501	6.0822	6.0742	5.5416
10	4.98	5.1740	5.4209	5.6365	5.4293
11	3.43	3.7788	4.2263	4.7539	5.0294
12	3.40	3.4758	3.7305	4.2123	4.7035
13	3.54	3.5272	3.6162	3.9434	4.4708
14	1.65	2.0254	2.4365	3.0260	3.9067
15	2.15	2.1251	2.2646	2.6756	3.5553
16	6.09	5.2970	4.5598	4.0414	4.0623
17	5.95	5.8194	5.3939	4.8048	4.4398
18	6.26	6.1719	5.9136	5.3869	4.8039
MAPE		20.795	24.546	30.613	36.6633
MAD		.8578	1.0216	1.2362	1.4307
MSD		1.6403	1.9071	2.3378	2.8048

   b. Based on the accuracy measures – choose an alpha of .2 for the 'best' forecast

19.32   If alpha is 1.0, then the forecast will always be equal to the first observation.

$$\hat{X}_{t+h} = X_1$$

19.34   Use .7 for level (alpha of .3) and .5 for trend (beta of .5)

Double Exponential Smoothing

Data	CanadaIP
Length	15.0000
NMissing	0

Smoothing Constants
Alpha (level): 0.7
Gamma (trend): 0.5
Accuracy Measures
MAPE: 4.7820
MAD: 4.1013
MSD: 28.0623

Row	Time	CanadaIP	Smooth	Predict	Error
1	1	79	77.148	72.825	6.17500
2	2	74	76.260	81.534	-7.53375
3	3	78	78.003	78.010	-0.00956
4	4	80	79.925	79.749	0.25104
5	5	83	82.628	81.759	1.24136
6	6	88	87.069	84.896	3.10398
7	7	85	86.627	90.424	-5.42363
8	8	87	87.325	88.084	-1.08364
9	9	79	81.821	88.402	-9.40237
10	10	84	82.682	79.607	4.39284
11	11	91	88.302	82.006	8.99391
12	12	100	97.232	90.774	9.22636
13	13	100	100.880	102.933	-2.93313
14	14	106	105.866	105.554	0.44562
15	15	112	111.609	110.697	1.30328

Row	Period	Forecast	Lower	Upper
1	16	116.896	106.847	126.944
2	17	122.182	109.496	134.868
3	18	127.469	111.916	143.021
4	19	132.755	114.212	151.298
5	20	138.042	116.437	159.647

19.36

Winters' Method for FoodPrice

Forecasts

Period	Forecast	Lower	Upper
15	125.448	124.599	126.297
16	126.466	125.531	127.402
17	126.967	125.927	128.007

19.38 $\hat{X}_n = 260.6644,\quad T_n = -8.6609$

Forecast for eight quarters:

Year	1	2	3	4
7	273.1269	230.6040	177.3303	232.1205
8	235.5794	197.7740	151.1529	196.5420

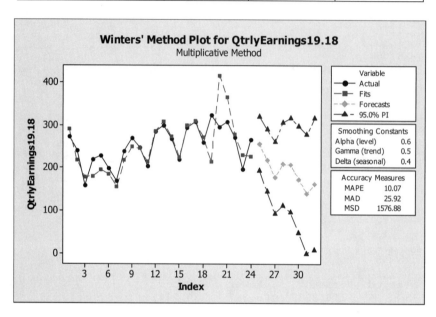

19.40   The data to be used for this exercise comes from Table 19.10: Index of Volume of Shares Traded:

Regression Analysis: Volume_Table19-10 versus Vol_lag1

```
The regression equation is
Volume_Table19-10 = 87.8 + 0.169 Vol_lag1
15 cases used 1 cases contain missing values

Predictor          Coef      SE Coef          T         P
Constant          87.85        30.45       2.88     0.013
Vol_lag1         0.1690       0.2855       0.59     0.564

S = 11.06       R-Sq = 2.6%       R-Sq(adj) = 0.0%
Analysis of Variance
Source             DF           SS          MS         F         P
Regression          1         42.9        42.9      0.35     0.564
Residual Error     13       1589.5       122.3
Total              14       1632.4
```

The first-order autoregressive model is

$\hat{y}_t = 87.85 + .169 y_{t-1} + a_t$

$y_{17} = 87.85 + .169(92) = 103.398$

$y_{18} = 87.85 + .169(103.398) = 105.324$

$y_{19} = 87.85 + .169(105.324) = 105.650$

$y_{20} = 87.85 + .169(105.650) = 105.705$

19.42

4th order model:

Regression Analysis: Starts versus Startlag1, Startlag2, ...

```
The regression equation is
Starts = 4.45 + 1.25 Startlag1 - 1.10 Startlag2 + 0.313 Startlag3
         - 0.064 Startlag4
20 cases used 4 cases contain missing values
Predictor        Coef      SE Coef         T        P
Constant        4.449       2.884       1.54    0.144
Startlag1      1.2517      0.2783       4.50    0.000
Startlag2     -1.0950      0.4182      -2.62    0.019
Startlag3      0.3131      0.4193       0.75    0.467
Startlag4     -0.0641      0.2935      -0.22    0.830

S = 1.042       R-Sq = 73.2%     R-Sq(adj) = 66.1%
```

$z - statistic \ for \ \phi_4 = -.218$. Fail to reject H_0 at the 10% level

3rd order model:

Regression Analysis: Starts versus Startlag1, Startlag2, ...

```
The regression equation is
Starts = 4.10 + 1.24 Startlag1 - 1.03 Startlag2 + 0.245 Startlag3
21 cases used 3 cases contain missing values
Predictor        Coef      SE Coef         T        P
Constant        4.100       2.183       1.88    0.078
Startlag1      1.2375      0.2509       4.93    0.000
Startlag2     -1.0325      0.2900      -3.56    0.002
Startlag3      0.2450      0.2695       0.91    0.376

S = 0.9808      R-Sq = 73.2%     R-Sq(adj) = 68.4%
```

$z - statistic \ for \ \phi_3 = .909$. Fail to reject H_0 at the 10% level

2nd order model:

Regression Analysis: Starts versus Startlag1, Startlag2

```
The regression equation is
Starts = 5.73 + 1.03 Startlag1 - 0.788 Startlag2
22 cases used 2 cases contain missing values
Predictor        Coef      SE Coef         T        P
Constant        5.728       1.245       4.60    0.000
Startlag       1.0332      0.1573       6.57    0.000
Startlag      -0.7877      0.1705      -4.62    0.000

S = 0.9765      R-Sq = 70.3%     R-Sq(adj) = 67.2%
```

$z - statistic \ for \ \phi_2 = -4.621$. Reject H_0 at the 10% level

1st order model:

Regression Analysis: Starts versus Startlag1

```
The regression equation is
Starts = 2.61 + 0.633 Startlag1
23 cases used 1 cases contain missing values

Predictor        Coef     SE Coef         T       P
Constant        2.614       1.451      1.80   0.086
Startlag       0.6333      0.1874      3.38   0.003

S = 1.376       R-Sq = 35.2%     R-Sq(adj) = 32.1%
```

Forecasts from the second order model:

$$\hat{y}_{25} = 6.776, \hat{y}_{26} = 9.103, \hat{y}_{27} = 9.792, \hat{y}_{28} = 8.670, \hat{y}_{29} = 6.968$$

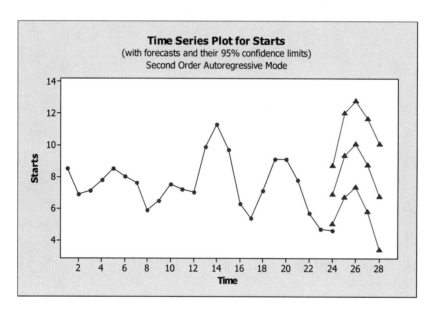

There would be no change if a significance level of 5% were used instead of 10%, the second order model z-statistics of -4.621 is significant at the 10% and 5% level.

19.44

3rd order model:

Regression Analysis: Earnings versus esp_lag1, esp_lag2, ...

```
The regression equation is
Earnings = 2.48 + 0.870 esp_lag1 - 0.272 esp_lag2 - 0.093 esp_lag3
15 cases used 3 cases contain missing values
Predictor        Coef     SE Coef         T       P
Constant        2.477       1.317      1.88   0.087
esp_la         0.8697      0.3030      2.87   0.015
esp_la        -0.2720      0.3928     -0.69   0.503
esp_la        -0.0932      0.3076     -0.30   0.768
S = 1.328       R-Sq = 51.7%     R-Sq(adj) = 38.5%
```

z − statistic for $\phi_3 = -.303$, Fail to reject H₀ *at the 10% level*

2nd order model:

Regression Analysis: Earnings versus esp_lag1, esp_lag2

```
The regression equation is
Earnings = 2.16 + 0.916 esp_lag1 - 0.349 esp_lag2
16 cases used 2 cases contain missing values
Predictor        Coef      SE Coef          T        P
Constant        2.158        1.033       2.09    0.057
esp_la         0.9161       0.2608       3.51    0.004
esp_la        -0.3489       0.2629      -1.33    0.207
S = 1.237      R-Sq = 52.4%      R-Sq(adj) = 45.0%
```

$z - statistic\ for\ \phi_2 = -1.327$, Fail to reject H$_0$ at the 10% level

1st order model:

Regression Analysis: Earnings versus esp_lag1

```
The regression equation is
Earnings = 1.57 + 0.696 esp_lag1
17 cases used 1 cases contain missing values
Predictor        Coef      SE Coef          T        P
Constant       1.5697       0.9342       1.68    0.114
esp_la         0.6962       0.1900       3.66    0.002
S = 1.234      R-Sq = 47.2%      R-Sq(adj) = 43.7%
```

$z - statistic\ for\ \phi_1 = 3.664$, Reject H$_0$ at the 10% level

Use the 1st order model for forecasting

$\hat{y}_{19} = 5.927, \hat{y}_{20} = 5.695, \hat{y}_{21} = 5.534, \hat{y}_{22} = 5.422$

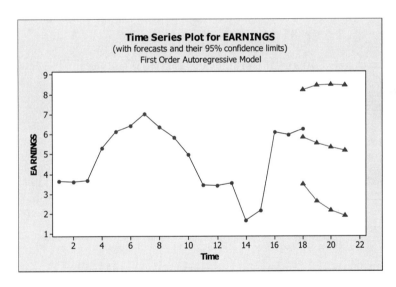

There would be no change if a significance level of 5% were used instead of 10%, the first order model z-statistic of 3.664 is significant at the 10% and 5% level.

19.46 $\hat{X}_{1996} = 202 + 1.1(951) - .48(923) + .17(867) = 952.45$

$\hat{X}_{1997} = 202 + 1.1(952.45) - .48(951) + .17(923) = 950.13$

$\hat{X}_{1998} = 202 + 1.1(950.13) - .48(952.45) + .17(951) = 951.64$

19.48

4th order model:

Regression Analysis: earndiff versus earnlag1, earnlag2, ...
```
The regression equation is
earndiff = 0.0941 - 0.936 earnlag1 - 0.547 earnlag2
           - 0.367 earnlag3 - 0.251 earnlag4
19 cases used 5 cases contain missing values
Predictor        Coef     SE Coef         T        P
Constant      0.09409     0.03251      2.89    0.012
earnlag1      -0.9358      0.2647     -3.53    0.003
earnlag2      -0.5471      0.3451     -1.59    0.135
earnlag3      -0.3674      0.2905     -1.26    0.227
earnlag4      -0.2514      0.2122     -1.19    0.256
S = 0.06788    R-Sq = 51.4%    R-Sq(adj) = 37.6%
```

T-statistic for $\phi_4 = -1.185$. Fail to reject H_0 at the 10% level

3rd order model:

Regression Analysis: earndiff versus earnlag1, earnlag2, ...
```
The regression equation is
earndiff = 0.0799 - 0.907 earnlag1 - 0.479 earnlag2
           - 0.173 earnlag3
20 cases used 4 cases contain missing values
Predictor        Coef     SE Coef         T        P
Constant      0.07994     0.02358      3.39    0.004
earnlag1      -0.9068      0.2466     -3.68    0.002
earnlag2      -0.4787      0.2601     -1.84    0.084
earnlag3      -0.1735      0.2051     -0.85    0.410
S = 0.06707    R-Sq = 46.9%    R-Sq(adj) = 37.0%
```

T-statistic for $\phi_3 = -.846$. Fail to reject H_0 at the 10% level

2nd order model:

Regression Analysis: earndiff versus earnlag1, earnlag2
```
The regression equation is
earndiff = 0.0596 - 0.704 earnlag1 - 0.286 earnlag2
21 cases used 3 cases contain missing values
Predictor        Coef     SE Coef         T        P
Constant      0.05961     0.01742      3.42    0.003
earnlag1      -0.7037      0.1943     -3.62    0.002
earnlag2      -0.2865      0.1923     -1.49    0.154
S = 0.06676    R-Sq = 43.4%    R-Sq(adj) = 37.2%
```

T-statistic for $\phi_2 = -1.490$. Fail to reject H_0 at the 10% level

1st order model:

Regression Analysis: earndiff versus earnlag1
```
The regression equation is
earndiff = 0.0399 - 0.592 earnlag1
22 cases used 2 cases contain missing values
Predictor       Coef     SE Coef        T        P
Constant      0.03995     0.01757     2.27    0.034
earnlag1      -0.5920      0.1814     -3.26    0.004
S = 0.07858    R-Sq = 34.7%    R-Sq(adj) = 31.5%
```

T-statistic for $\phi_1 = -3.263$. Reject H_0 at the 10% level

Use the 1st order model for forecasting

$\hat{y}_{25} = .070, \hat{y}_{26} = -.001, \hat{y}_{27} = .041$

19.50   Parts a,b,c:

Period	a. Unweighted	b. Laspeyres Price	c. Laspeyres Quantity
1	100.00	100.00	100.00
2	110.30	109.72	103.78
3	117.43	115.55	100.04
4	127.52	123.47	105.29
5	143.96	137.18	106.00
6	158.22	149.41	105.85

19.52   Forecasts are generated by analyzing each individual component; trend, seasonal and cyclical. Then, once each component has been analyzed and measured, the information is then incorporated into the forecasting model.

19.54   A seasonally adjusted time series is one that is free from the effects of seasonal influence. Government agencies expend large efforts on seasonal adjustments in order to gain a clearer picture of the underlying data pattern.

19.56   a.

Runs Test: Sales
```
Sales
K =   737.0000

    The observed number of runs =   10
    The expected number of runs =   13.0000
    12 Observations above K    12 below
            The test is significant at   0.2105
            Cannot reject at alpha = 0.05
```

b.

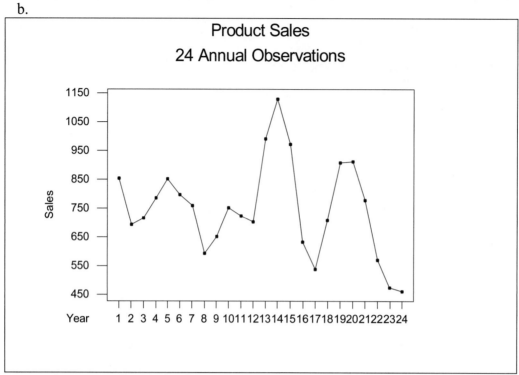

Product Sales
24 Annual Observations

Strong cyclical behavior as well as a slight downward trend

c.

Year	Sales	5pt MA
1	853	*
2	693	*
3	715	779.4
4	785	768.2
5	851	781.2
6	797	756.8
7	758	729.8
8	593	709.8
9	650	695.0
10	751	683.8
11	723	763.4
12	702	859.2
13	991	903.4
14	1129	885.0
15	972	852.2
16	631	795.6
17	538	751.2
18	708	739.2
19	907	768.4
20	912	774.6
21	777	727.6
22	569	638.0
23	473	*
24	459	*

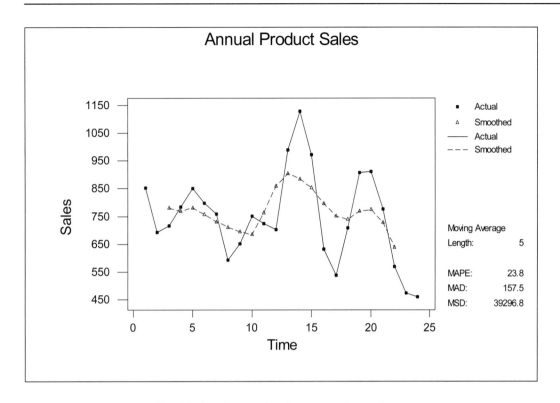

Strong cyclical behavior and a downward trend

19.58   a.

Moving average

```
Data        PriceIndex
Length      15.0000
NMissing    0

Moving Average
Length: 3

Accuracy Measures
MAPE:  5.6999
MAD:   6.1389
MSD:  84.4352
```

Row	Period	PriceIndex	AVER3	Predict	Error
1	1	79	*	*	*
2	2	87	85.000	*	*
3	3	89	88.667	*	*
4	4	90	89.000	85.000	5.0000
5	5	88	89.000	88.667	-0.6667
6	6	89	90.333	89.000	0.0000
7	7	94	91.667	89.000	5.0000
8	8	92	91.333	90.333	1.6667
9	9	88	92.000	91.667	-3.6667
10	10	96	100.333	91.333	4.6667
11	11	117	109.667	92.000	25.0000
12	12	116	115.667	100.333	15.6667
13	13	114	114.333	109.667	4.3333
14	14	113	112.000	115.667	-2.6667
15	15	109	*	114.333	-5.3333

b.

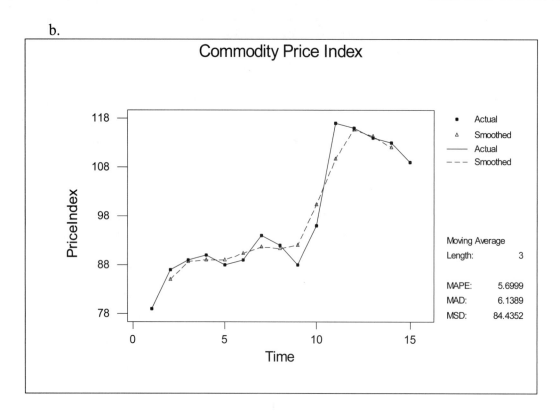

Strong upward trend and cyclical behavior

19.60

Double Exponential Smoothing
```
Data          PriceIndex
Length        15.0000
NMissing      0
Smoothing Constants
Alpha (level): 0.7
Gamma (trend): 0.6
Accuracy Measures
MAPE:  5.9448
MAD:   6.1265
MSD:  63.3177
```

Row	Time	PriceIndex	Smooth	Predict	Error
1	1	79	79.345	80.150	-1.1500
2	2	87	85.298	81.326	5.6737
3	3	89	89.199	89.662	-0.6621
4	4	90	90.985	93.285	-3.2848
5	5	88	89.708	93.692	-5.6920
6	6	89	89.307	90.024	-1.0235
7	7	94	92.558	89.193	4.8069
8	8	92	92.739	94.463	-2.4629
9	9	88	89.683	93.609	-5.6094
10	10	96	93.659	88.197	7.8026
11	11	117	110.535	95.451	21.5491
12	12	116	117.613	121.378	-5.3776
13	13	114	117.659	126.197	-12.1970
14	14	113	115.436	121.120	-8.1201
15	15	109	110.946	115.487	-6.4866

Row	Period	Forecast	Lower	Upper
1	16	108.272	93.2621	123.282
2	17	105.598	86.6480	124.549
3	18	102.925	79.6916	126.157
4	19	100.251	72.5514	127.950

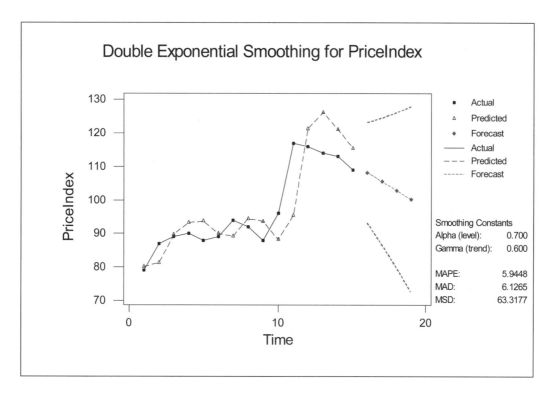

19.62

4th order model

Regression Analysis: Sales versus saleslag1, saleslag2, ...
```
The regression equation is
Sales = 435 + 1.26 saleslag1 - 1.10 saleslag2 + 0.321 saleslag3
            - 0.063 saleslag4
20 cases used 4 cases contain missing values
Predictor        Coef       SE Coef          T        P
Constant        434.9         287.5       1.51    0.151
saleslag       1.2626        0.2796       4.52    0.000
saleslag      -1.1016        0.4211      -2.62    0.019
saleslag       0.3210        0.4220       0.76    0.459
saleslag      -0.0634        0.2938      -0.22    0.832

S = 103.9      R-Sq = 73.3%      R-Sq(adj) = 66.2%
```

T-statistic for $\phi_4 = -.216$. Fail to reject H$_0$ at the 10% level

3rd order model

Regression Analysis: Sales versus saleslag1, saleslag2, ...
```
The regression equation is
Sales = 401 + 1.25 saleslag1 - 1.04 saleslag2 + 0.253 saleslag3
21 cases used 3 cases contain missing values
Predictor       Coef      SE Coef          T        P
Constant       400.7        217.8       1.84    0.083
saleslag      1.2484       0.2509       4.97    0.000
saleslag     -1.0394       0.2905      -3.58    0.002
saleslag      0.2532       0.2694       0.94    0.360

S = 97.76       R-Sq = 73.3%     R-Sq(adj) = 68.6%
```

T-statistic for $\phi_3 = .940$. Fail to reject H_0 at the 10% level

2nd order model

Regression Analysis: Sales versus saleslag1, saleslag2
```
The regression equation is
Sales = 568 + 1.04 saleslag1 - 0.785 saleslag2
22 cases used 2 cases contain missing values
Predictor       Coef      SE Coef          T        P
Constant       568.1        124.8       4.55    0.000
saleslag      1.0368       0.1580       6.56    0.000
saleslag     -0.7847       0.1710      -4.59    0.000

S = 97.72       R-Sq = 70.2%     R-Sq(adj) = 67.1%
```

T-statistic for $\phi_2 = -4.590$. Reject H_0 at the 10% level

Use the 2nd order model for forecasting

$\hat{y}_{25} = 672.829, \hat{y}_{26} = 905.554, \hat{y}_{27} = 979.039$

Chapter 20:

Additional Topics in Sampling

20.2 Answers should refer to each of the steps outlined in Figure 20.1

20.4 Answers should refer to each of the steps outlined in Figure 20.1

20.6 Answers should deal with issues such as (a) the identification of the correct population, (b) selection (nonresponse) bias, (c) response bias

20.8 Answers should deal with issues such as (a) the identification of the correct population, (b) selection (nonresponse) bias, (c) response bias

20.10 Within Minitab, go to Calc → Make Patterned Data... in order to generate a simple set of numbers of size 'n' or 'N'. Enter first value as 1, last value as the total number of stocks traded on the New York Stock Exchange. Go to Calc → Random Data → Sample from Columns... in order to generate a simple random sample of size 'n' from the number of all stocks. "Sample ____ rows from column(s):" For Exercise 20.10 enter __20__ as the number of rows to sample from. The results will be the observation numbers in the list to include in the sample.

20.12 Within Minitab, go to Calc → Make Patterned Data... in order to generate a simple set of numbers of size 'n' or 'N'. Enter first value as 1, last value as 12,723. Go to Calc → Random Data → Sample from Columns... in order to generate a simple random sample of size 'n'. "Sample ____ rows from column(s):" Enter __100__ as the number of rows to sample from. The results will be the observation numbers in the list to include in the sample.

20.14 $\bar{x} = 9.7, s = 6.2,\ \hat{\sigma}_{\bar{x}} = \sqrt{\dfrac{(s)^2}{n}\dfrac{N-n}{N}} = \sqrt{\dfrac{(6.2)^2}{50}\dfrac{139}{189}} = .7519$

$9.7 \pm 1.96\,(.7519)$ $(8.2262, 11.1738)$

20.16 $\hat{\sigma}_{\bar{x}} = \sqrt{\dfrac{(5.32)^2}{40}\dfrac{85}{125}} = .6936,\ \ 7.28 \pm 2.58\,(.6936)\ \ (5.4904, 9.0696)$

20.18 $\hat{\sigma}_{\bar{x}}^{\,2} = \dfrac{(s)^2}{n}\dfrac{N-n}{N} = \dfrac{s^2}{n}\left[1 - \dfrac{n}{N}\right] = s^2\left[\dfrac{1}{n} - \dfrac{1}{N}\right]$

20.20   95% confidence interval: using $\hat{\sigma}_{\bar{x}}^2 = \dfrac{s^2}{n}\dfrac{N-n}{N} = \dfrac{(43.27)^2}{60}\dfrac{760}{820}$

$N\bar{x} - Z_{\alpha/2}N\hat{\sigma}_{\bar{x}} < N\mu < N\bar{x} + Z_{\alpha/2}N\hat{\sigma}_{\bar{x}}$, where

$N\bar{x} = (820)(127.43) = 104,492.6$

$N\hat{\sigma}_{\bar{x}} = \sqrt{\dfrac{s^2}{n}N(N-n)} = \sqrt{\dfrac{(43.27)^2}{60}820(820-60)} = 4,409.8619$

$104,492.6 \pm 1.96(4409.8619)$

$95,849.2706 < \ N\mu\ < 113,135.9294$

20.22 $\bar{x} = 143/35 = 4.0857$

90% confidence interval:

$N\bar{x} - Z_{\alpha/2}N\hat{\sigma}_{\bar{x}} < N\mu < N\bar{x} + Z_{\alpha/2}N\hat{\sigma}_{\bar{x}}$, where

$N\bar{x} = (120)(4.0857) = 490.2857$

$N\hat{\sigma}_{\bar{x}} = \sqrt{\dfrac{s^2}{n}N(N-n)} = \sqrt{\dfrac{(3.1)^2}{35}120(120-35)} = 52.9210$

$490.2857 \pm 1.645(52.9210)$

$403.2307\ <\ N\mu\ <\ 577.3407$

20.24 $\hat{p} = 56/100 = .56$

$\sigma_{\hat{p}} = \sqrt{[\hat{p}(1-\hat{p})/(n-1)][(N-n)/N]}$

$= \sqrt{[(.56)(.44)/99][(420-100)/420]} = .0435$

90% confidence interval: $.56 \pm 1.645(.0435)$: .4884 up to .6316

20.26 $\hat{p} = 31/80 = .3875$

$\sigma_{\hat{p}} = \sqrt{[\hat{p}(1-\hat{p})/(n-1)][(N-n)/N]} = \sqrt{[(.3875)(.6125)/(79)][(420-80)/420]}$

$= .0493$

90% confidence interval: $.3875 \pm 1.645(.0493)$: .3064 up to .4686

$128.688 <\ Np\ < 196.812$ or between 129 and 197 students intend to take the final.

20.28   a. $\bar{x}_3 = 43.3$, $\hat{\sigma}^2_{\bar{x}_3} = \dfrac{s^2}{n}\dfrac{N-n}{N} = \dfrac{(12.3)^2}{50}\dfrac{208-50}{208} = 2.2984$

90% confidence interval: $43.3 \pm 1.645\sqrt{2.2984}$: 40.806 up to 45.794

b. $\bar{x}_{st} = \dfrac{1}{N}\sum_{j=1}^{k}N_j\bar{x}_j = \dfrac{152(27.6)+127(39.2)+208(43.3)}{487} = 37.3306$

c. $\hat{\sigma}^2_{\bar{x}_1} = \dfrac{(7.1)^2}{40} \dfrac{152-40}{152} = .9286$, $\hat{\sigma}^2_{\bar{x}_2} = \dfrac{(9.9)^2}{40} \dfrac{127-40}{127} = 1.6785$

$$\hat{\sigma}^2_{\bar{x}_{st}} = \frac{(152)^2(.9286)+(127)^2(1.6785)+(208)^2(2.2984)}{(487)^2} = .6239$$

90% confidence interval: $37.3306 \pm 1.645\sqrt{.6239}$:
36.0313 up to 38.6299
95% confidence interval: $37.3306 \pm 1.96\sqrt{.6239}$:
35.7825 up to 38.8787

20.30 a. $\hat{\sigma}^2_{\bar{x}_1} = \dfrac{s^2}{n} \dfrac{N-n}{N} = \dfrac{(1.04)^2}{50} \dfrac{632-50}{632} = .0199$; $3.12 \pm 1.96\sqrt{.0199}$:

2.8435 up to 3.3965

b. $\hat{\sigma}^2_{\bar{x}_2} = \dfrac{(.86)^2}{50} \dfrac{529-50}{529} = .0134$; $3.37 \pm 1.96\sqrt{.0134}$:

3.1431 up to 3.5969

c. $\hat{\sigma}^2_{\bar{x}_{st}} = \dfrac{(632)^2(.0199)+(529)^2(.0134)}{(1161)^2} = .0087$; $\bar{x}_{st} = 3.2339$

$3.2339 \pm 1.96\sqrt{.0087}$: 3.0513 up to 3.4166

20.32 a. $N\bar{x}_{st} = 237(120) + 198(150) + 131(180) = 81{,}720$

b. $\hat{\sigma}^2_{\bar{x}_1} = \dfrac{s^2}{n} \dfrac{N-n}{N} = \dfrac{93^2}{40} \dfrac{120-40}{120} = 144.15$,

$\hat{\sigma}^2_{\bar{x}_2} = \dfrac{64^2}{45} \dfrac{150-45}{150} = 63.7156$, $\hat{\sigma}^2_{\bar{x}_3} = \dfrac{47^2}{50} \dfrac{180-50}{180} = 31.9078$

$$\hat{\sigma}^2_{\bar{x}_{st}} = \frac{(120)^2(144.15)+(150)^2(63.71556)+(180)^2(31.9078)}{(450)^2} = 22.4354$$

95% confidence interval: $181.6(450) \pm 1.96\sqrt{22.4354}\,(450)$:
$77{,}542.3153 < N\mu < 85{,}897.6847$

20.34 a. $\hat{p}_{st} = [100\dfrac{6}{25} + 50\dfrac{14}{25}]/150 = .3467$

b. $\hat{\sigma}_{\hat{p}_1}^2 = \dfrac{\hat{p}_1(1-\hat{p}_1)}{n_1-1}\dfrac{N_1-n_1}{N_1} = \dfrac{.24(.76)}{25-1}\dfrac{100-25}{100} = .0057$

$\hat{\sigma}_{\hat{p}_2}^2 = \dfrac{.56(.44)}{25-1}\dfrac{50-25}{50} = .0051$,

$\hat{\sigma}_{\hat{p}_{st}}^2 = \dfrac{(100)^2(.0057)+(50)^2(.0051)}{(150)^2} = .0031$

90% confidence interval: $.3467 \pm 1.645\sqrt{.0031}$: .2550 up to .4383

95% confidence interval: $.3467 \pm 1.96\sqrt{.0031}$: .2375 up to .4559

20.36 a. $n_3 = \dfrac{208}{487}130 = 55.52 = 56$ observations

b. $n_3 = \left[\dfrac{208(12.3)}{152(7.1)+127(9.9)+208(12.3)}\right]130 = 67.95 = 68$ observations

20.38 a. $n_1 = \dfrac{632}{1161}100 = 54.43 = 55$ observations

b. $n_1 = \left[\dfrac{632(1.04)}{632(1.04)+529(.86)}\right]100 = 59.09 = 60$ observations

20.40 a. $n_2 = \dfrac{1031}{1395}100 = 73.91 = 74$ observations

b. $n_2 = \left[\dfrac{1031(219.9)}{364(87.3)+1031(219.9)}\right]100 = 87.71 = 88$ observations

20.42 How large n?

$n = \dfrac{N\sigma^2}{(N-1)\sigma_{\bar{x}}^2 + \sigma^2} = \dfrac{(400)(10,000)^2}{(399)(1215.8055)^2 + (10,000)^2} = 57.988$, take 58 observations

20.44 $\sigma_{\hat{p}} = \dfrac{.04}{1.645} = .0243$, $n = \dfrac{417(.25)}{416(.0243)^2 + .25} = 210.33 = 211$ observations

20.46 Proportional allocation: $\sigma_{\bar{x}} = \dfrac{500}{1.96} = 255.1020$

$\sum N_j \sigma_j^2 = 1150(4000)^2 + 2120(6000)^2 + 930(800000)^2 = 15424 \times 10^7$

$$n = \frac{15424 \times 10^7}{4200(255.1020)^2 + 15424 \times 10^7 / 4200} = 497.47 = 498 \text{ observations}$$

Optimal allocation:

$$\sum N_j \sigma_j = 1150(4000) + 2120(6000) + 930(8000) = 24760000$$

$$n = \frac{(24760000)^2 / 4200}{4200(255.1020)^2 + 15424 \times 10^7 / 4200} = 470.78 = 471 \text{ observations}$$

20.48   a. $\overline{x}_c = \dfrac{69(83) + 75(64) + \cdots + 71(98)}{497} = 91.6761$

b.

$$\hat{\sigma}_{\overline{X}_c}^2 = \frac{(52-8)}{52(8)(61.125)^2} \frac{(69)^2(83 - 91.67605634)^2 + \cdots + (71)^2(98 - 91.67605634)^2}{8-1}$$
$$= 66.409$$

99% confidence interval: $91.6761 \pm 2.58\sqrt{66.4090}$

70.6920 up to 112.6602

20.50   a. $\hat{p}_c = \dfrac{24 + \cdots + 34}{497} = .4507$

b.

$$\hat{\sigma}_{\hat{p}_c}^2 = \frac{52-8}{52(8)(62.125)^2} \frac{(69)^2\left(\dfrac{24}{69} - .4507\right)^2 + \cdots + (71)^2\left(\dfrac{34}{71} - .4507\right)^2}{8-1} = .0013$$

95% confidence interval: $.4507 \pm 1.96\sqrt{.0013}$: .38 up to .5214

20.52 $\sigma_{\overline{x}} = \dfrac{5000}{1.645} = 3039.5$, $n = \dfrac{720(37600)^2}{719(3039)^2 + (37600)^2} = 126.34 = 127$

observations.
Additional sample observations needed are 127-20 = 107

20.54 $\sigma_{\overline{x}} = \dfrac{20}{1.96} = 10.2$

$$n = \frac{(100(105) + 180(162) + 200(183))^2 / 480}{480(10.2)^2 + (100(105)^2 + 180(162)^2 + 200(183)^2) / 480} = 159.35 = 160$$

observations. Additional sample observations needed: 160-30 = 130

20.56   Discussion questions – various answers

20.58   a. $\bar{x} = \dfrac{747}{10} = 74.7$, s = 11.44, $\hat{\sigma}^2_{\bar{x}} = \dfrac{(11.44)^2}{10} \dfrac{90-10}{90} = 11.633$

90% confidence interval: $74.7 \pm 1.645 \sqrt{11.633}$: 69.089 up to 80.311

b. The interval would be wider; the z-score would increase to 1.96

20.60   a. $\hat{p} = \dfrac{38}{61} = .623$, $\hat{\sigma}^2_{\hat{p}} = \dfrac{.623(.377)}{61} \dfrac{100-61}{100} = .0015$

90% confidence interval: $.623 \pm 1.645 \sqrt{.0015}$: .559 up to .687

b.   If the sample information is not randomly selected, the resulting conclusions may be biased

20.62   a. $\bar{x}_{st} = 11.5845$

$\hat{\sigma}^2_{\bar{x}_1} = .7321$, $\hat{\sigma}^2_{\bar{x}_2} = 1.9053$, $\hat{\sigma}^2_{\bar{x}_3} = 1.7508$

$\hat{\sigma}^2_{\bar{x}_{st}} = \dfrac{(352)^2(.7321)+(287)^2(1.9053)+(331)^2(1.7508)}{(970)^2} = .4671$

99% confidence interval for managers in subdivision 1:
$9.2 \pm 2.575 \sqrt{.7321}$: 6.997 up to 11.403

b.   99% confidence interval for all managers:
$11.5845 \pm 2.575 \sqrt{.4671}$: 9.8247 up to 13.3444

20.64 $\hat{p}_1 = \dfrac{9}{20} = .45$, $\hat{p}_2 = \dfrac{15}{20} = .75$

$\hat{p}_{\hat{p}_{st}} = .63, \hat{\sigma}^2_{\hat{p}_1} = \dfrac{\hat{p}_1(1-\hat{p}_1)}{n_1-1} \dfrac{N_1-n_1}{N_1} = \dfrac{.45(.55)}{20-1} \dfrac{120-20}{120} = .0109$

$\hat{\sigma}^2_{\hat{p}_2} = \dfrac{\hat{p}_1(1-\hat{p}_1)}{n_1-1} \dfrac{N_1-n_1}{N_1} = \dfrac{.75(.25)}{20-1} \dfrac{180-20}{180} = .0088$

$\hat{\sigma}^2_{\hat{p}_{st}} = \dfrac{(120)^2(.0109)+(180)^2(.0088)}{(300)^2} = .0049$

90% confidence interval is:
$.63 \pm 1.645 \sqrt{.0049}$ or 0.5147 up to 0.7453

20.66   a. $n_1 = \dfrac{120}{300} 40 = 16$ observations

b. $n_1 = \left[\dfrac{120(.98)}{120(.98)+180(.56)}\right] 40 = 21.54 = 22$ observations

20.68 $\sigma_{\bar{x}} = \dfrac{2000}{1.645} = 1215.8$, $n = \dfrac{328(12000)^2}{327(1215.8)^2+(12000)^2} = 75.28$

= 76 observations

20.70 Various answers. Answers should include a discussion of the potential for stratification of the population. Because different counties utilize different ballots and ballot techniques, a stratification by county may prove reasonable. The method used by the county could also be utilized in the stratification – e.g., butterfly ballots and hand-punched vs. electronic ballots.

Chapter 21:

Statistical Decision Theory

21.2   D is dominated by C. Therefore, D is inadmissible.

21.4   a. D is dominated by C. Hence D is inadmissible and removed from
        further consideration.
        Maximin criterion would select production process C:

Actions	States of Nature			
Prod. Process	Low Demand	Moderate Demand	High Demand	Min Payoff
A	100,000	350,000	900,000	100,000
B	150,000	400,000	700,000	150,000
C	250,000	400,000	600,000	250,000

   b. Minimax regret criterion would select production process A:

Actions	States of Nature			
Prod. Process	Low Demand	Moderate Demand	High Demand	Max Regret
A	150,000	50,000	0	150,000
B	100,000	0	200,000	200,000
C	0	0	300,000	300,000

21.6

Actions	States of Nature			
Prod. Process	Low Demand	Moderate Demand	High Demand	Min Payoff
A	70,000	120,000	200,000	70,000
B	80,000	120,000	180,000	80,000
C	100,000	125,000	160,000	100,000
D*	100,000	120,000	150,000	Inadmissible
E	60,000	115,000	220,000	60,000

   *inadmissible

Therefore, production process C would be chosen using the Maximin
Criterion.

Actions   Regrets or Opportunity Loss Table

Prod. Process	Low Demand	Moderate Demand	High Demand	Max Regret
A	30,000	5,000	20,000	30,000
B	20,000	5,000	40,000	40,000
C	0	0	60,000	60,000
D*				Inadmissible
E	40,000	10,000	0	40,000

*inadmissible

Therefore, production process A would be chosen using the Minimax Regret Criterion.

21.8   Assume a situation with two states of nature and two actions. Let both actions be admissible. The payoff Matrix is:

Action	S1	S2
A1	M_{11}	M_{12}
A2	M_{21}	M_{22}

Then action A1 will be chosen by both the Maximin and the Minimax Regret Criteria if for: $M_{11} > M_{21}$ and $M_{12} < M_{22}$ and $(M_{11} - M_{21}) > (M_{22} - M_{12})$

21.10 a. Payoff table for students' decision-making problem

Actions	Offered Better Position	Not Offered Better Position
Interview	4500	-500
Don't Interview	0	0

b. EMV(Interview) = .05(4500) + .95(-500) = -250
EMV(Don't Interview) = 0
Therefore, the optimal action: Don't Interview

21.12 a. EMV(Certificate of Deposit) = 1200

EMV(Low risk stock fund) = .2(4300) + .5(1200) + .3(-600) = 1280

EMV(High risk stock fund) = .2(6600) + .5(800) + .3(-1500) = 1270

Therefore, the optimal action: Low risk stock fund

b. Decision tree

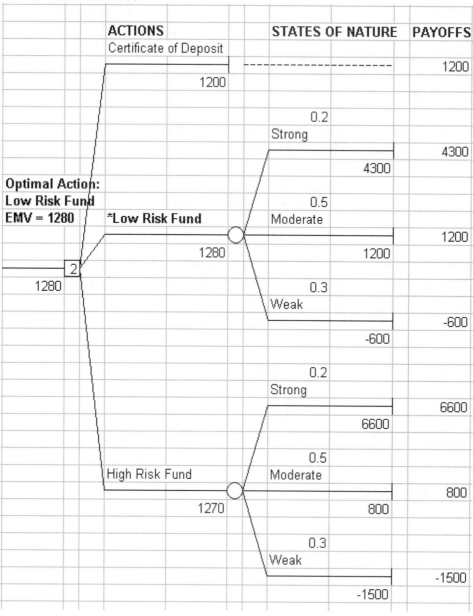

21.14 a. i) false ii) true iii) true
     b. No

21.16 a. EMV(New) = .4(130,000) + .4(60,000) + .2(-10,000) = 74,000
          EMV(Old) = .4(30,000) + .4(70,000) + .2(90,000) = 58,000
          Therefore, the optimal action: New center

     b. Decision tree

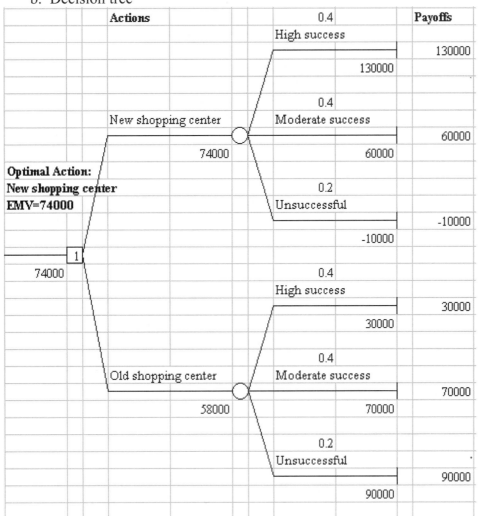

21.18   a. EMV(A) = 30,000 + 350,000p + 900,000(.7 – p) = 660,000 – 550,000p
            EMV(B) = 45,000 + 400,000p + 700,000(.7 – p) = 535,000 – 300,000p
            EMV(C) = 75,000 + 400,000p + 600,000(.7 – p) = 495,000 – 200,000p
            EMV(D) = 75,000 + 400,000p + 550,000(.7 – p) = 460,000 – 150,000p
            EMV(A) = 660 – 550p > 535 – 300p = EMV(B) when p < .5
            EMV(A) = 660 – 550p > 495 –200p = EMV(C) when p < .471
            EMV(A) = 660 – 550p > 460 – 150p = EMVA(D) when p < .5
            For p < .471, the EMV criterion chooses action A, same decision as in
            21.13.

b. EMV(A) = 170,000 + .3a > 415,000 = EMV(B) > EMV(C) > EMV(D)
    when a > 816,667

21.20 a. EMV(check) = .8(20,000 – 1,000) + .2(20,000 – 1,000 – 2,000) = 18,600
    EMV(not check) = .8(20,000) + .2(12,000) = 18,400
    Therefore, the optimal action: Check the process

b.   Decision tree

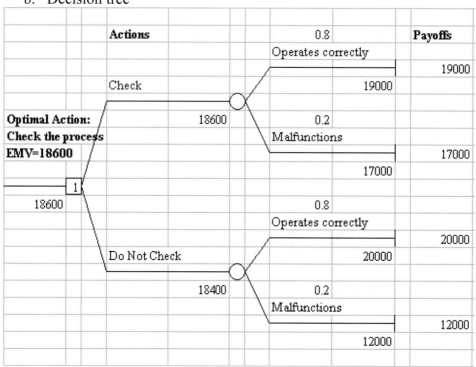

c. EMV(check) = 19,000p + 17,000(1 – p) > 20,000p + 12,000(1 – p)
    when p < 5/6 = .8333

21.22 a. payoff table for a car rental agency

Extra Ordering	6	7	8	9	10
0	0	-10	-20	-30	-40
1	-20	20	10	0	-10
2	-40	0	40	30	20
3	-60	-20	20	60	50
4	-80	-40	0	40	80

b. Per the EMV criterion, the optimal action is to order 2 extra cars:

Extra Orders

	6	7	8	9	10	EMV
0	0(.1)	-10(.3)	-20(.3)	-30(.2)	-40(.1)	-19
1	-20(.1)	20(.3)	10(.3)	0(.2)	-10(.1)	6
2	-40(.1)	0(.3)	40(.3)	30(.2)	20(.1)	16
3	-60(.1)	-20(.3)	20(.3)	60(.2)	50(.1)	11
4	-80(.1)	-40(.3)	0(.3)	40(.2)	80(.1)	-4

21.24   a. Action A1 is taken if $M_{11}p + M_{12}(1 - p) > M_{21}p + (1 - p)M_{22}$ or $p(M_{11} - M_{21}) > (1 - p)(M_{22} - M_{12})$

     b. Action A1 inadmissible implies that A1 will be chosen only if $p > 1$. In short, for part a. to be true, both payoffs of A1 cannot be less than the corresponding payoffs of A2.

21.26   a. Optimal action per the EMV criterion is action A

     b. $P(L \mid P) = \dfrac{(.5)(.3)}{(.5)(.3) + (.3)(.4) + (.1)(.3)} = \dfrac{.15}{.3} = .5$

$$P(M \mid P) = \dfrac{(.4)(.3)}{(.5)(.3) + (.3)(.4) + (.1)(.3)} = \dfrac{.12}{.3} = .4$$

$$P(H \mid P) = \dfrac{(.1)(.3)}{(.5)(.3) + (.3)(.4) + (.1)(.3)} = \dfrac{.03}{.3} = .1$$

     c. EMV(A) = .5(100,000)+.4(350,000)+.1(900,000) = 280,000
        EMV(B) = .5(150,000)+.4(400,000)+.1(700,000) = 305,000
        EMV(C) = .5(250,000)+.4(400,000)+.1(600,000) = 345,000
        Therefore, the optimal action: C

     d. $P(L \mid F) = \dfrac{(.3)(.3)}{(.3)(.3) + (.4)(.4) + (.2)(.3)} = \dfrac{.09}{.31} = .2903$

$$P(M \mid F) = \dfrac{(.4)(.4)}{(.3)(.3) + (.4)(.4) + (.2)(.3)} = \dfrac{.16}{.31} = .5161$$

$$P(H \mid F) = \dfrac{(.2)(.3)}{(.3)(.3) + (.4)(.4) + (.2)(.3)} = \dfrac{.06}{.31} = .1935$$

     e. EMV(A) = .2903(100,000)+.5161(350,000)+.1935 (900,000) = 383,815
        EMV(B) = .2903(150,000)+.5161(400,000)+.1935(700,000) = 385,435
        EMV(C) = .2903(250,000)+.5161(400,000)+.1935(600,000) = 395,115
        Therefore, the optimal action: C

f. $P(L \mid G) = \dfrac{(.2)(.3)}{(.2)(.3)+(.3)(.4)+(.7)(.3)} = \dfrac{.06}{.39} = .1538$

$P(M \mid G) = \dfrac{(.3)(.4)}{(.2)(.3)+(.3)(.4)+(.7)(.3)} = \dfrac{.12}{.39} = .3077$

$P(H \mid G) = \dfrac{(.7)(.3)}{(.2)(.3)+(.3)(.4)+(.7)(.3)} = \dfrac{.21}{.39} = .5385$

g. EMV(A) = .1538(100,000)+.3077(350,000)+.5385(900,000) = 607,692
EMV(B) = .1538(150,000)+.3077(400,000)+.5385(700,000) = 523,077
EMV(C) = .1538(250,000)+.3077(400,000)+.5385(600,000) = 484,615
Therefore, the optimal action: A

21.28 a. $P(E \mid P) = \dfrac{(.8)(.6)}{(.8)(.6)+(.1)(.4)} = \dfrac{.48}{.52} = .9231$

P(not E|P) = 1 − P(E|P) = 1 - .9231 = .0769

b. EMV(S) = .9231(50,000)+.0769(50,000) = 50,000
EMV(R) = .9231(125,000)+.0769(-10,000) = 114,615
Therefore, optimal action: retain

c. $P(E|N) = \dfrac{(.2)(.6)}{(.2)(.6)+(.9)(.4)} = \dfrac{.12}{.48} = .25$, P(not E|N) = .75

d. EMV(S) = .25(50,000)+.75(50,000) = 50,000
EMV(R) = .25(125,000)+.75(-10,000) = 23,750
Therefore, optimal action: sell

21.30 a. P(2 | 10%) = .01, P(1 | 10%) = .18, P(0 | 10%) = .81

b. P(2 | 30%) = .09, P(1 | 30%) = .42, P(0 | 30%) = .49

c. Probability of the states of 10% defective and 30% defective given:

# defective	10% defect	30% defect
2 defective	.308	.692
1 defective	.632	.368
0 defective	.869	.131

EMV of actions	check	Do not check
2 defective	17,616*	14,464
1 defective	18,264*	17,056
0 defective	18,737	18,952*

*optimal action given the circumstance

21.32 a. Perfect information is defined as the case where the decision maker is able to gain information to tell with certainty which state will occur
  b. The optimal action: Low risk stock fund (see Problem 21.12)
   EVPI = .2(6600 – 4300) + .5(0) + .3(1200 – (-600)) = 1000

21.34 Given that the optimal action is: New center
  EVPI = .4(0) + .4(70,000 – 60,000) + .2(90,000 – (-10,000)) = 24,000

21.36 The expected value of sample information is $\sum_{i=1}^{M} P(A_i)V_i$ where

$P(A_i) = \sum_{j=1}^{H} P(A_i \mid s_j)$. For perfect information,

$P(A_i \mid s_j) = 0$ for $i \neq j$ and $P(A_i \mid s_j) = 1$ for $i = j$, thus $P(A_i) = P(s_i)$

21.38 EVSI = .3(345,000 – 280,000) + .31(395,115 – 383,815) + .39(0) = 23,003

21.40 Given that the optimal action: retain the patent (see Problem 21.28)
  EVSI = .42(0) + .52(50,000 – 23,750) = 13,650

21.42 a. EVSI = .11(-600 – (-910)) + .89(0) = 34.1
  b. EVSI = .013(-600 – (-1540)) + .194(-600 – (-825)) + .793(0) = 55.87
  c. The difference = 21.77
  d. None
  e. 24.75

21.44 a.

Payoff	-10000	30000	60000	70000	90000	13000
Utility	0	35	60	70	85	100

  b. EU(New) = .4(100) + .4(60) + .2(0) = 64
   EU(Old) = .4(35) + .4(70) + .2(85) = 59
   Therefore, the optimal action: New center

21.46 94,000p – 16,000(1-p) = 0 ➔ p = 16 / 110

Payoff	-160000	0	94000
Utility	0	160 / 110	100

$$\text{Slope}(-16000,0) = \frac{160/110}{16000} = .00009$$

$$\text{Slope}(0,94000) = \frac{100 - 160/110}{94000} = .00105$$

Therefore, the contractor has a preference for risk

21.48 a. P(S1) = .3(.6) = .18, P(S2) = .42, P(S3) = .12, P(S4) = .28

   b. EMV(A1) = 460, EMV(A2) = 330, EMV(A3) = 0, EMV(A4) = 510
       Therefore, the optimal action: A4

   c. Draw the decision tree

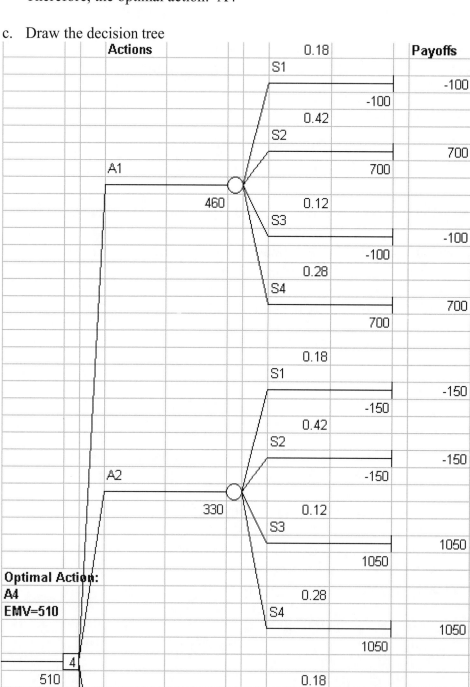

TreePlan (Continued for 21.48):

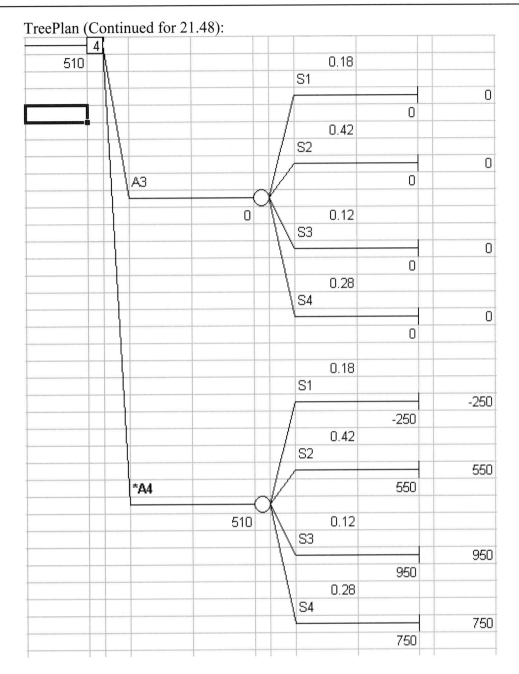

d. EVPI = .18(250) + .42(150) + .12(100) + .28(300) = 204

e. 79